I Know It
in My Heart

>>>>>>>>>>>>>

Always believe what you know in your heart +

Mary Reuffe

I Know It
in My Heart

WALKING THROUGH GRIEF
WITH A CHILD

A MEMOIR

MARY E. PLOUFFE, Ph.D.

SHE WRITES PRESS

Published 2017
Printed in the United States of America
ISBN: 978-1-63152-200-0 pbk
ISBN: 978-1-63152-201-7 ebk
Library of Congress Control Number: 2016957317

Cover design © Julie Metz, Ltd./metzdesign.com
Cover photo: "Margaret's Hands" © Jack Montgomery Photography
Interior design by Tabitha Lahr

For information, address:
She Writes Press
1563 Solano Ave #546
Berkeley, CA 94707

She Writes Press is a division of SparkPoint Studio, LLC.

HOW COULD I EVER KNOW? (from "The Secret Garden")
Lyrics by MARSHA NORMAN Music by LUCY SIMON
Copyright © 1991, 1992 ABCDE PUBLISHING LTD. and CALOUGIE MUSIC
All Rights Administered by WB MUSIC CORP.
All Rights Reserved
Used By Permission of ALFRED MUSIC

No More (from INTO THE WOODS)
Words and Music by Stephen Sondheim
© 1987 RILTING MUSIC, INC.
All Rights Administered by WB MUSIC CORP.
All Rights Reserved Used by Permission
Reprinted by Permission of Hal Leonard LLC

For Martha

Seeds

When you are trying to be a writer in Maine, people throw seeds at you.

They know the soil here is rocky, boulder-filled like the coastline, so they keep throwing them. Handfuls sometimes.

Occasionally, one finds a crack, a tiny crag between the boulders, and germinates, shooting something green and persistent and impossibly beautiful.

So many people have done that for me.

....

Joan Dempsey listened to a haiku I wrote about peeling potatoes, and said, "You are a writer. I want to be your friend."

Suzanne Strempek Shea waved a few journal fragments in the air and said, "Do you have an agent?"

Ted Deppe cried two long poet's tears the night I read on the coast of Ireland.

....

I didn't believe them, mind you, but the seeds got caught in my Keens.

So I sat down and kept writing.

....

Susan Conley taught me how to make a story come alive with scene and dialogue and didn't even flinch when I said, "Oh, I get it. You want me to write all the stuff I skip when I'm reading."

Monica Wood introduced me to the "naked narrator in a lab coat" who would become my voice.

All these seeds found earth and surrounded me with living shoots, green and growing.

....

Total strangers invited me to join writing groups, and read my work with kindness. They watered those shoots, pruned the ones that prickled, and nurtured my garden while I wrote.

It took years, but the shoots became trees to lean against, ferns to dry my tears, and flowers to give me hope.

....

I knew I had a story. Martha and Herb and Liamarie gave me that.

But the writer who tells it owes everything to those seeds. What works in this book grew from them. What does not is mine alone.

....

So come to Maine if you want to be a writer. Know that you will be surrounded by kindness and wisdom and encouragement and skill.

And look closely as you walk my garden. If, in my story, you find comfort or compassion or companionship, take those seeds and bring them home.

....

Spread them wide and plant them deep, so my debt will be repaid.

Contents

>>>>>>>>>>>>

SECTION III: GRIEVING

SECTION IV: GROWING

EPILOGUE

Prologue

Winslow Park

There's a small town park about a mile from my home. It sits on a long narrow peninsula where the Harraseeket River and the ocean meet. One side looks out to a scattering of islands in Casco Bay, then beyond to open ocean. The other side borders an inlet with a view of Harraseeket Harbor, and the small cove around the corner where my house sits, hidden behind the hemlocks. When the tide is in, red and yellow kayaks dot the cove. But a few hours later, blue herons will bend their backs alongside clam diggers in the mud.

The trail along the inlet weaves deep into the pine forest, tracing the water's edge as you head to the point. In summer a hundred campsites fill with tents and RVs and people who plant flowers outside their campers for a two-week stay. But mostly when I go there, the park is empty. I can walk along open ocean, buffeted by crisp winds in the fall, or track footprints in winter snow. Or I can take the inlet trail where spring mud is deep, and I am sheltered from the ocean winds. I never tire of this place.

I walk to the point, where a few benches capture the view. I always head to the same one. It is pebbled granite, thick and solid, with a tall angled back. It sits at the tip of the peninsula, with the best view of the boats moored in Harraseeket Harbor and the traffic of sailors squeezing through the small channel that links the ocean with the river's mouth.

Engraved in the back of the bench is the name of a young woman who grew up just a few miles from me. I know her parents. Her brother played baseball with my son. Her name and the dates of her birth and death are engraved beneath several carefully chosen, loving adjectives. I read them every time I'm there, but they never stick. What always sticks is her story . . . a vibrant young woman celebrating her twenty-third birthday on a camping trip with two close friends in western Maine woods not seventy miles from this spot. A storm, a tree falls. She is killed instantly, her friends untouched.

I remember her mother speaking to the crowd that overflowed the South Freeport Church onto its chair-filled front lawn. "I don't know how we are standing today," she said, "but I think it is because you are all standing with us."

I know why I go to this bench. It is not to honor her loss, though I do. It is not to remember my community of friends and neighbors grieving together and supporting her family, and building this bench in her memory. It is none of these things.

This is, for me, a monument to randomness. To the simple truth that we do not decide our fate. And to the concrete, overwhelming truth that beauty sits with horror, and I must find a way to bear them both.

The Favor

It was one of those late summer nights, an August night in Maine when dusk brings a hint of fall air. The phone rang, and I reached for the receiver on the wall beside my kitchen table, trading hands so I could keep sweeping up the dinner crumbs as we talked. I knew it would be Martha, so we didn't bother with "Hello," just started the conversation where we'd left off so many times in the past few weeks.

"I think I'm going to do it," she began. "I think I have to."

"OK," I said quickly. I remember feeling relief.

"I need you to take Liamarie if you can. It should be three, maybe four weeks."

"Of course," I said instantly. "Of course I'll take Liamarie."

I never even asked my husband or my children.

A simple conversation between sisters. A favor she knew I would grant before she asked, so neither one of us wasted much emotion on the moment. And neither one of us could have imagined where that favor would take us.

Martha had breast cancer. Since her diagnosis in January, she had done everything the doctors advised: surgery, chemotherapy, radiation. By all standard measures her treatment was done. But there was one more option they wanted to her to consider. It was risky, and all the research wasn't in yet, but preliminary results looked promising, and her participation in a Johns Hopkins study would add to the knowledge base.

The truth is, I never doubted what she would decide. I knew she'd do her own research and hear all the warnings, but I also knew two things her doctors did not know. Being on the front lines in a cause she believed in was familiar territory. It would not scare her. She had spent her twenties and thirties on the front lines of more causes than I could count.

More importantly, if any treatment held the promise of letting her raise her three-year-old daughter, the child she had spent nine years trying to conceive, she would take it.

What she was asking of me was easy, nothing more than most sisters would do for one another, and I remember being pretty confident about doing it. Liamarie was a good kid, an easy kid, with spunk and energy just like her mother. Two of my three children were still at home, and, at ten and fifteen, they had crazy-busy schedules that would provide lots of distraction for their three-year-old cousin. We could sweep Liamarie up for a month of Maine adventure and return her to her family no worse for the wear. Or so I thought. As a clinical psychologist who treated both children and adults, I had no doubt I could do this for Martha, and do it well. It was simple.

Reflecting on that scene now, I feel a bit foolish. Because nothing about the weeks and months and years that followed was simple. Nothing followed the script we had imagined. Liamarie's three-week visit grew into months, while the treatment we hoped would extend her mother's life took it instead.

This is our story. The earliest pieces were written on tear-stained journals at 3:00 A.M., when my grief and sadness made sleep impossible. At first, I wrote to survive. To find a place to put my feelings so I could get up, and make breakfast, and walk the short distance across the garage and up the stairs to my office to do my job. Nothing in my life prepared me for the onslaught of feelings that Martha's death evoked. Not my father's death when I was nineteen. Not all my years of training, or the hundreds of hours I spent walking others though grief in my clinical practice. I needed to write to keep myself functioning as my world fractured around me.

Later I wrote for Liamarie, hoping to give her memories of her mother that would be rich and detailed, and accessible to her when she was grown. I wanted her to know how much her mother loved her, and how we had tried to cushion her trauma.

And there was another reason. After Martha's death, I looked for materials to guide me, and to help my brother-in-law with Liamarie's grief. But what we found was dispassionate, analytical, completely out of touch with what we were feeling: the desperateness of a wounded parent trying to cradle a grieving child. I was making it up as I went along, using all my clinical skills and a heaping dose of parenting intuition to do the best I could for Liamarie. I needed to write about that as well, to remember what I was learning along the way.

But ultimately, I wrote this because I know that if Martha could have given me instructions before she died, she would have asked me to use her story to make a difference. "It is what it is; don't waste it," she would have insisted. I'm glad we never had that conversation, because I would have resisted. I am a solitary soul, reserved and private. I do not share easily. Being a therapist has only reinforced that temperament, that inclination to focus on the feelings of others and not on my own. Besides, in the midst of my pain, I could not have imagined how to turn our tragedy into anything of value.

But as years passed after Martha's death, I saw in Liamarie's eyes the same challenge. She was teaching me so much about love and resilience, this tiny child. From age three, when she had no words for her confusion and despair, through her pre-teen years, I was learning at every turn. I began to wonder if our family's path through this powerful human experience might be worth sharing.

One afternoon, perhaps five years after Martha's death, Liamarie and I were laughing at some silliness I cannot remember. We were sitting on a couch, giggling and pushing at each other like puppies. I thought of Martha, imagined her laughing with us as she watched. Liamarie must have seen an expression cross my face. Suddenly, she spoke.

"It's OK, Mary Beth. Mama wants us to be happy." She patted my arm. "I know it in my heart."

Her words stayed with me. Maybe that is the real story, I thought, the one I do want to tell. Not just how we got through the horror. How we got back.

Section I

Remembering

Of two sisters, one is always the watcher, one the dancer.
—Louise Gluck

Chapter 1

The Portal

Traumatic memories break all the rules. They do not sit logically, sequenced in a familiar pattern of beginning to middle to end. They do not separate fact from feeling, emotion from understanding, sensation from experience. Instead, everything exists together, a cacophony of images and sounds, space and time, terrors and truths. No wonder we push them away.

There is often only one gentle way in. A portal that binds what lies behind, holding it at bay, so that you can enter carefully, so that you will not be swallowed. When the memory is triggered, you go there first, hoping it will hold you and give you a chance to breathe, to decide whether to enter. Even now, so many years after my sister's death, this is true for me. Martha's name, her face, and her story all take me instantly to one place. Telling the story can only begin there.

It is the room in which she died.

It was a small room at the end of a long corridor. It was barely big enough for the hospital bed, access for staff to walk on both sides, and the collection of machines keeping her alive. Several IV poles feeding her fluids and antibiotics, a cardiac monitor, and the ventilator pump with its flashing red LED display are the ones I can remember now. There may have been more. They were like sentries, standing guard to her right and left. When I stood at the end of the bed, they framed her face.

Next to the doorway, a rectangular glass cutout in the wall provided a view of the corridor. Disembodied heads floated by a second or two before visitors appeared in the doorway, as if a spirit were announcing each arrival. Nurses heading in the other direction, down the corridor to a patient's room, glanced in quickly but rarely slowed their steps. On that side of the wall, the world moved fast.

There was only one chair in the room, a small straight-backed chair with wooden arms and a seat upholstered in institutional beige. Usually, it was pushed in the corner. I sat in it when I was alone, when things were quiet.

Mostly, things were noisy: beeping machines scoring her progress, measuring her vital signs. If her oxygen level dropped for any reason—a twisted line, a shift in her body position—the monitor began its sharp rhythmic *beep beep beep beep*, demanding attention until someone reset it. Just across from her doorway, the nurses' station buzzed with activity: white flashes, intercom static, phones ringing, and always the muffled voices that rose and fell, wafting into our room. When I sat in the chair, I closed my eyes, letting the sounds, the smells, the antiseptic taste of the air settle in around me. When I close my eyes now, it is all still there.

Martha made no sound. No whimper, no words. But her body spoke. Sometimes it thrashed, fought, strained to pull itself up and away from the bed. Sometimes it was perfectly still. Once, only once, I saw a nurse wipe a tear that slid from her left eye.

There was one large window in the room. Its view was just another brick wall across the courtyard, but it had a wide sill, almost two feet deep, where I could toss my bag or hoist myself up to sit. From that perch, I could see everything: Martha's full length stretched out on the bed, her straight auburn hair gone, her strong athletic body lying beneath white sheets that bled a sea of lines and tubes. Looking down, I was a child in an oversize chair, watching something not real, a picture that would turn itself off any moment. I could pretend up there, but I could not ground myself, could not stay in touch with the psychologist part of me, who was used to hospitals, to reading charts, to conferencing with a team. I had to jump down and stand when the doctors came in.

Off in the corner of the room was a picture of Liamarie, Martha's three-and-a-half-year-old daughter. An 8x10 portrait taken at day care and set in a simple frame. She was posed and smiling, wearing a dark plaid cotton dress with puffy sleeves and a Peter Pan collar, and looking nothing like the spirited dynamo who had been living with me for months. *No way,* I always thought when I glanced at the dress. *She wouldn't keep that on for two minutes at my house.* "Too itchy," she would have said. "Not comfy."

Herb, Martha's husband, is there too. But in my mind's eye picture of that room, he is unusually silent, clutching an executive leather folder in his hands and looking over at me with an expression I cannot read.

White-clad doctors and nurses float in and out, but they have no faces. Not a single one.

No matter how I try, I can't add much to the picture. Pieces are missing, never recorded, or lost to the trauma of what was. Mostly I remember Martha, lying in that bed. Strong, brave, determined-to-live Martha.

This is the portal, this room in the transplant unit at Johns Hopkins. The pictures from that room never change. They do not overwhelm me now, but if I stay long with the images, I can slide easily into a replay of the confusion, the knowing and the not knowing, the belief and unbelief that lived there. This is how I remember.

Chapter 2

Family

>>>>>>>>>>>>

Memory not only stores meaning; it also creates it. Alfred Adler faithfully recorded each patient's earliest memory, believing it held the crystallization of that person's beliefs about the world and his or her role in it. Am I weak or powerful, loveable or easily rejected? Go back to the earliest memory for the template, he advised.

Recent understanding of memory complicates this idea, though it does not cancel out its truth. We need language to encode memory, words to store what happened and what it means. Before age three the architecture of the brain is set up to take in new learning but not to encode it with the language of meaning that holds it, glues it in time. That's why we all learn our colors, but few of us remember when or how.

Emotions play a key role. The first things stored permanently are rarely mundane. They are events that have emotional meaning, that stand out and grab our attention. Maybe they set our compass, but I am not sure of that.

My own earliest memory is the day my parents brought Martha home from the hospital, a week after she was born. It is sharp and distinct, stored in the sepia tones of a 50's photograph in my head. My parents stood together just inside the front door, where the glass-curtained window filtered sunlight into the living room. My father wore his dark business suit and fedora hat. My mother still had her coat on, and was leaning in to him and holding a small pale pink bundle too high for me to see. They shared a glance, then my father looked down and said, "Martha Ann or Anne Marie. You and Eddie can choose."

Eddie turned to face me. With his fiery red hair and face full of freckles, he looked like a Dublin postcard come alive, but that day he had no impish grin. "This is in-portant," he said. "We have to talk alone." He led me into the bedroom just a few feet away, leaving my parents behind. I already knew my answer but didn't say a thing. He walked solemnly down the narrow corridor between two twin beds, then turned to face me. I tickled my fingers across the bumpy Queen Ann bedspread, waiting for him to start.

"We should pick Martha Ann," he said. "She was born on Washington's Birthday, and Daddy says Martha was Mrs. Washington's name." I looked blank. "George Washington was our first president," he explained. "We talked about that in kindergarten."

I didn't know anything about that, but I was glad I didn't have to argue. "Anne Marie is used," I said. "That's our cousin's name. She's a whole new baby and needs a whole new name."

Martha grew into a wiry towhead, with skinny arms and legs and huge round eyes. She moved fast, took risks, and seemed afraid of nothing. My mother called her a "runner," and I can still hear her frantic "Where is your sister? Where did she go now?" and taste the mix of guilt and annoyance I felt every time she escaped home and headed down the road to adventure.

There were three and a half years between us, but personality separated us more than age. I was introspective, a watcher of all the Irish Catholic subtext that flowed through my father's big extended family. And I was painfully self-conscious, chubby, moody, and too curious for my own good. Childhood seemed a burden I wanted to cast off as soon as possible. A place where grown-ups didn't take me seriously, and rebuffed my efforts to understand. They wanted me to be carefree and happy, and I was neither. But I was deeply insulted by the expectation, and annoyed when they called me cute or charming.

Martha was the polar opposite. She had her own agenda, and couldn't care less what adults were doing unless it interfered with her plans. But she was a natural comic and happy to take center stage to perform. "Martha, give us a fashion show," my mother asked when company arrived and, at eight or nine, Martha agreed happily, entertaining a roomful of adults with nothing but a sheet and her imagination. Between appearances, she hid behind a door to rearrange her garb.

"Presenting ... the world famous Queen of Sheba!" She flew out and paraded across the room, her toga flying behind. While the audience roared, she scurried back behind the door.

"And now, the world's oldest bag lady," she croaked. Creeping out, bent like an ancient crone with the sheet draped over her head, she waddled across the room, an imaginary cane in hand.

I watched from the corner of the room, laughing with everyone else, and wondering at her imagination and her confidence. Martha loved making the world laugh. I could never quite separate it from feeling laughed at and somehow inadequate.

I was in middle school before I knew anyone who was not Irish. My father was the youngest of ten children, "seven who made it to adulthood," he always added, as if that was a good percentage. Our New England mill town was divided into neighborhoods, each with its own name ... The Acre ... The Highlands ... Belvedere. And when I asked what they were, I was likely to get, "That's where the French, or the Italians, or the Jewish people live," as an answer. My small neighborhood parochial school was filled with Murphys and O'Briens and Flanagans. In March of my fifth grade year, my friend Mary Margaret and I hatched a plan.

"Everyone's going to wear green on St. Patrick's Day," she said. "Let's wear orange!"

That night at the dinner table, I shared the joke, giggling, and my soft-spoken grandfather transformed, flew to his feet in a rage and roared up the stairs to his room, screaming words I could not understand in his thick brogue ... *Orangemen ... starvation ... dying* ... I burst into tears, no idea what I had done. My mother ran after him. "Pa, she doesn't know, she's just a child."

I learned that night what it meant to be raised in Ireland, as my grandparents were, and what deep and unspoken loyalties lay beneath the surface. "But I just thought orange was a color the Irish don't like," I cried to my mother. "Why didn't you tell me?"

"I know, I know, and Grandpa will forgive you. It is Ireland's history, and a sad one, and we just don't talk about it. But it means a lot to the old folks," was her answer. "Now go up and see him."

I climbed the stairs feeling terrible, and couldn't stop the tears as I tried to speak.

"Sure, gurl, your bladder's gettin' too close to your eyes," my grandfather said gently, and took my hand. "Nothin' to say now, it's over. Don't be cryin' now." I knew he had forgiven me, but it was weeks before I could think of it without shame.

"A bit of the dark Irish soul in that one," I heard him say to my mother later.

"Oh, Pa, she's fine; leave her be."

....

To say that Martha and I were close growing up would be the Irish truth, the one that ignores feelings as long as everything looks good on the surface. We rarely fought, and got along well enough when we had to, but we were never each other's first choice.

I was a reader, a music lover, a bit of a dreamer. I had no difficulty making friends, and they were a happy distraction from my real life, the one inside my head. But I did not crave companions, and I preferred my time alone. Martha had a wide circle of friends, and no interest in mine. Choosing a book over an invitation made no sense to her. *People . . . action . . . adventure,* her expressions said. *What is there to decide?*

My mother did her best to hide it, but she was disappointed.

"Do you know how lucky you are to have one another? I was an only child. I would have done anything to have a sister." Her lament made me feel guilty and sad for her, but no different about Martha. The truth was, Martha and I were happy with our differences. They freed us both. I was relieved not to have a sister tagging along behind me. She was free to chart her own course, and perfectly comfortable being who she was.

By adolescence we were about the same height, but there the similarity ended. She was broad-shouldered, lean and strong, with long-fingered hands and hard, elegant nails I envied. Her large light blue eyes sat front and center on her face, framed by straight copper-red hair.

I was softer, rounder, with deep-set azure eyes and dark ash-blonde hair that curled easily and streaked in the sun. "I know that you're the pretty one," she said one Easter Sunday morning when she caught me admiring myself in the mirror. "But your nose keeps you from being beautiful." There was not a trace of envy in her voice.

By the time she was a teenager, "I'll do it, but I don't like it," was her answer to my parents' rules. Then, with her hands on her hips, she'd tell them why. Why it was not fair, or necessary, or just plain not what she wanted. The whole thing never made much sense to me. If you were going to obey, why complicate it with a lot of argument? A few times I tried to intervene. "You're just making things harder." I argued, "Just do it and be quiet."

"No way," she insisted. "If I have to do it, they have to listen to me." Hearing her out was the price of compliance. And occasionally she won. After one year at Notre Dame Academy, the all-girls high school I fit into so well, she stood in the living room and challenged my parents. "OK, I did what you asked. I tried it, and I don't like it." She went to Lowell High the following year.

But not everything went so easily.

She was probably thirteen the Sunday morning she came downstairs and announced, "I don't think I'm going to Mass anymore. I'm not sure I believe all this God stuff."

"Well, believe what you like," my father answered calmly, "but get your coat on. As long as you're living under my roof, you're going to church with your family. It won't do you any harm." It was a quiet ride to church that day, and I climbed the circular staircase up to the choir loft shaking my head. By then, church was a place for me to sing, and I never questioned singing.

So, I have few memories of sharing secrets on the bed, of giggling about boys or swapping sweaters as we moved through school. But something passed between us when my father died.

Martha stood in the back hall and opened the door for me as I rushed in. She was a month shy of her sixteenth birthday, and already dressed in a dark wool dress for the wake, which began in less than an hour. A January snowstorm had turned my four-hour trip from college in New York to more than seven hours, an endless ride for me, sitting in the back seat of a car driven by two silent uncles who could barely answer my simple questions about my father's sudden and unexpected death.

My mother waited in the kitchen. I could see her out of the corner of my eye, standing in front of the sink in a short sleeved black dress, her face a mask of confusion and pain. Both arms were encased in heavy white casts, only her finger tips exposed, the result of a fall just two weeks before that broke both wrists.

I stopped when I saw Martha's face and barked an order.

"Go upstairs to mom's room. In the bottom left hand drawer you'll find some black stockings. I need those."

She looked confused and tilted her head. "Do you know what happened?"

"Yes, I know." I said, and held her glance for a moment.

"OK." She nodded, and headed quickly up the stairs.

We wrapped the casts together.

Chapter 3

Bookends

≫≫≫≫≫≫≫

Who were you before all this happened?

It's a question I often ask in my office when people tell me their stories of trauma. Like a coded language, it only makes sense to those who understand. They sit back and nod for a moment before answering. I let this silence be, give it time to say what we do not need words to convey. Trauma changes us. Whether it destroys or strengthens, devastates or empowers, it changes who we are.

One woman rifled through her bag, and pulled out a photo in response to my question.

"Here," she said, thrusting the photo across and into my hands. "That's who I was. I want her back."

My bookend was simple. I was a mid-forties clinical psychologist with a busy private practice and a part-time position teaching psychiatric residents at Maine Medical Center. My husband Bill and I were bonded in two tasks we shared with equal fervor: raising our three children and caring for our long-widowed elderly mothers. "You are a strong person. You do not crumble," Bill had complimented me once. Most of the time I felt that, and when I did not feel it, I leaned on believing it.

And if I had to pull out a photo to show who we all were before this happened, it would be one taken at Christmas 1996, just a month before Martha's diagnosis. My house had been Christmas Central for our families for years by then, and it was filled. We were milling around the living room, enjoying the winter light from the long row of glass skylights that cut deep into the ceiling and turned towering pines into a backdrop the full length of the room. Bill grabbed his camera and coaxed my mother: "Come on Mary, you've got all your children and grandchildren here. That doesn't happen very often. Sit in the middle, and let's get a picture."

My mother still had Martha's new hiking boots, a Christmas gift, on her feet. "I like these, I might just get some," she'd said minutes before. We laughed a bit too enthusiastically, and she shot us an annoyed glance.

Ed and I sat on opposite sides of Mom, and our children filled in around us on the long white living room couch. Ed's daughter and mine were in fifth grade that year, and had lots to chatter about behind Margaret's closed door. Matt was delighted to have his big brother home from college, and I was glad to see Justin relaxing a bit. At fifteen and twenty, my boys dwarfed their grandmother, and scooted out as soon as the picture was taken, eager to get back to a game of winter whiffle ball on the driveway. "Be careful of the ice!" I yelled, but no one listened.

Martha sat on the edge of couch, tall and straight, holding her daughter. Her smile was broad and open. I look at that picture now, and see one of the last unguarded expressions on her face . . . pure joy . . . with Liamarie on her lap and no hint of illness in her eyes.

"I've got my whole family," Liamarie crowed, spreading her arms wide with satisfaction.

"Yes, you do," Martha said with a laugh, "but it's time to get ready for bed."

"Not now, Mama."

"Oh yes, now. Come on upstairs, and brush your teeth."

Suddenly, Liamarie was on her feet. "I don't want to, and I don't have to!" Hands on her hips, she looked defiantly at her mother, daring her to battle.

"Liamarie?" Herb's voice joined from the kitchen. He'd hidden himself quickly out of view. "That can't be *my* daughter, Liamarie, *can* it?" His voice was a stage whisper, astonished and horrified. Liamarie giggled.

"Well, OK," she conceded, "but you have to read . . ."

"Have to? Is that how you ask, young lady?" Martha's voice faded as they headed up the stairs.

....

Thirteen of us sat around the Christmas table that year, including Bill's brother Paul, and both grandmothers. Bill cut the turkey. There were homemade breads, three kinds of cranberry sauce, and way too many vegetables. Our plates overflowed.

Martha and I handled the kitchen, and she provided fast and efficient counterpoint to my wishful indecision. While I searched for the Christmas bowl I planned to use for potatoes, she put them on the table in whatever was handy with a firm, "Forget it, it's done."

This is as good as it gets.

I remember that thought, and wanting to stay with it. We don't get many Hallmark card moments in our lives, I reminded myself, and this is one of them. Drink it in. But another thought kept intruding.

Two of these women will not be here next year.

I was annoyed with myself, but I couldn't seem to shake it.

At eighty-four and eighty-nine, the grandmothers were the likely candidates. Bill's mother had battled cancer for ten years by then, and her body was tiring from the effort. My mother was younger, but a rapidly weakening heart had put her on a first name basis with the EMTs in nearby Yarmouth, where she still had her own tiny condo. "Jerry's the nice one," she'd told me earlier that day. "You don't have to rush when he calls you. He'll take good care of me till you get there."

But they are here and able to enjoy the holiday, I chastised myself.

"Mary Beth, Mary Beth, can you read me a story?" Liamarie interrupted from upstairs.

"Of course, if Mama says it's OK."

"Can you read two?" she added, before Martha could reply.

Two of these women . . .

"Here I come!" I yelled.

Chapter 4

Liamarie

That Christmas, Liamarie took center stage the moment she arrived. Martha and Herb were just inside the kitchen doorway, Liamarie in her mother's arms and Herb loaded down with packages. Justin bounded over to help, tucking bags filled with gifts under his arms and smiling at his little cousin.

"Hi, Liamarie," Justin reached out to take her hand. "Merry Christmas!"

Liamarie pulled back and scowled.

"You remember Justin," Martha coaxed. "He came and stayed with us a few months ago." Liamarie remembered all right. She'd come down early one morning to find Justin and his college roommate, both well over six feet tall, in sleeping bags on the floor. "Mama, Mama, giant mens in the living room!" she screamed as she ran back up the stairs.

Now, from the safety of her mother's arms, she pointed her tiny index finger up close to Justin's nose. "You are *too big!*" she announced in a loud voice. She glared at him, determined not to be cowed, this two-and-a-half-year-old who was barely twenty pounds herself. Martha turned quickly to hide her laughter.

"Gee, I wonder where she gets that from," I said.

Liamarie was a sprite of a child, delicate in build, small boned, and slender. I could circle her thigh with my thumb and index finger, span her buttocks with my palm. But she was lithe, flexible, and coordinated; totally in charge of her tiny body. Compared to my own children, who always topped the growth charts, she seemed miniature, a powerhouse of energy and enthusiasm, intelligence and stubbornness, yet never above the 30th percentile in height and weight.

But she was whip fast and quick with words, startling those who heard her. Full sentences at two, with extra words thrown in whether she was sure of them or not. Just a week before that Christmas visit, she'd stormed into her parents' room when she heard raised voices. "Put that voice down. Don't you talk bad manners to my Papa." She glared at Martha, who couldn't wait to call and share the story.

The first thing you noticed was her eyes. They were too big for her face, too milk-chocolaty brown for a child. There was an old-soulness to them that caught and captured you. *I know things you don't think I know*, they seemed to say. *Don't try to fool me.*

The eyes were familiar. The color was not her mother's soft blue-gold, but the gaze and expression were so like my little sister of a generation ago—wide eyed, wondering, and ready for adventure. And the broad deep forehead was just like her mom's. The top half of her face was all Martha. Then she smiled. Herb's exuberant grin appeared; his lips and chin surrounding perfectly straight teeth. Herb saw Martha in Liamarie's smile, but to me, it was her dad's unflagging excitement, his enthusiastic energy that was mirrored in her wide smile and the roundness it brought to her eyes.

Her hair was chestnut brown from the day it sprouted, no evolution from towhead to burnished red-copper like her mother's, not a strand suggesting it would become her father's sleek black. Warm brown, the color of wild horses in the wind.

But it was not really looks or personality that gave Liamarie center stage. The truth is the whole family was still a bit amazed that she existed. We still looked at her in wonder, grateful and a bit astonished that this tiny child had found a way to be.

Martha and Herb met in the early seventies, when college campuses were on fire. Martha was captured by the causes: the anti-war and civil rights protests that turned her from a theater major at a small Catholic women's college in New Haven to a student of geography and labor movements at Boston University; a red-haired Irish Catholic girl who went to Black Panther meetings at night.

Herb was at Boston College, a first generation Latino New Yorker, whose parents were raised in Colombia and Ecuador. He flipped easily from English to Spanish in staccato conversation that never lost its Latin American fire. He was exuberant, excitable, and endlessly optimistic against her more analytic determination. But they shared a passion for social change, and his intellect and creativity made them a good team. "He's got a hundred ideas a day," she told me laughingly when I first met him a few years later. "Ten of them are brilliant and three of those might actually work. My job is to get us from one hundred to three."

My relationship with Martha during her twenties was tense, and mostly silent. Her political work sat between us like a sore. After my father's death, Martha's increasingly radical choices terrified my mother, and her grief focused in on them. She told herself that my father would have known how to "stop all this nonsense," and "talk some sense into her," that none of this would have happened had he lived. I was never sure of that, but I felt her blended grief and fear like a sword inside me. I had no idea what to do when she called me frantically to report what Martha was up to in college, and felt completely inept at influencing my strong-willed sister. Mostly I was sad for my mother, and felt just as I had as a child, annoyed and guilty that I could not take away her pain.

The tension came to a head one summer afternoon in 1975 when Martha arrived at the new apartment Bill and I had in eastern Connecticut. He'd finished law school a few months before and taken a position in a small-town practice in Putnam. My head was filled with finding a job, meeting the community, and being the wife of the new young lawyer in town whom everyone wanted to meet.

But I was delighted she was coming and sensed she had big news to share. She'd come to tell me that she and Herb were serious and thinking about marriage. "He's shorter than I am," she said wryly, and we giggled like teenagers, "but he's so smart, and so determined, and God, he makes me laugh." *This was what I missed*, I thought, what I noticed other girls sharing over the phone in college. It felt good.

Then she saw the papers on my coffee table, articles she had sent weeks before.

"So, what did you think?" she began.

"I haven't finished them," I admitted. "I haven't had time."

Suddenly she was furious. "Dammit, this is important. Don't you care what is happening in the world?"

"Look, Martha, it's not my world, this political stuff. And frankly, some of it seems pretty nuts to me. Sometimes I feel like you're getting brainwashed with some theories I don't read about anywhere else."

"You witch!" she screamed.

We both froze, shocked and silent. This broke all the rules: all the Irish family rules of respect, suppression of anger, and avoidance of conflict. Neither one of us knew what to do next. We retreated into polite silence for the rest of the visit.

Though I could not have verbalized it then, I think we struck a deal in that silence. I would watch, and support when I could, and love my sister if not her choices. She would focus on what we did share and leave her politics at the doorstep. Most of the time it worked. I watched a lot. I watched her move to Germany for two years, after getting married in 1980, to work with organized labor. I watched her join a radical labor party here in the States, whose views seemed a mix of paranoia and politics that made no sense to me. Once, I watched her get led away in handcuffs on the nightly news.

I wondered if Martha and Herb might forgo having children, if politics might be their life. But, as she approached her thirties, the desire to have a family was growing. I could feel it in her more frequent phone calls as my own children arrived. Martha wanted to know every detail, every funny story. The politics that had kept us so far apart in our twenties was gradually supplanted by what we had in common: the desire to be a mom.

Martha was in her mid-thirties when they decided to have a child. She was forty-three when Liamarie was born. Nine years of trying and failing. Nine years of miscarriages and pregnancies that disappeared at ultrasound, absorbed somehow into nothingness. Nine years that included one episode of gestational trophoblastic disease, a rare and unusual circumstance in which pregnancy produces a tumor in the uterus.

"It's rarely malignant," she told me on the phone. "I'll just need a D and C and we can try again."

But hers was malignant, and that meant "chemo-light," as she called it. A car picked her up at noon from her job as a paralegal at a large D.C., law firm, took her to GW University Hospital where she read while the IV flowed. By 2:00 p.m. she was back at her desk.

Nothing dissuaded her, and while they kept trying to conceive, they also began adoption applications. "We want five kids, a houseful!" Herb would say with characteristic exaggeration while I rolled my eyes and Martha grinned. "I mean, at least five!"

When Liamarie arrived in May of 1994, I traveled to Virginia with Margaret, then a first grader, to help and to celebrate. Herb was exploding with pride and found a way to insert the words "my daughter" into every sentence until he had us laughing hysterically. He prowled the house trying to catch every event, every expression, with his camera.

"My daughter is having her diaper changed." *Click.*

"Did you see that? See, my daughter smiled!" *Click.*

When he left to get more pictures printed, I found Martha sitting quietly with Liamarie in her arms, looking at her in wonder. "I never knew," she said, "I really never knew."

....

Martha went to her death with the same determined spirit, the same driven intensity that gave her that moment. Martha never changed. That is not true for the rest of us. It is not true for me, or Herb or Liamarie, or the others who lived through her illness and survived her death. We are all changed.

I believe that we need two bookends. The one we start with and the one at the other end of trauma. The second is embedded with seeds of the first, but is never exactly the same. It's some new version, some transformed self that comes after life has beaten you down. And whether it's nearly a mirror-image or unrecognizable, you need to know its strength. You need to understand how it will bear the weight. You need to figure out how it can hold your life together.

Chapter 5

The Numbers

It was a cold January afternoon, less than a month after that Christmas photo was taken, that I answered Martha's phone call, standing in my kitchen.

Her voice was strained, frightened, anxious. "I have a tumor," she said. "I'm at the surgeon's office, and I don't like her expression. She just did a needle biopsy . . . without anesthesia."

"What—when—you can't be serious," I said.

"Oh, I'm serious," she went on. "I found a lump and saw my OB an hour ago. She called a surgeon in the same building, and she worked me in. I'm telling you I don't like her expression."

After we hung up I stood in my kitchen, staring at the phone, still in my hand. *This can't be happening to her. Not now. Not again.* I was angry. Raw, purple anger. I remember thinking: *This should be mine. If there is any fairness in the world, this should be mine.*

A week after that surgeon's visit, lab reports confirmed her suspicions. The results were stark. Martha's tumor was malignant and very large. I took this call sitting at my office desk. "Of course, they want to do a mastectomy right away," she said, "and then after that, we'll talk about the rest." She was not crying, but her voice was flat and discouraged.

"What can I do?" I asked helplessly. "Is there anything?"

"There is one thing," she replied. "Could you tell Mom? I don't think I can get through that."

"Of course, I'll go over there tonight." Then I said something I no longer remember, something to give permission to the sadness. "What brings me to tears is the adoption," she said. "This will destroy our chances to adopt."

The response startled me at first, but as soon as she said it, I knew that it was true.

They had just reactivated their adoption request with the Colombian agency that had offered them a toddler the same month Liamarie was born. The timing then was terrible. They knew that a three-month stay was the minimum required to satisfy Colombia's adoption requirements. Three months in a country with limited medical care and facilities. No matter how much they wanted another child, it was not a risk they were willing to take with a newborn baby. So, they passed up the opportunity to adopt a two-year-old boy with dark hair and eyes. Herb couldn't resist looking at the folder and seeing the child they were letting go. Martha couldn't bear to open the envelope. "Vincenzo," she had whispered to me then. Vincent. It was our father's name.

....

I went to Virginia in mid-February when Martha had her mastectomy. Liamarie was excited about my visit and too young to worry about the "bad spot" the doctors were getting rid of for Mama. She paraded me proudly into her day care and explained the locker setup with care. "Now the juice has to go on this shelf, and my lunch box goes on this side."

In the midst of my own anxiety, I was grateful that Liamarie and I had an easy bond. Perhaps it was because I was there so early in her life, or simply that she was an open and extroverted child. But after her last visit to Maine, she had told Martha, "Guess what, Mama? I have another mother."

"Oh *no*, Liamarie, you *do*?

Liamarie grinned at her mother's distress.

"Don't worry, Mama. It's OK, it's Mary Beth."

We fell quickly into a routine. I dropped her at day care, visited Martha, and then picked her up to join Herb for dinner. Each night, after we read *Bambi*, her favorite story, she dragged out the choice of a second book as long as she could. Then she gave me my instructions. "You have to lie down on the bed with me 'cause my mama is not here."

It was not until the third night that the tears finally came. Even then she tried to spare my feelings. "Mary Beth, I love you very much," she sobbed, "but I want my mama to come home."

....

Martha called them "the numbers." It was a dismissive term, usually spoken with mild annoyance and irritation. "You just have to get past the numbers," she said, "and get on with what you need to do next." Perhaps that was her way of coping as her numbers were revealed. They were seldom positive, more often discouraging and scary if you stayed long with their implications.

"Seven positive lymph nodes out of seventeen," the lab report came back after the surgery. That was the first set of numbers. Then a few weeks later, the full pathology report. The cell analysis typing and staging all read like a recipe for disaster. In almost every category, she had the result that was more highly correlated with recurrence. Her tumor was very large, and aggressive.

We were stunned. How could a tumor two inches long have been missed on her last mammogram, only six months earlier? It had to have been there. The radiologists reviewed that mammogram and found nothing.

I wrote quickly on the small notepad on my kitchen table when she called just after her meeting with the oncology team at Fairfax Hospital. She was businesslike, and I could tell she was reading from her notes.

"They're calling it a very aggressive disease. I've got a six out of nine Elston score. That's how they grade these things, and that means a high probability that it could spread. It's hormone-negative and that's not good; there's cell structure stuff, and chemical analysis."

"Wait, you're going too fast," I started to say, but she talked right over me.

"My cell structure is unorganized, not what you want," she went on. "And the DNA analysis is what gives me the Elston score." She started to read me some chemical terms—anemploid, diploid—but I had stopped writing. "Well, the bottom line is I've got the ones correlated with a higher rate of recurrence and a likelihood of spread. Not all, but most. The tumor is Stage III, N1, M0 . . . The N1 means it has spread to the nodes, and M0 means they haven't found it anywhere else. Without treatment, my odds of recurrence are 80 percent."

We were both silent for a moment. I turned to a new page on the notepad.

"So they want me to do two rounds of chemo, one they called the 'bad stuff,' followed by regular chemo, then radiation. And then, after that, he said we'll talk about a bone marrow transplant."

"A bone marrow transplant?" I asked incredulously.

"Yeah, some new program at Johns Hopkins. I can't think about that now—maybe if I have a recurrence, I don't know. Look, I've got to get out of here and organize these notes so I can do some research," she said. "I'll call you later."

I hung up the phone and looked down at the notes I had taken. My tiny handwriting filled the page, but all I could see then were the two dark underlines I'd put beneath that number, 80 percent, and the black inked loon at the top of the notepad looking back at me.

I could hear Matt's footsteps taking the stairs by twos as he came up from his room. I folded the sheets into my palm, then once again neatly, and tucked them into my jeans pocket. Matt came around the corner and saw the expression on my face. "Are you OK, Mom?"

"Uh-huh," I mumbled, and turned away.

Chapter 6

Decisions

≫≫≫≫≫≫≫≫≫

"So what do you think I should do about my hair?"

"What do you mean?"

"With Liamarie. I think it might scare her when it starts falling out."

Martha's surgical recovery had gone well, and chemo was about to begin. She had returned to her usual proactive action mode. "You're the psychologist. How do you think she'll react?"

I flashed suddenly on the day I picked up then two-year-old Justin at day care at UConn, when I was doing my doctoral work. Between classes, I'd gotten a new short haircut. Justin looked confused and angry, then began to shriek, "Not my mom, not my mom, not my mom," until I took his face in my hands and soothed him with my voice.

"Well, she's almost three. She'll probably be fine if it's falling out gradually, but you definitely should prepare her. She'll take her cues from you. If she sees you're upset about it, she's more likely to be."

"I think I'm going to shave it before chemo starts. I'll tell her the medicine will make it fall out, and I don't want the mess. That will make sense to her."

The control will be good for both of you, I thought.

I waited for the phone call later that night to see how the conversation had gone.

"Well," Martha said, "it didn't go the way I expected. I told her I was going to let the hairdresser shave my head. I explained about the medicine. She was pretty calm, and asked me a couple of questions, like would it grow back, and would it be the same color. Then she said, 'OK, Mama, me too!' Now, she's mad at me. She thinks it's not fair that I get to shave my head and I won't let her."

A few days later Martha called again, after the hairdresser visit was over.

"How did she react when she saw you?" I asked.

"She made me laugh," Martha said. "She ran her hand back and forth over my scalp and announced. 'You are a ball, and I am going to bounce you!'"

As Martha's chemo began in early March, here in Maine we'd gotten our own bad news. Bill's mother's cancer had returned, and this time the surgeon was gentle but clear. He would do one final surgery, but it would not stop the disease. This was the last intervention.

Peggy's surgery was more complicated than expected, and she was hospitalized for weeks this time, before being discharged to a nursing home. Caring for her meant I could not help Martha as she went through her chemotherapy. She relied on her wide circle of friends, who adored her and were happy to provide rides, childcare, and whatever else she needed. We spoke almost every day.

"This is the year from hell, you think?" she joked.

"You bet," I said. "But it's got to get better."

"Not yet, I'm afraid. Herb's got to go to Las Vegas. They want him to set up a new operation out there. So he'll be back and forth for a while."

"Las Vegas? How's that going to work?"

"We'll just have to make it work. And anyway, it's only temporary."

"But while you are doing chemotherapy?"

"Look, it is what it is," she said. A familiar phrase I'd heard her use over and over since her diagnosis. "It is what it is," she said impatiently to anyone who complained.

"I wish I could be there."

"Well, I've got friends who offer to do things I wouldn't even ask family to do," she replied. "I'm pretty lucky there. How is Peggy?"

"Hanging on. Just hanging on."

....

That spring, Herb's trips to Las Vegas became more frequent, and, by late April, they could see the handwriting on the wall. "They promised him when he took this job that the company was not moving." Martha said one night. "But it's not looking good."

"You mean you might have to move?"

"I mean his job might be in Las Vegas permanently. And I'm in the middle of chemo. We can't move. Besides, I'm still fighting to get my hospital bills paid. We certainly can't change insurance companies now."

From the beginning of her cancer diagnosis, Martha's experience with insurance had been a nightmare. Though her surgery was immediately approved, payments to her doctors and hospital were delayed for months. She began getting requests from the insurance company demanding "lists of all doctor, nurse, and physician assistant appointments," along with "reasons, prescriptions, and diagnoses" from August 1996 to February 1997. She could not understand why they wanted records that pre-dated and had nothing to do with her breast cancer, but they were insistent that nothing would be paid until they were received. Initially, they refused to explain, but after some pressure, they admitted they were trying to cancel her coverage on the basis of a preexisting condition. Any preexisting condition.

"Isn't there a law against that?" I asked.

"Yeah," she answered. "It's supposed to let you move from one policy to another without all this hassle when you change jobs, but it doesn't go into effect until next January. They keep telling me until then they're entitled to investigate."

"So what do they think they'll find?" I was still confused. "Do they think you delayed getting treatment for breast cancer?

"No, my coverage never lapsed; it just transferred when Herb changed jobs. What they're looking for is an excuse, anything I forgot to report on the application, anything they can use to say the application was 'not truthful' and therefore fraudulent."

From February to May she cooperated, sending what they requested. When she called to check on progress, agents professed ignorance. On numerous occasions, she was put on hold in the middle of the call and transferred to an unidentified voice mail extension: "This is extension 2467, please leave a message." She called it the black hole.

In June, with no bills paid, she received a new request for the same information. She was furious, and tired of apologizing to her doctors. She filed a claim with the Attorney General's office and the Virginia Bureau of Insurance, asking them to investigate the company's actions. They intervened, and her claim was settled, her bills paid in full. The process brought out the crusader in her. "How can people who are *really* sick deal with this? I have the energy and the knowledge to fight them, but what about those who have neither?" She was appalled at the insensitivity and inefficiency of it all.

So when Herb's company finally confirmed that the executive offices were moving to Las Vegas, insurance was the first thing on Martha's mind. There was no way she was going to risk another insurance change. He had to go.

So, in the spring of 1997, Herb relocated to Las Vegas, bought a condo in the small neighboring town of Henderson, and never missed a beat in his job. Martha became a single parent of a three-year-old back in Virginia, coordinating chemotherapy with child care. Every third week, she flew with her daughter to Las Vegas. "There's chemo week, then exhaustion week, then a week when I have a bit of energy. I'm going to go out on those weeks and set up the condo. I don't know how long we'll stay there, but for now it's home, and after my treatment is over, I'll recuperate out there."

"Great" I said, trying to be positive. "I've never been to Las Vegas, so we'll come out when you're done. I'm curious to see it."

"It's faux city, faux . . . faux . . . faux . . . not a thing on the strip is real. It's just awful. I swear when God decides to turn this place to salt, the light on the Luxor Hotel will be there to guide his aim."

....

As chemotherapy progressed, Martha's treatment team at Fairfax Hospital began talking to her more and more about the transplant program at Johns Hopkins.

"Just getting in is a long process," Martha told me one night. "My cancer has to be bad enough for the insurance company to decide it's a good bet I'll have recurrences that will cost them more later on if they don't pay for this. That's the actuarial part. Then, once they say yes, I'd have to go through a bunch of tests at Johns Hopkins so the transplant team is convinced I'm healthy enough to get through it."

"So, you're considering it?"

"I'm just going to take it one step at a time."

My own days were full: seeing people in my office or teaching residents at Maine Medical Center, and then stopping at the nursing home to visit my mother-in-law before heading to a soccer game or to take my turn at the carpool. By early May, the doctors told us Peggy's time was limited. "Three, maybe four weeks, I expect. You can visit anytime." She'd been moved once again, to a place only ten minutes from home, so Bill stopped on his way home each night, and I tried to visit earlier in the day.

I was often tired, but Peggy's greeting always cheered me. "Oh, you've come so far. Did you take the ferry?" At first I tried to orient her, to remind her she was not on Prince Edward Island, on the farm where she was raised. But the gentle hills of the island soon captured me too, and I'd settle in and describe the red earth, the potato fields, and the patchwork green farmland rolling down to the ocean, the images we both loved so well.

Martha phoned each evening, and I looked forward to the call, taking it in my bedroom. The kids did homework, and I had some time with my sister. On good days she was excited, talking about the condo and the process of decorating and making peace with a move there. On more somber days, we went back in time and opened topics we had never explored. She spoke about what it was like to be at home with my mother after my father died. She was only a junior in high school, that day when he left for work, collapsed with a cerebral hemorrhage at a luncheon meeting, and was gone by 9:00 P.M.

"I remember thinking I will never let myself be so dependent on another human being," she said one night. I thought guiltily that Ed and I had the freedom to go back to college, and just our own loss to navigate. She was the one at home, with only a teenager's ability to make sense of my mother's overwhelming grief.

"Were you mad at us for leaving?" I asked.

"No, it just was what it was. I was the one there."

She spoke about how much it had meant to her that I had called and sent packages when she spent a month in jail during her protest days for what was, for her, a matter of principle and a decision to protect others from prosecution.

"But you did nothing wrong," I argued at the time.

"I know," she said, "but I can do this, and if it will close the case, I should."

We talked about so many things, but always ended with her concerns about Liamarie. She worried that her chemo-fatigue and low energy were frightening Liamarie, and that her early images of her mother would always be tarnished. "These years are so important," she said. "I want to be a good role model for her, but some days I just can't."

"Look, you can't worry about that now."

"I let her sleep in with me yesterday. I was just so exhausted, afraid I'd fall asleep first and not hear her if she woke. It's not right."

"It's what needs to be right now. Better she is with you and feels safe. We can fix that later."

Our relationship grew in those months, and I felt closer to her than ever before. All the differences of personality and politics were submerged by the realities of life and death, holding on and letting go, that were playing themselves out in our lives.

....

It was a very hot week, just before the Fourth of July, when Martha came to visit.

My three children and I stood in the kitchen to greet them, and she led the parade, dropping luggage and tote bags on the floor and reaching enthusiastically to hug each of the kids. Herb and Liamarie followed just behind. She set the tone in one movement, reaching up and pulling off her short auburn wig to reveal a completely bald head. "There, let's get that over with," she announced, and the kids were momentarily stunned. "It's going to be too hot all week for me to be wearing that thing." Herb and Liamarie burst out laughing, and the tension was gone.

Since her mastectomy, Martha had undergone twelve cycles of chemotherapy: four of what her doctors called "the bad stuff," Adriamycin, followed by eight rounds of CMF, the more standard recipe of three drugs they described as "a breeze by comparison." When she came to visit, she was lobbying her treatment team to move up her radiation, overlapping it with the last few chemo rounds, so that she could head to Las Vegas and some late-summer freedom with her family.

To look at her, you would hardly know what she had been through. She was slender, much thinner than usual, but she celebrated that by wearing skinny jeans and tank tops, and taunting me a bit. "Hey, you've got to get something good out of this, right?" From the moment of her dramatic entry, I could see the relief on my children's faces. She was still strong; she moved fast; she gave orders to anyone who'd listen. Martha was OK.

Herb took over the kitchen on nights we didn't grill, and whipped up dinner with ease. Martha and I scoured the Freeport outlets looking for bargains. That year, we had a special task: trying to find something smaller than the size 2 underpants that slid down over Liamarie's hips. "I like my princess panties, Mama, but you need to get some that will stay up!" she complained.

And, as always, Maine worked its own magic: the clear, black star-filled skies, the wind through the hemlocks playing solo accompaniment to evening's rest. Martha and Herb slept deeply, woke late in the morning, and slowed their usual city pace. On the night of the Fourth, we headed out to see the fireworks. Stepping into the breezeway, Liamarie on her hip, Martha looked up to see a doe standing just outside on the patio, not four feet away.

"It's Bambi," she whispered to Liamarie.

Liamarie froze, delighted, and whispered back, "Where is Faline?"

"I don't see her," Martha said quietly.

Liamarie scanned the yard. "I think she's in the thicket," she whispered.

....

Later that week Martha and I sat on the patio out back, and she broached the subject of her treatment. "I could quit here. After this radiation, if my cancer is gone, I could just say that's it. But they still want me to consider a transplant. I guess I'm a pretty good candidate."

She had brought a folder full of materials, articles about ongoing transplant studies and the protocol of the procedure at Johns Hopkins. We looked at some of them together. "I'd be part of a research program, a phase II study, she explained. "The phase II studies try variations of the protocol, different drug combinations, or different dosages, to see what works best. But the truth is they still aren't sure the whole transplant thing works. There have been some good results in other countries, but some of the US results are not so great. They don't know yet, really."

I listened and tried not to take a side. "You've done a lot already," I said hesitantly.

"But they'll never know if it works, if people like me don't volunteer," she replied. "And what if my cancer comes back, and I said no to this? Will I be able to live with myself if I didn't at least try?" We both knew the answer to that question, and I said nothing. She sat quietly, her wide-brimmed hat covering her bald head and shielding her face so I could not see her expression.

"I'm so sick of reading about five-year survival rates. That's all they talk about in the damn numbers conversations. It's so frustrating. Five years is nothing. I need twenty. I need twenty years to raise Liamarie."

A few weeks later, she had her first interview with the transplant team at Johns Hopkins. It was preliminary, a chance for her to get her questions answered about the procedure. "Well, they're certainly not trying to sell me," she said sarcastically when she called me afterward to report. "I was hoping they'd be more encouraging, try to convince me to do it." But instead the dialogue was stark:

Will this improve my odds of long-term survival?
We don't know yet; preliminary studies are positive.

What are the dangers of the transplant itself?
Major organ failure, which can be fatal.

Is there anything that predicts that? Age, overall heath, whatever?
No.

What is the survival rate for the procedure?
95 percent nationwide, 98 percent here at Johns Hopkins.

When Martha was first diagnosed, the mention of a transplant had shocked us both. We associated transplants with last-ditch efforts, final extraordinary measures taken for those who would otherwise surely die. But this was different. The transplant her doctors were recommending was no last-ditch effort. It was, instead, a final step in her treatment, a step they hoped would prevent recurrence of her cancer.

It would be an autologous transplant, using Martha's own bone marrow, not marrow from another donor. The marrow is taken by leukapheresis, a procedure that separates stem cells from her blood. These stem cells would be treated and stored while she underwent high-dose chemotherapy. This would kill both cancerous and normal cells, including the remaining stem cells in her bone marrow. Finally, she would be reinfused with the harvested stem cells to reconstitute the marrow, replenish white blood cells, and slowly reestablish the immune system.

This was not a pleasant procedure. It had many side effects, and patients were isolated to reduce their risks while the immune system was fragile.

The phase II clinical study at Johns Hopkins was designed to see whether this stem cell transplant procedure would increase long-term survival rates for patients with high-risk primary tumors when it was done as part of the initial treatment plan, before any recurrence. The study also included a second treatment regimen, immediately following the transplant, in which graft-versus-host disease was induced with the drugs gamma interferon and cyclosporine A. This powerful immune reaction, it was hoped, would kill any remaining tumor cells in her marrow.

We talked about this all through the summer.

She read everything, did her own research, and came to her own conclusions. "They know how to treat the initial tumor," she said one night, "but not the recurrence. If this thing comes back, the odds are against me." The odds were already not great. After surgery, chemo, and radiation, her chances of recurrence were still 40 to 50 percent. Eight months of aggressive treatment just to get to fifty-fifty odds.

Again and again she came back to one statement. "I need twenty years, not five. I need twenty years to raise Liamarie." In the end, that would be the only number that mattered.

So, that late August night when Martha called and began with the simple words, "I think I'm going to do it. I think I have to," I was relieved. Relieved that the debate was over, relieved that her decision was made, relieved that she was willing to do one more thing that might keep her alive.

And though we had not talked about it before this, as soon as she added, "I need you to take Liamarie if you can," there was no need to consider. It made perfect sense for Liamarie to come to Maine. There was no support system in Las Vegas, no day care, no familiar faces, no one to be family while Herb worked. So that too was an easy answer, and in giving it, I was relieved again.

Finally, I was able to do something to help.

Chapter 7

Fall

>>>>>>>>>>>>>>>

To participate in the transplant study at Johns Hopkins, three things were necessary. First, the tumor had to be aggressive enough that recurrence was both likely and potentially lethal. Second, conventional treatment had to have successfully removed all traces of the tumor. Finally, a thorough medical screening was required to rule out any other underlying conditions that might make the transplant procedure too risky.

"So there's a whole list of tests I have to go through. MRIs, bone scans, kidney screenings, that kind of stuff," she told me one evening in September. "It will be weeks before I know. But we got insurance clearance to start anyway."

I knew they had just overcome another unexpected hurdle. After moving to Las Vegas, Herb's company had changed insurers. The new insurance company had to review and agree to the transplant. As an executive, Herb was in on all the meetings, and made sure Martha's situation was addressed. Yes, they would continue her coverage. Yes, they would cover a bone marrow transplant done at one of five "centers of excellence" which met their approval. Yes, Johns Hopkins was one of these. And yes, they would put it all in writing. We all breathed a sigh of relief.

"So what is Hopkins looking for?"

"Well, signs of recurrence, of course. If that's already happened, they'll reject me. But mostly it's other stuff—kidney, heart problems, anything we don't know about that might make me a bad risk."

I wondered how it felt to have everything about your body examined so closely. Are you worthy of being saved? Are you a good enough specimen for us to invest in? I didn't say any of that.

Martha's attitude was different. Now that she had approval, she saw it as her job to pass all the screenings. They were "just hoops I have to jump through," and she went through the process as though determination alone could dictate the results. We talked most nights, but she spoke mostly about logistics: getting rides for herself when the test required it, getting rides for Liamarie when she could not get back in time to pick her up.

"I'm going to owe my friends big time when this is over. Every time they switch a test time, I'm on the phone changing schedules."

The hospital would not give Martha an admission date until she had passed all the tests, but as each result came back positive, I began to relax. Then, one night, her voice was different.

"There's something on my lung scan. They're having someone else look at it. It might be nothing."

I could feel the rumblings underneath. *They can't stop this now. They can't take this chance away from her.* Having the transplant had become the goal, and I felt the shift. The transplant now meant recovery. With it she will be well. Without it? I knew this was emotion, not fact, but it was powerful nonetheless. If they took this chance away from her, I wasn't sure we could ever go back to believing that the conventional treatment she'd had would be enough. We didn't talk about it, but we both felt it. A few days later, the results were in.

"It's just a little scarring," she reported, "probably from my smoking days, but anyway they said it should be fine. No reason to cancel." I could hear the relief in her voice. "Next week I'll go in for the leukopheresis and some outpatient preliminary stuff, and then it looks like I'll be admitted November 4."

....

The day before Martha was to drive up for the first of the leukopheresis procedures, we spoke on the phone at about 4:00 P.M.

"Are you ready for this?" I asked.

"Yeah, I think so. Pheresis is pretty easy, and I'm hoping they can get enough stem cells that way. Sometimes, after all the treatment I've had, the numbers drop too low. If that happens, they'll have to go in and do a bone marrow harvest. I'd like to avoid that if I can. But you know, I actually feel like I've won something here. I'm kind of excited."

I laughed. "Yeah, you won alright . . . the chance to get your immune system destroyed, then brought back to life again. Congratulations!" But we were both laughing by then.

"Well, I'm heading to bed early," she said. "I've got to be at Hopkins at 6:00 A.M."

Just before 9:00 P.M. she called again.

"What's up?" I asked, thinking she had some last minute question.

"They just called me. They've withdrawn approval."

"What? Who?" I asked, dumbfounded. "The hospital?"

"No, the insurance company's central office in California. A secretary just called. She says the medical director has decided that the transplant is not medically necessary. And get this, it's 5:30 P.M. there, so he's left for the day, and, 'unavailable to discuss it with me.'"

"The night before the procedure is to begin?" I screamed. "They can't be serious! There is a special level in hell for these guys, I swear."

"Yeah, Dante would have described it in detail if he'd known about managed care. But right now I've got to figure out what to do."

"What can you do? Did you call Hopkins?"

"Yes, but they can't advocate; it's up to me."

"What will you do?"

"I don't know, but I know one thing. I'm going to fight."

Martha went into action mode, faxing the central office every document, every x-ray, every report she had, papering their offices for the next few days. Several exhausting days later, they reversed themselves again. The procedure was approved.

In the meantime, however, all her dates had to be redrafted at Hopkins. Operating room time, scarce and precious, had to be rebooked in case a bone marrow harvest was necessary, admission dates dropped back, and all her plans for support services reworked. Now her schedule took her right into the holidays. The hope that she would be over the transplant itself by Christmas was gone. In fact, as the hospital printed out the new itinerary, it showed she would enter the hospital in mid-November and her stem cell reinfusion would take place Christmas Eve.

Is it cynical of me to believe this was the insurance company's ploy to see if she would back away from the procedure? I don't think so. Insurers thrive on tactics of delay and denial, knowing that—facts aside—a certain number of people will simply give up, go away, or die in the face of the frustration. Some will be too sick to fight. Those who are ambivalent may take the refusal as a sign that they are not meant to proceed. Some percentage will inevitably have their disease progress beyond the point where the procedure is possible or safe. Many will not know how to fight, will not have the intelligence or the stamina or the resources to persist. And all of these sad facts, every single one of them, saves them money and increases their profits.

To those who feel I am too harsh, I offer this: Not one piece of data, not one report, review, test result, or lab study Martha faxed to them in the days following her refusal was new. Every page was already in their files. The only piece of data they didn't have was whether they could intimidate this patient into giving up.

....

Halloween afternoon I stood in the kitchen with Margaret who, at ten and a half, was within an inch of my height. I braided her long, dark hair, and the tips of the braids, tied with white grosgrain bows, fell to her waist. With her clear blue eyes, she was the spitting image of Judy Garland, dressed in Dorothy's blue and white checked pinafore from *The Wizard of Oz*. We had difficulty finding shoes in her size, but scoured the thrift shops until we found some red leather kitten heels she could just manage to balance. I covered them with glue and sprinkled them with red glitter. She was leaving a trail of red sparkles as she skipped through the kitchen, and we made final touches to her costume.

Just then the phone rang. It was the nursing home. Peggy had passed away, quietly and comfortably, just a few moments earlier, with a nurse and hospice volunteer at her side.

"There was no time to call, no warning," the nurse explained. "She just left us."

Her funeral on Wednesday, November 7, was in Natick, Massachusetts, where Bill had grown up. It was good to see his two brothers and to grieve together, but my gratitude that day was not just for the end of Peggy's suffering. It was for more selfish reasons. Martha was bringing Liamarie to Maine later that week.

Martha had done a good job preparing Liamarie for her time in Maine. "Papa has to work in Las Vegas, and I need to go to the hospital for a few weeks. So you will stay with Mary Beth and Bill in Maine." At first Liamarie resisted in her usual self-assured way. "No, Mama, I don't think I will do that. I will stay with you." But slowly, gradually, Martha convinced her that this was the best plan.

"But I will miss you," Liamarie said.

"I will miss you too, but when this is done I will be *all done* with the doctor stuff, and then we can be together all the time."

"Will Margaret and Matt and Justin be there?"

"Not Justin, he's back at college. But Matt and Margaret will be."

"But I want Justin to reach me to the sky!" She had finally made friends with her big cousin over the summer when he swooped her up over his head so she could touch the ceiling beams. Over and over, she approached, leaning against his leg, asking, "Can we do it again?" and squealing with delight each time she flew.

Martha laughed. "Well, maybe when he comes home for Thanksgiving."

My children were prepped to make Liamarie feel welcome, and she quickly caught their excitement. Matt and Margaret took her downstairs to the playroom while Martha and I talked. The big futon in the playroom doubled as a guest bed.

"She can sleep with you downstairs while you are here, but I'll move her up to Margaret's room when you go," I suggested.

"That should work. She really wants to sleep with Margaret, you know."

"I know. And that should help with the transition. I'll put a cot in there, and since it's just down the hall, I will hear her if she gets up."

Martha was looking down now. "I am so grateful ..." she began. "Don't be silly," I interrupted, "this is going to be fun!"

....

I tried to arrange my office schedule for the next few days so that Martha and Liamarie had the house to themselves. Martha had brought along a set of ballet videos, professional performances of *The Nutcracker, Swan Lake*, and a few others. Liamarie loved these, and when I came down from the office, I found Martha resting on the couch, and Liamarie swirling around the family room. "Watch me, Mama, watch me dance!"

Three days later we rode to the airport, and Liamarie gave her mother a big kiss.

"Have fun," Martha said as she hugged her.

"You have fun too, Mama."

Late the next afternoon, Martha called again. "My blood count is too low. They want me to wait a week." She was annoyed. "I guess it's not uncommon after the pheresis, but it was OK before that. What do you think I should do? I hate to move Liamarie now that she's settled in."

"Come back," I said. "It'll just be a week." So she flew back to Maine.

But the next week, the results had only improved a little, still not high enough to begin. The hospital counseled patience. "Give it some time," they said, "and you'll get there. We don't want to start you until the count is where it should be."

So again she flew back to Maine. This became a pattern: Martha spending a few days at a time here with her daughter and flying back to Baltimore at the end of each week for the blood work, assuming each time that the transplant would begin. The process was frustrating. The magic number of white cells was 2000. Although they had been up to 2700 before the pheresis, they dropped sharply after that, and each week was a disappointment: 1500, 1700, climbing but never making the cutoff. Finally, I called Peggy's oncologist, who agreed to do the blood work here in Maine so that Martha could avoid the costly flights back and forth. All through November and December this continued. The tension was rising. It was difficult to be patient and relaxed, to enjoy another "Mama visit" with Liamarie when we all felt like horses in the starting gate waiting for the gun to fire, waiting for the race to begin.

Finally, it was Christmas again. *So different from last year*, I thought. Peggy was not with us, and her absence was palpable, but the tension of Martha's upcoming transplant superseded that. Herb flew out from Las Vegas, and Martha ordered a huge Virginia ham and a dwarf hemlock for our garden. "Something green," she said, "to remind us of spring when this will all be over."

Christmas night, after all the gifts were opened, Martha and Herb prepared to leave. They were taking a few days together in Virginia before he headed back to Las Vegas. Her blood counts were almost there now, and climbing, so we all thought this was it, the last time we'd be together before the transplant. Liamarie and Margaret snuggled, watching television on the couch. The kisses and hugs were longer and more emotional for the adults, but for Liamarie it was just another of "Mama's visits" that was coming to an end, and she was reluctant to be interrupted. I noticed Margaret taking in the scene and hugging her little cousin.

That night Liamarie slept like a baby. When I heard crying and ran the short distance down the hall, it was Margaret, sobbing in her bed. I gathered her up, and we went down to the family room. She was up all night, vomiting and sobbing, struggling to put into words the sadness, fear, and loss she was feeling for her little cousin. She had just turned eleven, and she knew how long a month was, had some sense of how serious a transplant was. "It's so sad, Mumma," she sobbed in my arms. "It's so sad. I couldn't be away from you so long. How can she do it, Mumma?" I rocked and held her for hours, until the light began to rise in the window.

Caught between childhood and adolescence, feeling her cousin's pain but unable to distance herself from it, Margaret's place was unique. This was going to be especially hard for her. I tried to reassure her that Liamarie was blessed with ignorance, that time and distance and what her mother was experiencing were not real for her. She knew only that her mama was going to the hospital for a while, and she would be having an adventure with us. "The best thing we can do is to help her feel safe and loved. I know you can help me do that," I whispered over and over.

Martha was with us one more time. She had her blood drawn in South Portland on January 2. After two weeks of holiday break, we were hoping for a good result. But when she came out, her face was drawn. "They're still down. I knew they would be." We were silent all the way home. I wondered how long the team would let this continue, postponing and postponing her admission. We did not have to wait long to find out. When the team got the results, they called her. I watched her take the call in my kitchen, her face intent and concerned. It was Monday afternoon.

"They want me to fly back tomorrow and meet with the team on Wednesday," she said as she hung up the phone. "The nurse won't tell me what Dr. Kennedy is thinking. Just says they want to talk about it." All evening she practiced her arguments with me. "If not now, why not try again in a month? If he says never, I'm going to fight it. It *can't* be never. That makes no sense."

When she called after the Wednesday meeting, I could hear the relief in her voice. "We're going ahead. More tests tomorrow and I'll be admitted on Friday."

She was so upbeat I hated to ask. "What about the counts?"

"Close enough. He thinks it will be fine."

Section II

Bonding

There is something that you must always remember, you are braver than you believe, stronger than you seem, and smarter than you think.

—Christopher Robin to Winnie the Pooh
A. A. Milne

Chapter 8

Attachment

❯❯❯❯❯❯❯❯❯❯❯

"I'm disappeared," Liamarie ran into my bedroom, hid behind the low rack of jackets in the eaves closet, or squeezed into the small space between Bill's dresser and the wall. I heard her giggling. Then, in a stage whisper, "What's that word again?"

"Reappeared," I whispered back from just outside the door. And out she popped, arms outstretched, delighted with her magic. "I'm reappeared!"

A child therapy supervisor warned me once: Never do anything with a three-year-old that you are not willing to do at least five hundred times. Repetition, repetition, repetition. That is the work of learning and processing emotions in this age group. Liamarie loved this game. People disappear and reappear. Though I knew it was pretty typical preschool play, I sensed it had meaning on a deeper level. Now that her mother's transplant process had begun, there would be no more visits. Martha was in isolation, and only Herb was allowed the occasional face-to-face visit. But she had a phone right by her bed, and most days she answered it on the first or second ring. Always her first question was about Liamarie.

"Look," I told Martha, "she's doing fine. It's pretty amazing with all you've been through this past year. But I don't really see a lot to worry about." I knew Martha needed this reassurance, wanted to hear that her daughter had not been damaged by the illness and all it had taken from their lives, but I meant it. "My job is to send her back to you as emotionally healthy as she was when she came," I said one afternoon. I would remember those words time and again, in the months and years to come, when Liamarie's big brown eyes looked up at me for answers.

Missing is a different experience for young children. It is not an ever-present reality, an awareness of absence that looms like a shadow, coloring every moment, as it is for adults. Children focus on the now, their attention absorbed by its immediacy. Unless the need for Mom or the expectation of Mom's presence occurs, they can be unaware of missing her when occupied and happy.

Three-year-olds also have little internalized visual or verbal memory. So, it is not the thought or picture of Mom that brings feelings of separation and sadness. Rather, sensory memory rules, and sensation triggers loss. A hurt, a fall, or the feeling of crawling into bed, associated with a mother's warm touch—all these bring out the craving for Mom.

So it was for Liamarie. She felt safe and happy during the day and rarely talked about missing her mom. It was usually at bedtime or when she was tired that we heard, "I miss my mom." As her body wound down and needed comfort and closeness, the pull for her mother was there. At first I suggested phone calls, but these were rarely soothing.

"Hi, Mama, I love you and I miss you, want to talk to your sister?" she'd say in one long breath and hand me the phone. I tried coaching her ahead of time, reminding her of songs or day care projects she might share, but she rarely wanted to talk more than a few seconds. I knew these were precious calls for Martha, who never tired of Liamarie's voice.

When Martha called, it was the same. Liamarie was unlikely to jump up, reluctant to be interrupted if she was having fun. Loneliness at three is very self-focused. If I am feeling it, I want soothing. If I am not, I do not want to be pulled into it or forced to acknowledge it. "I'm watching *Mary Poppins* . . . don't bother me," was a not-uncommon reply. And though I could feel Martha's disappointment, she understood.

"It's OK, don't make her come. If she's OK, I'm OK."

Words have little power to soothe at three. Words soothe because they generate internal images and calming feelings associated with those images. For adults, the familiar cadence of a loved one's voice brings not only the mind's eye picture of the beloved but also sensations of safety or relaxation or affection. These are fragile at three, just beginning to be formed. The voice on the phone is familiar but not always soothing. Without the ability to see and touch, phone calls can be overstimulating, disruptive, and unsettling.

Remember the emotional language of preschoolers, I reminded myself. It is about touch and holding and presence. And language itself is less about words, and more about rhythm and cadence, and tones that signal comfort, safety, and love. When Liamarie was lonely, she wanted soothing, but it needed to be in the moment. She needed to be hugged or snuggled. She needed arms around her and a calm voice reading a familiar book or singing a lullaby. Fortunately, we had lots of arms willing to do that, and her cousins were old enough to be a part of the team.

The days went well. She adjusted to First Step, the day care that opened its doors and found room for her the minute I explained the situation. It was just a few miles away in the center of the village. Margaret had attended from age two through kindergarten, and I knew almost all the staff, who were kind, loving, and nurturing. Liamarie loved the idea that her big cousin Margaret had gone there, and when we visited, she oriented herself by asking Jackie, the director, "Was Margaret in this room, and this room? Did Margaret play with this dress-up box?" Jackie remembered Margaret more than most, because her own daughter and Margaret had been best friends in their preschool days. So she had lots of stories to tell Liamarie about when her cousin was here, what she had liked, and what she'd played with. It all helped to make Liamarie feel this was just another extension of her Maine home and family. I trusted Jackie to keep a special eye on Liamarie and communicate any signs of stress she saw.

Liamarie made friends easily and came home chattering about "the sames and the differents" between this day care and the one in Virginia. She didn't resist going or question that she had to go to "school," just like Margaret and Matt, so Bill and I could work. The familiarity of a group setting was reassuring, one of the things unchanged in her routine, and that was good.

Within the first few days at day care, Liamarie confided to her teacher, "I'm here because my mama's in the hospital in Virginia." When she was asked how it felt, she answered calmly, "I miss her, but it's OK, because Mary Beth and Margaret are taking care of me."

I watched her negotiate the attachment. She emptied her backpack at the end of the day, pulling out the picture she had made in school to show me. Then she paused, deciding whether it was for her mom, for herself to bring home to Virginia, or for me. Often her answer was, "It's for me and my mom," as though she needed to reinforce their connection, their togetherness. Sometimes the pictures could go on my refrigerator, but the ones for her mom we kept in a special folder, safe for the future.

One afternoon, another child at day care was crying, missing his mother. Liamarie comforted him and said, reassuringly, "I know. I miss Mary Beth, too." It was only natural that, in that setting, I was the "mom" to be missed, the one who dropped off and picked up at the end of the day, the one whose hugs were most recently felt. I never told Martha that story, afraid she might feel hurt, or feel Liamarie's adjustment was too good. I knew that was not true. She was a healthy child who knew she needed mothering and was able to accept it in the moment. There was no doubt she would want her real mom back when Martha was well.

Bedtime was a bit more challenging. I promised Martha that I would try to shape Liamarie's sleep pattern, but I expected it to be a challenge. There was no doubt Liamarie's energy, her high-strung nature, and her "can't miss anything" personality contributed to the problem of her settling down at night. But the real problem was that, in the past six months, Martha, too exhausted to do otherwise, had broken all the rules. With Herb gone to Las Vegas for long stretches, Martha was a single parent going through her second round of chemotherapy, with radiation on top of that. By evening she had no energy for a fight. Sometimes it was a matter of safety. Letting Liamarie sleep with her meant that she would not resist the bedtime process, would not roam if her mother fell asleep first. So after a few unsuccessful tries at getting Liamarie into her own bed, Martha would give in and give up. Bedtime lost its meaning, and this three-year-old was often still up at 10:00 or 11:00 P.M.

Some days were spent in bed as well, snuggling with her daughter, reading books, playing simple games among the bedclothes. Sometimes this was all the energy Martha could summon in the face of global fatigue and nausea that she tried to hide from Liamarie. Bed became their playground, a place of interaction, not a place where you go to turn off your energy and rest.

All the cues we attach to sleep behavior—quiet sounds, soft lights, low stimulation—are there to teach the child's nervous system how to turn itself down gradually. The gentle rituals of bedtime create a pathway for the brain to learn to quiet itself, to lower alertness and reduce attention. Before this is learned, babies sometimes have to cry themselves to sleep, to exhaust themselves by turning up the central nervous system to full alert until it collapses and shuts down to sleep. Slowly, gradually, with the rituals of holding and rocking and singing lullabies, we teach our infants the cues that signal their neurology to let go into sleep deliberately, gently, in response to the touch of soft bedclothes, the lowering of the lights, the closing of your eyes.

I knew that making bed their playground went against all of this, but there was no way I was going to challenge what was happening. Whenever we spoke, I could feel in Martha's voice such a mix of emotion—sadness that this was Liamarie's experience of her mother, determination to parent with structure, fear that Liamarie might be damaged by her lack of energy and by the constant reminders that "Mama is sick."

More than anything, I could see her pull back from conflict whenever it could be avoided. *I don't want you to remember your childhood like this . . . I don't want you to remember me like this*, her expression said silently. It came too close to the fear we avoided addressing, so we did not speak about it.

Instead, she confessed, "I've just given in. I'm being a poor parent."

"No, you're not," I insisted. "We can fix bedtime later. Right now it is more important that her time with you is comfortable and as normal as you can make it. That's the best way to keep her emotionally intact through all of this." We both believed that whatever disciplinary price she paid for that could be recovered later. There was always later. For now, just get through the best you can.

As soon as Liamarie arrived, I began to shape her schedule. Because she could not tell time, bedtime was whenever we announced it, whenever we drew the bath, gathered the books, and signaled the beginning of the process. Initially, I waited until 10:00 P.M. to begin, looking for signs of fatigue that would lessen her resistance. Gradually working the time back by fifteen minutes every night or two, we had her in bed between 8:00 and 8:30 in a few weeks.

The ritual involved one or two stories, then a series of songs I sang, lying on Margaret's bed until Liamarie went off to sleep on the cot next to me. I went back to all the old favorites I had sung to my own children: "Sing a Song of Sixpence," "Oh What a Beautiful Morning," "I've Been Working on the Railroad," "She'll Be Coming Round the Mountain When She Comes," "Row, Row, Row Your Boat," and always, at the end, the Irish lullaby, "Too-Ra-Loo-Ra-Loo-Ra," that my own mother had sung to us as children. They had to be sung in the same order each night, and she corrected me if I got it wrong. "Can you sing another one?" she'd ask, and I found the series getting longer and longer until I realized she was using it to stay awake. So I let myself finish the songs and begin deep, slow breathing, lying still and not responding to the whispered, "Mary Beth, Mary Beth, are you awake?" Soothed by my quiet breathing, she would usually fall asleep within a few minutes.

The familiar, the known, the predictable is so much a part of what is soothing, and I watched her body relax as we went through the ritual. Initially I tried duplicating things I had heard her do with her mom, but I quickly realized this was overstimulating and too painful. She wanted soothing, she wanted ritual, but it needed to be different enough that it did not always trigger thoughts of Mom and feelings of separation. So we created our own. The tape that Martha had made, a recording of Liamarie's favorite stories in her mother's voice, was put aside. I found a children's book of ballet stories, and it became a bedtime favorite. I climbed under the covers with her, and let her pick one or two each night. *The Nutcracker*, *Swan Lake*, she loved them all, but *Coppelia* was her favorite. The story of the wooden doll that comes to life was hard for her to follow, with its subterfuge and trickery, but she laughed and asked over and over again how Swanhilda made the wooden doll dance. And often, as her eyes began to close, an arm floated gently up over the covers in a graceful arc.

Chapter 9

Negotiating Family

﹥﹥﹥﹥﹥﹥﹥﹥﹥﹥﹥

"Supercalifragilisticexpialidocious. If you say it loud enough it's something quite atrocious."

I could hear Margaret's voice singing with the CD the moment I opened the door from my office and began to walk across the garage.

And Liamarie, laughing and trying to imitate. "Do it again, do it again. Supercaxi . . . Oh no!"

In a week, she had that mastered and pleaded to put *Mary Poppins* on the sound system at full blast whenever Margaret was home. Margaret was usually happy to oblige, and they sang and danced around the family room until they both collapsed. Margaret was clearly Liamarie's favorite; she was still young enough at eleven to play a few rounds of Memory or Chutes and Ladders with enthusiasm. For Margaret, it was a chance to play board games, even if they were not ones she would have chosen, and she was glad to have someone not too big or too busy to play. But there was another side to this. I could see the look shift on Margaret's face when she was tired or just needed to be alone. She did not know how to extricate herself, did not know how to say "no." The change in Margaret's life was the largest, I realized with some concern: a little sister sharing her room, a younger child suddenly taking our attention and wanting hers endlessly as well. And the crushing look on Liamarie's face when Margaret headed out the door with friends left them both miserable.

Negotiating a relationship with Matt was a bit more difficult.

Matt was harder to catch. At fifteen and a half, he was on his high school soccer team and in a band, and his frenetic comings and goings initially confused her.

"Where he going now? Why he leaving again? What he doing?" she asked in amazement. The facts never seemed to satisfy. Finally, I said, "He's a teenager, Liamarie," an explanation I offered with a shoulder shrug that implied this was a mysterious state that could not be understood. She adopted that gesture and phrase with a mix of awe and annoyance, as she watched him run in, grab his athletic bag or his guitar, and head out the door within seconds. "He's a teenager. There he goes again."

But when Matt was home, she descended quietly to his room, on its own mid-level between the first floor and the basement. She opened the door cautiously and peeked in.

"It's Victoria Picklebottom!" he announced when he saw her, and she pretended outrage.

"No, I'm not. I'm Liamarie!"

"Oh, you're not Victoria Picklebottom? Are you sure? Now, what's your name again?"

"I'm Liamarie; you know that, I'm Liamarie!"

It was their own little ritual that signaled she was welcome to enter his kingdom. Later, I'd find her sitting on his bed, saucer-eyed, giant headphones swallowing her head as she listened to him play on his keyboard.

She toyed with making herself a Plouffe, adding our name to hers, and telling me, "There are six people in this family . . . you have two boys and two girls." She switched to calling my children her brothers and sisters, and I always agreed, supporting her right to adopt us as her own. This was not about learning relationships. It was about feeling safe, feeling she belonged, feeling she was loved and cared for. And in that way she was right . . . we were a family of six, and I had four children.

Justin was back in college, a senior by then, and we were used to his not being home. Liamarie seemed to find his absence distressing and reassuring at the same time.

"Why he lives there?" she asked. "Why you let him go?"

But again, it was not the facts she wanted. How could he be my son and be living away from me? Sons are supposed to be with their parents. How could we be without him, and was he happy being so far away? These were the questions she really needed answered.

"I have a brother named Matt, and a sister named Margaret . . . *and* I have a big brother named Justin, and *he* lives at Princeton," she repeated regularly as she embedded herself in our family. Perhaps it helped to know that others, too, live far away from those they love, and that they are still family.

Liamarie's connection with Bill was a bit more gradual. He is more reserved than her dad, quieter and harder to read. So she watched him, always willing to accept his offers to play, but clearly negotiating his calmer style. He did not push, but waited for her to come to him. One morning as he left for work, she asked, "Can I give you a hug?"

"Oh, Liamarie, I would love that. I just love hugs," he answered and gathered her up, swinging her from side to side. After he left, she snuggled up to me with a question. "Does he like kisses too?"

In time their special connection revolved around pizza. In our family, Bill is the only one who can eat cheese. The rest of us have a sensitivity that makes eating cheese lead almost instantly to nausea and vomiting. Even the smell can leave us feeling ill, so Bill is reduced to eating the occasional pizza by himself, preferably at the other end of the house.

Now he had a pal. Once a week, he came home from work and called, "Where's my pizza buddy?" And she would come running.

"Come on, Liamarie, they don't know what they're missing."

"They're missing *pizza*, but I'm not!"

She'd come home riding on his shoulders, squealing with delight at being "up so high . . . higher than my papa!"

With each of us, she found a way to attach, a way to connect and feel loved.

I watched her closely for signs of stress, and restricted eating was one. She was a tiny child with a tiny appetite, but her food intake concerned me. I conceded to the occasional trip to McDonalds to encourage her. She sat in a booster seat, thrilled with her McNugget Happy Meal, chatting away with anyone who passed. One night a stranger asked, "Are you visiting for the weekend?"

"Nope," she piped up before we could answer, "I'm here because my mama is in the hospital and Papa's in Las Vegas *again!*" The poor woman's face fell, and she rushed away embarrassed, while we sat laughing hysterically and trying to explain to Liamarie why her dramatic comment was so funny.

This is one resilient child.

I soothed myself with that thought in the early weeks of her visit.

She's resilient, she's attaching to all of us, and her development is not disrupted by all of this. It's just continuing in a different environment for a little while.

Chapter 10

The Ice Storm

>>>>>>>>>>>>>>>

If you ask anyone in Maine about January 1998, they answer automatically, "Oh yes, the ice storm."

Snow and ice don't faze us here in Maine. We move around them in our lives, and move them around our landscape with a comfort and competence that is impressive. The neighbor who plows my driveway heaps the snow up near my office entrance. Some years the pile is fifteen or twenty feet high, and Bill has to carve the walkway path from a mountain that looms over it, creating a tunnel in the deepest of February weather. When out-of-staters complain, we respond with a quizzical look. "This is Maine. This is winter. What did you expect?"

But January 1998 was different. Like our personal Hurricane Katrina, the ice storm of 1998 broke all the rules. For more than a week, steady freezing rain fell over eastern Ontario, northern New York State, and northern New England. High winds and the weight of ice felled millions of trees. Power lines were decimated for miles; not only were the wires destroyed, but the poles and transoms and beams that supported transmission lines were tossed like sticks on the ground. Cars in parking lots became coated with ice so thick it was impossible to free them. Seven hundred thousand of Maine's 1.2 million people were without power for days, many for weeks. Crews from all over the country were dispatched to rebuild transmission lines and clear damage, a process that took months after the storm was over.

The initial predictions seemed hard to believe, and as they

increased in intensity, I chose to ignore them. We were on the southern end of all of this, I reasoned. The worst of the storm was north of us, and even as the reports became increasingly dire, I refused to be concerned. We often lose power for a day or two, but with woodstoves for backup heat, we usually hunker down and stay put until it is restored. Besides, I was too preoccupied to pay much attention to the warnings. We had a more important agenda. Martha had finally been admitted to Johns Hopkins, and the transplant was about to begin.

We lost our power on Thursday, day four of the storm, but still made no plans to leave the house. Early Friday morning Martha called. "I thought you were in surgery?" I said. That was the day of the bone marrow harvest. Her pheresis had not produced enough stem cells, and they were going into bone to gather more. If the harvest didn't yield enough stem cells, the transplant would be canceled. It was the last hurdle.

"I'm in the OR waiting room," she replied, "and I'm watching the TV on the wall. They just said Maine is having the biggest storm of the century! Are you guys OK?"

Damn, she does not need to be worried about this. "We're fine," I insisted. "I'll call you later today to hear the results. Don't worry about us."

But at 2:00 P.M. the phone lines went dead. Losing phone coverage was rare, and that really got my attention. The extent of the storm was becoming clearer, and I realized that we could be far down on the repair list for Central Maine Power Company. There was no telling when we would get power again.

I was able to reach Bill at work. "Find me a hotel room. We need a phone. Martha doesn't need to be worried about us while she's going through this," I said. But as he went down the list of hotel chains, the answer was the same. Hotels were already booked from Brunswick to the New Hampshire border. Finally, he tried the Harraseeket Inn, a lovely but expensive hotel here in Freeport. Yes, they had room and a special power-outage rate for locals.

There was something eerie about the next five days. We were cramped in one room, but it was elegant and luxurious. A mahogany bar and four-poster bed were the centerpiece, but cots for three kids filled the rest of the space. Bill and Matt ventured out each day across treacherous roads to feed the fire at home so we would avoid frozen pipes, while Liamarie, Margaret, and I enjoyed the indoor pool or hung out in the elegant wood paneled lobby, where a six-foot, stuffed polar bear sat at the grand piano, paws on the keys, as if waiting for the conductor's baton. We listened to radio reports each day detailing the extensive damage and the efforts of repair crews from all over the country heading north to help. Schools were closed; businesses were closed. Outside looked like a wasteland—trees down, darkness except for the main street of Freeport where L.L.Bean's presence seemed to reassure us all that we would get through this. "Open 24 Hours a Day, 365 Days a Year," the sign on the door said. And it was.

Liamarie adjusted to this change with typical three-year-old aplomb. "Why we have no less-trickety?" she asked, but happily accepted the cramped quarters at the inn. *This child would have loved a big family,* I recall thinking, as she reveled in having us all around her, sharing one room.

We walked to church, just a few doors down from the hotel, that Sunday morning. The heat was out, so the congregation was small and shivering through the quick Mass. A friend stopped me as we exited. "How are you holding up?" she asked.

"Oh we're fine. Hanging out at the Harraseeket Inn."

"Lucky you," she replied.

Bill swooped Liamarie up on his shoulders to speed the walk back.

"You love being up there, don't you? Up higher than your papa." I repeated Liamarie's description as she rode.

"Wait, wait . . . Bill, kneel down," she said suddenly.

"Do you want to get off?" he asked.

"No! But I have to tell Mary Beth a secret. Just kneel down."

Bill's strong hiker's legs crouched so she could lean over to me and whisper. "I am *way* higher than my papa," she said. "Papa is short . . ." then quickly, "but don't tell him!"

"OK," I whispered back. "It's our secret."

We were back at home for a few days when the weather hit again, knocking out power and sending us back to the Harraseeket Inn where Liamarie, perched on the registration counter, charmed a lobby full of guests and staff with her booming announcement: "We're here 'cause we have no less-trickety *again!*"

I realize now that the craziness of the external world helped us counter the days of the transplant itself. While Martha began the high-dose chemotherapy regimen, we were in winter survival mode, when simple tasks became complicated and filled most of our days and nights. There was not a lot of time to reflect on what was happening in the transplant room in Baltimore. Getting to the grocery store, keeping the woodstove fed, adjusting the children's schedules filled all the available time. My own practice was on hold, as my office had no heat, and I had no other place to see people. Phone calls kept me in touch with those who might be in trouble. External stressors like this consolidate strengths in some, distracting them from their difficulties. For others, the effect is the opposite, and fragile coping skills can be stressed beyond their breaking point. Keeping on top of my practice in the midst of this chaos was one more juggling ball in the air.

Bill and I took the three kids up to the Sunday River ski resort for our twenty-sixth wedding anniversary weekend in mid-January. But even there, the effects of the storm were evident. The hotel was functioning on auxiliary power, services were limited, and the sense of being in the grip of winter weather was evident. We left Matt babysitting in the room to steal a quick anniversary dinner downstairs in the elegant main dining room. Mid-meal, the power failed, and, for an instant, we were sitting in the dark. An eerie yellowish light appeared from emergency lamps along the wall, and cast an unappetizing tint on our food.

"The kids will be scared. Let's go," I said, and we left quickly, following ghostly gray-green lighting up the back staircase, feeling our way back to the room.

While my children had mixed feelings about the disruption of their schedules that lasted through most of January, Liamarie seemed to take it all in stride. By the end of the month, she'd begun asking, "What hotel are we going to this weekend?" She seemed genuinely disappointed when the answer was "none."

For me, the month flew by. Martha's procedure was going smoothly. Herb flew in from Las Vegas when he could and was the only one allowed any level of visitation while the transplant was in process. I did not worry, or wonder, or carry much anxiety from day to day. Martha was doing her part; I was doing mine. That was, I thought, all we needed.

Toward the end of January, I spoke with Martha about Liamarie.

"She's asking when she will go home, more and more now. I think she needs a date."

"I can't really be sure. Once I finish the inpatient part, I have to do the second phase. I want to do it from home if they'll let me, so I can commute. I bought a plane ticket for her that's dated February 14. I thought maybe I could move it up if I got home sooner, but that might actually not be too far off."

"I don't think it matters when it is, just that she knows it's real. The 14th sounds good to me. I'll call and book myself on that flight when things are more certain."

Long-distance time has no meaning at three. The future is a vague and open construct, next month no different from "when I grow up" in the mind of a very young child. What does matter is the certainty, the guarantee, the security of knowing that something important will happen, that the adults who are taking care of you will make it happen.

So we gave her the date: February 14, Valentine's Day. We believed it was the furthest date possible, and since it had a big heart on our kitchen wall calendar, Liamarie was happy we picked it for her "going home day."

"I'm going home on the one-four day," Liamarie announced every morning as the winter progressed. We circled it on the calendar, and it reassured her to stand on a kitchen chair, touch the number and remind herself that the visit had an end.

In early February, we decided it was a good date. Martha would be discharged on the 7th or 8th, have a week at home while she commuted to the Johns Hopkins outpatient department to begin phase two of the treatment, then hopefully be ready for Liamarie to return for good. But when I called to book my ticket on the same flight, there were no seats left. We had to change our tickets to the 15th. Liamarie was not happy. "Why not the one-four day? Why do I have to go on the one-five day now?" she argued. She listened to my explanations, but the look on her face said *don't do this again.*

Chapter 11

February 1998

>>>>>>>>>>>>

February began so well. The transplant was going smoothly. Our calls, once or twice a day, found Martha cheerily answering her own phone. Only the slight softening of her voice betrayed the process she was enduring. "It's doable," was her phrase for it all. "It's not that bad."

When I thought her treatment would happen before Christmas, I had wrapped individual ornaments, each with a funny limerick attached, for her to open when she needed her spirits lifted. There was the angel whose hair was just Martha's color, and the teasing poem that suggested it might be grey when this was over and it grew back. There was the chubby angel, telling her to enjoy the temporary skinniness that was making her big sister jealous. And the miniature Steinbach nutcracker to remind her of the one she'd brought me back from Germany.

"You're making me pretty popular around here. The nurses all want to come in to see what I opened and read the poem. You're pretty good at this."

"Yeah, I might consider a career at Hallmark after this is over. Do you think they have a satire division?"

Some days her mouth was sore from side effects, and her voice would catch with a quick pain, but she didn't like talking about it. When I prodded she said, "Yeah, the side effects stink. It's pretty much what they said it would be, but it's OK, really, I can do this. So tell me what my brilliant daughter did today."

Later, I learned that her dismissal of the side effects was

not just courage, but truth. She "sailed through the transplant," in the words of the nurses who attended her last month. This was always said with a hollow echo of wonder in their voices, as they watched her dying.

I felt closer to Martha during this month than ever before. I knew intuitively what she needed to hear when we talked. She knew she could say anything, and I would be there to listen. So in the familiar language of intimacy, silence was more soothing than words. Just hearing each other's breath or sitting with a simple thought brought us both comfort. One afternoon she completed forms for a study the social work department was conducting. "They asked me if I wanted someone to talk to," she said, "but I told them I was all set. I've got you."

Turning the calendar to February was a celebration in our house. Liamarie climbed on the kitchen chair at breakfast and pointed at her "going home" day with excitement. "It's on the *now* page, not the *next* page!" She loved looking up and seeing that red heart with big circles around it. We were all relieved that the end was in sight.

Liamarie's adjustment to us had, not surprisingly, been easier than our adjustment to having her here. The constant energy, the need for attention that comes with being three and a half was not always easy to accept. The novelty had worn off for my children, and been replaced with an unspoken wish to return to their own lives and agendas.

It had been especially hard on Margaret. Liamarie was in her room, in her toys, in her bed . . . . She'd have been in her back pocket if she could. I alerted Dr. Sue, our pediatrician, when I brought Margaret in for a checkup. "Can you talk with her? I think she's really struggling."

Dr. Sue was direct. "Margaret, having a three-year-old in your home is like being nibbled to death by ducklings. But the good thing is they're indestructible. Just tell her 'no' and she'll bounce back and find someone else to play with or something else to do." Margaret looked doubtful. The first part made sense. She knew the feeling of nibble, nibble every few seconds. But she never quite believed the indestructible part. "Mumma, I don't want to be mean," she said to me on the way home. I could see her caught, closest in age, identifying more with Liamarie's reality than any of us could.

Early in the visit she came to me quietly to say, "I'm not going to make it, Mumma." I hugged her and tried to reassure. But by February she knew she would. She knew the worst was over and the end was in sight. And we were all so proud of her efforts. In spite of the strain, she never made Liamarie feel she was unwelcome. Margaret had grown up a lot in the process.

Liamarie was showing some signs of stress herself. Once the transplant began, there were no "Mama visits," and the support those occasional breaks had provided was gone.

"But when is she coming for a visit?"

"She can't right now, but when she's done, you'll get to go home and be with her all the time." For adults the beginning implies the end. The process soothes and reassures. Not so for children.

"But why can't she see me now? She came before. Why the doctors won't let her? I want to see her *now*." The psychologist in me knew better, but I kept trying to use words to reassure. She could respond to my tone, but at three and a half, she wanted what she wanted, and she wanted this to be over.

There were other signs of stress as well. Her sleep was more disturbed. It was rare that she made it through the night without waking. Margaret tried to soothe her, but it was an adult Liamarie needed; only my presence—holding her, rocking her—would finally let her relax enough to rest. We moved Margaret to Justin's room so she could sleep through the night. I slept in Margaret's bed to be close when Liamarie awoke. And the ritual of songs, the already long list, grew as her tension increased. I knew all the verses of "Oh What a Beautiful Morning" and by now so did she. No matter how exhausted she was, if I skipped one, she would whisper, eyes closed, "statues," or "music" to signal me not to forget. Over and over, the same rituals, both of us tiring with the effort. One night she stopped me, opening her eyes and turning her face to me after I sang the simple verse:

Sing a song of sixpence, a pocket full of rye,
Four and twenty blackbirds baked in a pie
When the pie was opened the birds began to sing
Now wasn't that a tasty dish to set before the king.

"What's the next part?" she asked.

"I'm not sure. I think there are more verses, but that's the only one I know."

"But what does it mean?"

"I don't know, love, but I bet the king was surprised."

"Maybe the blackbirds were too," she said quietly.

························

Liamarie's behavior at day care held, but in early February I began to see changes at home. She was a strong-willed child but rarely had tantrums. Occasionally, she stopped us with an only child's fury that we had decided something without consulting her. "Get in the car; I'll explain there," is the mantra of large families, and she was not used to it. "*Wait!*" she yelled, "*I want to know why!*" Fortunately, when she got the respect she needed, she complied. She was not inherently oppositional and rarely fell apart over nothing. So the day she blew up over the Jell-O was a signal for me.

Liamarie hated Jell-O, did not like its "squiggly-ness," and would not try it, even though her cousins approved. She did, however, like the color green better than any other color. The afternoon I made red Jell-O, the floodgates opened. For almost a half-hour she ranted at me. "*I want green, not red! You know I like green, green, green—not red, green! Why did you make it red?*" she screamed, flailing her arms and racing around the kitchen. All my best efforts to soothe her were for naught. The anger in her voice made it clear. It was time. She needed to go home.

She wasn't the only one. February's arrival also meant the end of Martha's inpatient treatment. Reinfusion of the stem cells had gone well, side effects were receding, and her patience was wearing thin. She wanted as early a discharge as possible and pushed to set a date. On February 5 she had a low-grade fever. It had to be normal for twenty-four hours before they'd let her go. We spoke that afternoon.

"I'm going to put ice cubes on my head," she joked. "I have to get out of here."

Herb was coming home from Las Vegas on Saturday, February 8, but when her doctor suggested she might leave Friday, she jumped at the chance. A close friend was willing to pick her up and stay overnight until Herb arrived. "I can't wait to sleep in my own bed. I'm going as soon as they let me."

She was discharged on Friday, February 7. Phase two of the treatment was still ahead of her, but she was going home, finally going home.

She has survived the worst of this, I thought.

Chapter 12

I Love You

>>>>>>>>>>>>

It was Sunday morning. There was the brief ritual resistance from the kids about church and my ritual response, "Yes, we're going; you're going; let's go." The phone rang just as we headed out the door. Matt picked it up and handed it to me quickly. "It's Martha, and she doesn't sound too good."

"I'm at the Reston ER. Last night was horrible. I was up coughing all night, and my fever is 102. They want me to go back to Johns Hopkins." This last part was the hardest for her to say, and her voice was flat, devastated, hollow with disappointment.

"Then go," I said, trying to be calm. "Do what they advise. They know how to deal with this at Hopkins." My voice got firm, and I could feel myself go into big sister mode. "It's OK, we can deal with this. Just go and get well." There was a long silence.

"I love you," she said. I wanted to scream. *Don't tell me you love me; don't say anything that sounds like goodbye. Don't even think we need to do that right now.*

"Just go and get well," I said quickly.

Later that afternoon I went up to my bedroom and called Johns Hopkins. Herb put her on the phone. She was breathing with difficulty and gasped her report of the plans for testing the next day.

"Lavage of lungs . . . see what's causing the infection." Her breathing was uneven.

"Don't talk," I interrupted. "Herb can tell me later."

I tried to distract her with some story about Liamarie, but her breathing suddenly worsened. I could hear her gasping and stopped. "Do you need to rest?"

"Yes. I better get off the phone," she panted.

This time I said it. "I love you."

I lay on my bed for a while, fighting the panic.

Oh God, don't let this be what we both fear it is at this moment.

Chapter 13

ARDS

≫≫≫≫≫≫≫≫≫≫

Adult Respiratory Distress Syndrome. It doesn't sound so intimidating. Distress is something temporary, like stomach acid after a hot chili or anxiety about a late airline flight. You don't die from "distress"; you get over it, or it resolves itself over time.

Syndrome is a familiar word to me as well, though not quite so benign. In medical terms it refers to a condition rather than a disease process, a set of symptoms that go together to present a clinical picture. The implication is that we do not know much about one of two essential questions: what causes it and how to treat it. Sometimes the first is known, as in the case of genetic syndromes related to chromosome damage. We know what causes them, but until recently, genetic damage has been considered irreparable.

Sometimes we know nothing about etiology, and "syndrome" is a convenient way of describing a set of symptoms that occur together as a group. Labeling it seems to make it more manageable, but this is often deceptive. When we don't know why something occurs, treatment is at best a trial and error process. If you are lucky, science has invested in that process and produced some answers. Often, however, they are partial answers with less than ideal outcomes. In graduate school I learned to be cautious when I read the word "syndrome." For me it came to mean a condition that we probably know little about and can't really fix.

This simplistic definition certainly fits ARDS. It can occur suddenly, after an accident or shock. It can occur with pneumonia or other respiratory illness preceding it. But it can also occur in otherwise healthy lungs. It can occur in the elderly or severely ill patient with multi-symptom organ failure, or in a young healthy twenty-year-old brought in to the ER with fractures from an automobile accident. It does not happen alone, like a heart attack. Some shock to the system precedes it, setting the stage for the body to flip a switch that turns it on. It doesn't give warning of its arrival, however, and when that switch is thrown, the body is in a struggle for survival.

Unlike respiratory infection, which fills the lungs, blocking their efficiency, ARDS is an assault on the lung tissue itself, the fibrous material that must expand, absorb, and hold the air we breathe to extract oxygen from it. When ARDS hits, the lungs "bleed out," losing their absorbency, rigidifying and calcifying so that they cannot inflate and deflate. The body cannot get the oxygen it needs to survive.

The information about the recovery process is equally disturbing. Sometimes it heals, and the lungs repair themselves. Sometimes there is permanent lung damage. Often it is fatal. We know very little about how to predict which cases will heal, which will not. There are few guidelines to tell us, and almost no landmarks to watch for as you move ahead.

This is what happened to Martha, suddenly and without warning, on Monday, February 9. Sitting in her bed at Johns Hopkins, with Herb at her side, Martha's lungs went into ARDS. There would be no lavage of the lungs, as planned for later in the day; no methodical series of tests to determine what had spiked such a high fever. Suddenly at 2:00 P.M., she turned blue, and before Herb could get out of his chair, the team descended.

Chapter 14

The Injury

〉〉〉〉〉〉〉〉〉〉〉〉〉

Herb's voice on my answering machine Monday terrified me. "Call me as soon as you can. Things are not good. I need to fill you in." When I reached him, I could hear the tension in his voice, but he was controlled and trying to be positive.

He began with the good news. "Her white cell count is rising, her platelets are good, so the transplant is taking. But Dr. Kennedy says she's got explosive galloping pneumonia. It's completely invaded her lungs. She can't breathe on her own, so they've sedated her and put her on a vent. Dr. Kennedy says she's very unstable right now. He's only seen a couple of cases like this, with total organ failure of the lungs, and they need to find out what the infection is first. It could be viral or bacterial; they just don't know. They're going to treat her for everything.

"Please be ready to come right away," Herb continued. "If I need to make a decision about life support, I cannot do that alone. I need your help."

I called Bill from the car, as I headed to day care to pick up Liamarie. All I could say was, "Come home now, it's bad." I rode to the day care center, rocking in my seat and pleading in a sing-song voice, "Don't let her die, don't let her die, don't let her die."

The next day the news was better. "She's less stressed, and the ventilator is down to 40 percent oxygen. They're going to try to wean her from the vent and see if she can breathe on her own. They want to use a SIMV system, so she can start to take some breaths along with the vent. It's like training wheels for her to get back to breathing on her own," Herb explained. This was all new to me, and I took notes on my office pad, next to appointment cancellations and referrals.

In every call over the next few days, Herb told me her oxygen level, what antibiotic they were trying, and what tests they hoped to perform when they could get her off the vent. This was not his usual manner, this businesslike executive report, but I found it reassuring. I wanted to believe it meant things were under control and secure. But I could not get those words out of my mind: total organ failure of the lungs. And then I remembered. I'd read that phrase before in the materials Martha had brought this summer.

It was on the list of potentially fatal side effects.

I began to learn the language of pulmonary disease. The oxygen level pumped in by the ventilator changed from hour to hour and we began to define "progress" in percentiles. "She was at 70 percent oxygen this morning, only 60 percent tonight . . . that's good. They'll wean her from the vent in a day or two as the percentiles go down," Herb reported.

SIMV stands for Synchronized Intermittent Mandatory Ventilation, a system that allows a patient to begin taking spontaneous breaths through a valve, while also receiving mandatory breaths from the machine. Her oxygen demand had to be below 50 percent for her to begin the weaning process.

At first Herb was focused on her sedation. When she crashed and was put on life support, she had to be heavily sedated. He was desperate to communicate with her, to connect and know that she understood what was happening.

"I just want to talk with her and let her know we'll get through this."

Most of all he wanted her guidance about Liamarie. Should she come home as planned on February 15? Should we leave her in Maine? Did she want to see her? "I just need to talk with her," he repeated again and again, and I could hear the pain in his voice. So each day, the doctors would try to lighten her sedation, to see if Martha would wake. But each time they tried, her vital signs became unstable. Her blood pressure dropped, her oxygen levels peaked. It was too dangerous, the doctors told him. After a few days, they stopped trying.

For the next few days, the news was mixed. All the diagnostic tests were coming back negative, the identity of the infection no clearer. But she was holding her own, and the doctors told Herb that they were still "working toward a full recovery." I wrote those words down and read them over and over to myself. The stress of so many medications was pressuring her kidneys, so diuretics were added. Each report seemed to contain some good news and some bad. One test came back midweek, and Herb called to say, "It's not some wild and crazy terrorist virus" they thought it might be, but her kidneys were worse and they might have to do dialysis. Up and down, good news and bad. Her condition seemed so fragile, and it was hard to read between the lines of all the facts to understand what they meant for the future.

Then Friday, he called again. This time there was no pretense of good news. "Her oxygen level is up to 80 percent. Her lung x-ray looks worse. The team is meeting at 5:30 P.M., and they want me there."

I could feel the fear in his voice.

I knew I needed to see Martha for myself, to put some real pictures and emotions to the percentages and status reports. I needed to get my own reading on what the prognosis was. And now Herb wanted me to come, and to bring Liamarie. Whatever was ahead, he knew he needed to reconnect with his daughter, and soon. "I've been away so much. I need her to feel secure with me. I need you to bring her home."

I flew in with Liamarie on Sunday night. It was bitter cold and spitting rain. Herb looked exhausted when we arrived at the house. He had been at the hospital all day. He took over putting Liamarie to bed, and I left to head up to Johns Hopkins. George, a good friend of Martha's who had worked with her for years, was there to drive me. The look on his face said more than I wanted to know. He was quiet and spoke very little on the way up. Yes, he'd gone up with Herb earlier this week. No, things did not sound good. We sat in silence for the long rainy trip up the highway from Herndon to Baltimore. Finally, the exit. He took a wrong turn at the end of the ramp, and for a few minutes we found ourselves lost in the inner city neighborhood. "I'm sorry," he mumbled.

Just get me there, I thought, impatiently, *just get me there.*

That night as I walked into the transplant unit for the first time, I was hoping for something to reassure me, to give me some reason to be positive. I am comfortable in hospitals, have worked in them for years, and read their subtle signals well. As I walked briskly down the long corridor toward her room, I noticed two things. First, the silence from the nurses. No one approached me as I headed toward her room. No one greeted me or stepped forward. Then, "It's her sister," I heard one whisper.

I looked over at the nurses' station and saw their expressions just before I stepped through her doorway. And for a second I thought, *You are in a movie.* They had that look, that braced and hardened look the actors get when the script reads, "We'd better go talk to the family."

There were no doctors there that night, no one to break the tension as I entered Martha's room. I thought I knew what I would see, and I did not expect to be squeamish. I'd seen many patients on vents, and the machines were familiar equipment to me. In a veterans hospital clinical placement years before, I had learned to mask my reactions to open war wounds on the legs of young soldiers, and to stifle the horror one feels seeing a nineteen-year-old newly quadriplegic man in a halo cast and rotating bed. So I turned the corner into room 360 without hesitation.

But this. This was nothing like what I expected. Martha was not sedated, not by any definition I knew. No quiet, deep sleep, muscles relaxed and pain erased by unconsciousness. She was thrashing in slow motion.

They had tied her arms and hands to the side rails, but her legs were unrestrained. She pulled them up, bending her knees one at a time, lifting one leg over the side rail as the top half of her body continued to roll, her head arching and weaving slow circles in rhythm with her limbs. Her face was contorted, and her head and shoulders pulled forward then sank back. The straining, pulling motion repeated itself, legs climbing over the side rails, head rotating back, over and over as I watched in horror. It was a slow-motion video of someone writhing in pain. The expressions, the movements were all there, caricatured, like a mime performing for an audience. And there was no sound . . . no voice . . . no moan . . . no whimper . . . nothing to tell me she was in there and trying to communicate.

I said nothing, but the words flooding my brain were *athetoid movement, chorieform movement*. Brain damage. I'd seen this movement pattern before when I worked with patients with encephalitis and brain insults. It has a rolling symmetry to it, like an excruciatingly slow-motion dance. Days later, I'd ask the question directly, and the staff would try to reassure me. No, they would say, we intubated right away. No chance for damage to her brain. But that night I did not dare ask. I knew that I wouldn't believe them.

When I approached the bed, I thought she was orienting to my voice. I stood by the railing and her head pulled up, moving toward me. Her eyes, only half open, seemed to look at me. But her pupils did not focus, and the rotation continued. Her head turned away and continued its wide circular path. I touched her hand but there was no response, no grasping in return, nothing to suggest she could feel my presence.

This was so much worse than what I expected. This was what Herb was trying to avoid telling me, maybe avoiding knowing himself. This was our worst nightmare.

George stayed back, saying nothing as I stroked Martha's hand. I stood by the bed, frozen, for some time. Then a nurse approached. "I'm going to change her IV now," she said quietly. "Let me know if you have any questions."

I stepped aside toward the chair and nodded.

"You're her sister, right? It's OK if you want to read the chart."

"Not now, thanks."

And then she left. One more sign. Not one word of reassurance. No "Don't worry. We've seen this before, be patient." Nothing; just silence.

Before I left, another nurse came in to take vital signs. She smiled cautiously at me.

"So," I asked tentatively, "what is next?"

I don't remember her full answer, only the first few words. The cold hypothetical that I would hear over and over again in the weeks to come. "Well, if her lungs begin to heal . . ."

I did not know it then. I could not read the caution in her words. But the truth was pretty simple. Stopping the infection was only the first step. It meant reducing further damage. But it was not the infection that really concerned them. Like a flood that overruns a town in the night, ARDS had swept through her lungs ferociously, virulently, wreaking havoc on the walls, the structures, the very fibers of her lung tissue. The important question was not what caused the flood. The important question was whether there was anything left standing in its wake.

....

After we left Martha's room, George and I sat silently in a dark basement cafeteria for more than an hour. It was midnight by then, and a few night workers swept the floor behind me. George waited for me to speak, but I could barely look at him. He tried, this gentle man who hardly knew me, to ease my pain. "She saved my life once," he said softly. I looked over at him quickly, knowing I should ask when or how, but I could not speak. "Really she did, I mean it," he added. I looked at him. No words got past the images of Martha thrashing in that bed.

And as I wrestled with my own emotions, one question kept echoing:

What about Liamarie?

Chapter 15

Saying Goodbye

>>>>>>>>>>>>>

Herb was waiting for me when I got back that night, and we stayed up late, crying together and talking through the decisions ahead. He'd been struggling since Monday with questions he needed to answer. Should we bring Liamarie into that room? Would it help Martha to see her daughter? I was still reeling from the images in my head. I could not think straight.

"What have you told Liamarie?" Herb asked.

"Not much. I told her Monday that there was a tube in Mama's mouth to help her breathe so she couldn't talk on the phone right now. She was not happy."

I had tried to be calm, but I couldn't quell the tremor in my voice. Liamarie had looked at me angrily and walked out of the room. And the atmosphere in my house was charged. The background of reassuring adult voices—chattering with her mom, laughing, breathing the sense of normalcy into the air—was suddenly silent. I believed that she knew, no matter what we told her, that something was terribly, terribly wrong.

"And on the plane back here, she didn't ask. I kept telling her you would be here and happy to see her. But I didn't make any promises about Martha; I just said we'd have to see."

"I want to bring her up tomorrow. See how it goes. I have some friends who will ride up with us and stay with Liamarie while we visit."

The next day we drove to Baltimore, and Liamarie waited in the lobby while Herb and I went up to the third floor. Martha was a little quieter today, but still struggling and unresponsive when we approached. A nurse was changing her IV bag.

"Are you bringing her daughter up?" she asked casually.

Neutrality is an impossible standard for nurses. No matter how well they mask their tone, their expression, or their language, we read into their words all the expectations and questions we are struggling with ourselves. Should we let Liamarie see her mother like this? Would it serve any useful purpose? If this is a low point in Martha's eventual recovery, shouldn't Liamarie be protected from the trauma of the tubes, the needles, and more importantly, the inaccessibility of her mom? But if she was dying, shouldn't she and her daughter have an opportunity to say goodbye?

Denial does not protect children. Their imaginations conjure up fantasies far worse that what caring adults can explain, in simple terms, about even the most difficult situations. What they need is the feeling that *we* understand, that grown-ups are in control. This, more than any explanation of facts, settles their fears and helps them tolerate difficult stressors.

But very young children are also powerfully visual, and the impact of what is seen can be overwhelming. Most of us still remember the most frightening things we saw in childhood. They live in us, frozen in the terror of a picture we cannot understand. When language is too new, too limited a tool for self-soothing, the picture has no context, no perspective. It *is* how it *feels*, and that is terrifying. And that is how it is stored. Even years later, the memory kicks us emotionally, and we struggle to engage the adult language and understanding that quiet it.

As I stood in the doorway, trying to see the hospital room though Liamarie's eyes, I flashed back more than a decade. Matt was just two years old, and I took him to Munjoy Hill in Portland to watch the July Fourth fireworks overlooking the ocean. He loved the crowd, the noise, and the energy of the experience. But the instant the fireworks began, he stiffened, shocked by the display, and curled himself into a ball in my arms, hands over his ad buried in my chest. We were trapped by the crowd and ot leave. I held him close, whispering explanations of what was happening. He never moved and gave no sign of response to my words. I wrapped my jacket over his head, and he softened as I enveloped him with my body, wrapping him in tactile protection. His first protection was visual. Then all the other senses shut down . . . ears blocked, nose buried against the familiar smell of Mom. The young child retreats into darkness as a way of feeling safe.

Secondary to the sensory shutdown is tactile soothing. Terrified children jump into their parents' arms for safety, knowing the parent is bigger and will fight the threat if necessary. But this is not all. They seek the warmth, the touch, the tactile stroking and soothing stimulation of the hug. Strong arms holding their fear, containing their alarm reaction, and communicating the message of quieting, calming, and soothing that is imprinted from early infancy.

During this process, words are stored silently. Terrified children ask few questions in the midst of their fear. But they do hear your voice, its tone more important than its content. "It's OK . . . you are safe . . . I can protect you . . ." are messages sent with voice level and vocal pacing, as much as with words themselves. Explanations return later, as they did with Matt. For days afterward he repeated his mantra— "Up in the sky . . . red blue yellow . . . big boom . . . can't hurt you,"—processing the experience over and over from his highchair to anyone who would listen.

The visual impact in Martha's room was overwhelming, even to an adult. I tried to see it through Liamarie's eyes. If we brought her in, she would see her mother bald, eyes half open but unseeing, arms struggling against restraints, legs pushing and pulling as if she were trying to walk away in place. Tubes and IV lines emerged from every corner of the covers. The bright blue vent tube protruded from her mouth and was held in place with a piece of masking tape that extended, like a moustache, across her face.

We could soften some of this. Certainly we could turban her head, and maybe, with extra sedation, calm her grimacing and writhing.

But we could do nothing about the most important fact: her mother could not soothe her in any way. She could not respond, comfort, and console her child with voice or touch or even with a simple expression.

So that nurse's simple question—"Are you bringing her daughter up?"—was not so simple. Herb and I looked at one another.

"We're trying to decide," he said.

The nurse offered Herb a piece of flexible ventilator tubing and some surgical tape.

"Show her these," she said. "It might help."

Herb left and went down to the lobby. He sat on the floor with Liamarie, exploring the idea of a visit with her mom. She sat quietly, playing with the plastic, as Herb explained what Mama would look like, and how this tube would be coming out of her mouth, and a big piece of tape would be holding it in place. Silently she fingered the materials, and then said softly, "No, it would be too scary for me."

I was still upstairs, watching Martha and struggling with my own feelings. But it was Herb's daughter, Herb's decision. I needed to let him take the lead.

When I joined them in the lobby a few minutes later, Liamarie was still sitting quietly on the floor. Herb was standing now, and he told me what had happened.

I crouched down to be at eye level with Liamarie. She still held the blue pleated tubing in one hand. She was waving it, testing its flexibility, but her expression said she was done. She looked over at me without smiling.

"Too scary," I repeated softly.

She nodded and rose to her feet. She handed the materials back to her dad without a word, then reached over and took my hand.

....

I didn't sleep much that night. I wasn't upset with Liamarie's choice not to see her mother. Herb and I were both relieved that she was so clear. It gave us more time to think. We both knew this could not be Liamarie's decision. If Martha died, it would be a choice we would have to live with for a lifetime. And no three-year-old could understand the implications of that.

What kept me up was the concept of death. Object constancy, object permanence, Piagetian experiments with toddlers invaded my dreams that night. *Cognitive development in toddlers and young children*, I thought when I awoke. You need to read up on this.

But Liamarie did not give me the chance. The next morning, when Herb left for the hospital, she pulled me into the living room. "Play Ken and Barbie with me," she asked, and I cringed. Not my strong suit. I was not a fan of these precocious dolls for young children, but now was not the time to worry about the politics of child rearing.

She led me over to a big dollhouse set up in the corner of the living room. It was an older Playschool house, designed for small figures, but that did not seem to matter. I sat on the floor, and she picked up the two dolls from a pile of toys in the corner. "OK, Barbie and Ken are going dancing," she announced. She grabbed the figures rather roughly, and stuffed them in a blue plastic convertible car. She didn't bother to change Barbie's clothes, though she was in pants and a casual top. Whoosh. Liamarie shot the car across the room. She got up, retrieved the car and came back to the house.

"Now they come home and go to bed." She grabbed the car and removed the dolls, leaving Ken unceremoniously on the floor, and laying Barbie across the tiny bed, too small for the oversize figure. I had not yet said a word.

"And in the night she dies," Liamarie offered tentatively, articulating slowly. "But then she wakes up in the morning, right?" Suddenly I realized where this was going.

"Yes, love, toys are pretend so they can do that."

"And people, too." she insisted.

"No, Liamarie, not people."

"Why not people?"

"People are not pretend "

"So if Mama dies, she can come back to life again too?"

"No, love. No, she can't."

"I don't want to play this anymore," she said firmly, and walked away.

Chapter 16

Johns Hopkins

>>>>>>>>>>>

Herb and I agreed on a plan. We would alternate, one of us spending the day at the hospital, the other home with Liamarie. If there were important treatment team meetings, he would go. I sat with a map that night, confirming the path up the highway, nervous about finding my way into the parking garage. The next day I made my first trip alone.

Johns Hopkins University Hospital is a huge three-hospital complex embedded in Baltimore's inner city, surrounded by streets filled with poverty, violence, and fear. It's a straight shot up the highway from Herndon, but once I took the hospital exit, the inner city feeling surrounded me. Bags of trash lined the streets; a few sad staggering souls stared at me as I drove past. Every time I went, I held my breath between the highway and the parking garage, praying I didn't get a flat tire.

Each of my visits began the same way. I walked in the hospital's main entrance, headed to a long white desk where I gave her name and room number to get a visitor's pass. It was so different from Maine, I thought, where I often strolled into the medical center to teach a class or meet with residents without anyone slowing me down. Here, my entrance was cordoned through a gauntlet, two rows of uniformed security guards lining the path from the doorway to the desk. There was no way to go around them. They tried to look like greeters, smiling and gesturing each of us to move forward, but the weapons hanging from their belts made it clear they were on alert. I always wondered briefly what terror they were expecting, what violence they thought might come through these doors. But my mind couldn't be bothered with the question, and my heart rate increased as I approached the information desk.

At first, they looked up her name and room number on a list while I waited impatiently. Later, they just handed me the pass. Either I, or, more likely, her name, had become familiar to them. The last week of her life, their expressions seemed to shift, a cross between pity and compassion falling across their faces as they handed me the pass, then averted their eyes. Maybe I just imagined that.

I turned left down a hallway, gripping my pass, then walked quickly by the lobby chairs. They were usually filled with a mixture of pajama-clad patients and visitors in street clothes. The reflection in the glass-walled lobby doubled their number, and in the first week I was reassured watching these families, imagining when we might be among them, getting Martha out of the close quarters of her small room and one step closer to home.

Just beyond this was the gift shop. I did not go in there. I wanted to avoid the balloons tied to the cash register, blaring "Get Well Soon" or "It's a Boy" in their vivid colors. *There is nothing I can bring her*, I remember thinking. *Nothing.*

The flower shop was next. Each time I passed it, I was reminded that transplant patients can't have flowers, at least not real ones, nothing that could bring in germs or bacteria. In Martha's room, only one red silk arrangement sat on the windowsill. "Nothing living beyond this point," read the sign on the heavy doors that framed the entrance to the transplant unit. I was startled the first time I saw it. I always thought they could have phrased it better.

Just after the florist shop, I turned right and came immediately to the elevators. The bulletin board on the opposite wall was filled with flyers: a "Living with Cancer" lecture; a support group meeting for families. Many seemed permanent, faded and torn over time, but I looked for new additions if the elevator was delayed, something new, something to encourage me that things can change. But when the elevator came and its door closed behind me, a hard gray wall inserted itself between me and all those colorful messages of hope.

Getting off at the third floor, I headed right again, and made a U-turn around the elevator. There were offices ahead of me when the elevator door opened, but I never really processed the labels on them, something about lead on one of them, a reference I never understood. I was so intent then on making that U-turn and heading toward room 360. My heartbeat was rapid but steady. Two large heavy doors greeted me around the corner, and it took a lot of effort to open them. This was the transplant unit.

I passed the room she'd been in for the transplant itself, only two doors down. I wouldn't let myself look at it. It was that room I had called, sometimes two or three times a day, to see how it was going, to hear her saying, "This is doable, it really is," or to share some funny story about Liamarie. Mostly I called for myself, to quiet that panic that occasionally invaded my thoughts about the future. The future. There was always a future. We didn't talk about her not surviving this procedure. The numbers made that seem self-indulgent and morbid. A 98 percent survival rate, I always told myself. Relax.

But that room seemed part of another world now. A world filled with confidence and hope and expectation. I could not even look in, afraid a living, breathing Martha might look back, and I would fall.

Martha's room was at the end of the hall, right across from the nurses' station. The preferential location was hardly necessary, since a nurse or doctor was with her almost all the time. Sometimes they sat quietly with me, or busied themselves checking and rechecking her chart and telling me about the most recent medication trial. That first week a few nurses stopped by on their own time, people who had cared for Martha a few weeks before. "Oh, you're the one who sent the poems," one nurse said. "We had a lot of fun with those." Another told me about Martha reorganizing a procedure, insisting that something be done her way. She laughed as she told the story, "She was right, actually. It was better." It felt good to know they knew her as she was, not only as this unconscious, unresponsive patient with us now. But the look of wounded wonder on their faces always unsettled me. *How could this have happened? How could this be true?* it seemed to say. I always slowed a bit in the hallway just before I entered the room, bracing for what was to come. Martha's feet were the first things I saw when I rounded the corner. The first week I was there, they were a measure for me. I held my breath until I saw if she was pulling her knees up or climbing, trying to put her leg over the side rails of her bed. If her feet were quiet, I would sigh with relief. I hated to watch her struggle.

It made no sense to me. If she understood what had happened to her lungs she would have done anything to cooperate with treatment. If she knew that her struggle was doing her harm, she wouldn't have moved a muscle. I had watched her endure painful and intrusive procedures, without complaint or squeamishness, for more than a year now. I believed she had so much willpower she would have done anything to be still if it meant getting well. The doctors reassured me that all patients struggled, that it was a natural response against the intubation tube going down her throat and inflating her lungs. I didn't believe them. They had to sedate her, they said. It was standard procedure.

But was it sedation, I wondered, that so confused her that she could not know she needed to rest, to work with the machine that was trying to give her lungs a chance to heal? If she understood, she wouldn't fight. She was never one to panic, and no tube down her throat would change that.

That's what terrified me the first time I saw her. What if she doesn't understand? What if they didn't intubate soon enough to prevent damage to her brain? The slow rolling motion of her head and shoulders was eerily familiar, not easy to forget. I remembered a ten-year-old boy with meningitis, writhing on the pediatric bed, emitting a strange piecing squeal. Martha made no sound but her movement was the same. I knew it could mean brain inflammation, even permanent neurological damage.

After a few visits, I found the courage to ask. The staff tried to reassure me, "No, no signs of brain injury. She was right here when it happened. We intubated immediately." I wanted to believe them, but I could not dismiss what I was seeing. So I kept asking. Finally, as time progressed, they admitted what I knew was true: "We really won't be able to tell if there are neurological problems until she wakes up."

The alternative explanation for her thrashing was no better. Was the pain so bad that she had no control over her struggle? Would I have seen rough and jerky movements except for the dulling effects of so many tranquilizers and sedatives? She seemed behind veils of heavy, thick air as she turned her head from one side to the other, slowly, rhythmically rolling her chin and shoulders away from one another, pulling her head through the fog.

In the first week, there were times I thought she was orienting to my voice. I spoke and she seemed to turn toward the sound. My heart skipped a beat as her face approached mine. I willed it to stop, desperate for a sign of recognition. But her eyes never responded, never deliberately opened. Some days her eyes were half open, and I wanted to believe that she was looking at me as I tried to get through, but her pupils never focused, and in time, I doubted that as well.

Almost immediately I found myself using hypnotic language as I spoke to her, the slow rhythmic vocal pacing, and the quieting suggestions of a hypnotic induction. A few months before, I had made her a relaxation tape, my voice walking her through progressive muscle relaxation and visual images to relax her while she went through chemotherapy. I remembered some of those images now and repeated them, sitting close to her face and speaking softly. I wanted so much to think I could soothe her, using the strength of my voice to lead her to rest. But the more I tried, the more convinced I became that whatever was guiding her movements, directing the straining, pulling motion of her arms and legs, the tightening of her jaw and jutting of her chin was internal, not external. I don't think my voice ever got through.

If my voice did anything, it made things worse. Her blood pressure spiked and the vent flashed "Assist" and began beeping at me. She struggled against the equipment then, and I found myself backing away, afraid I was hurting her with my need to help. One afternoon, as I watched, a nurse asked another visitor to stop stroking Martha's arm. "Sometimes people in this state find it an irritant," she offered, and we watched as Martha quieted when it stopped. We realized that our need to speak, to touch, to connect could be disturbing instead of soothing. We needed to learn to back off and just be with her, quietly and without touch, to demonstrate our presence.

So I learned to close my eyes and speak to her silently, sending messages of love, of strength, of healing. But I felt so useless, facing this strong rigid body in a battle I could only watch, and whose outcome I could not influence.

Was it pain? Was she in such agony she could not stop writhing no matter how hard she tried? When they did begin morphine, almost two weeks after the initial injury, she quieted. Her breathing was more even, and, as the morphine increased, the muscles in her face, neck, and shoulders relaxed. *Oh God*, I thought, *have we all been so stupid? Have we let her writhe in pain, sedated but not soothed for two long weeks?* But I was so grateful I could not hold the anger. I just wanted to look at her face at peace and be glad.

On the days Herb made the Baltimore trip, I stayed with Liamarie. Part of each day, she took my hand and led me to play. I was grateful for my play therapy training. It signaled me the moment her tone shifted and the play took an important turn.

One afternoon it was the ballet story of *Coppelia*.

"You are Swanhilda, and I will be Coppelia," she began, handing me the small ballerina figures.

I was surprised at how much of the story she remembered.

"And now Coppelia comes to life . . . you make her dance."

I knew she hadn't really understood the convoluted story, the pretense of Swanhilda donning the costume and fooling Dr. Coppelius into believing he had cast a magic spell and made his beloved wooden doll dance. I wasn't sure how to proceed.

"Yes, in the magic of the story, Coppelia can dance," I began. "And she comes to life. She is wooden, and she comes to life."

"That's how it seems, doesn't it?"

"No, it *is*. She *does* come to life," she insisted angrily.

Over and over again, with fairy tales like Snow White and Sleeping Beauty, we returned to the same concern. Stories have magic. People die and come back to life. Each time she discovered this, it gave her hope.

"Yes, love, stories are pretend, and pretend is like magic."

"And people too, people have magic too."

And each time, I had to take that hope away.

"No, Liamarie, not that kind of magic."

February 22 was Martha's forty-seventh birthday. I sat quietly, watching her breathe, watching the red light on the oxygen monitor, go up and down . . . 60 percent, 65 percent, 70 percent. By then, it was not changing much. It dropped occasionally for a few hours but never long enough for the nurses to change their demeanor. By now, everyone expected the vent to stay. No one was talking about removal. The focus was entirely on the infection, and the panoply of drugs they were trying, one after the other. Each day, a new doctor would arrive, someone from infectious diseases or pulmonary disease or sometimes a painfully young-looking resident, to tell us what new antiviral or antifungal they were going to try. The antibiotics had been exhausted first, and now they were reaching, searching for any unique medication that might hit her infection. When Herb was there, they quizzed him over and over. Had they ever been to Africa? Where had they traveled in South America? I felt helpless with these questions. They reminded me of how little I knew about her life.

But when I walked in that morning, there was no staff, and I was grateful. No buzzing of activity. No questions. I sat silently. *It's her birthday*, I thought, *and no one knows*. It seemed silly to feel bad about this in the midst of all these efforts to save her life, but I suddenly wanted to tell someone, to make this day special in some way. I pulled my chair back toward the wall, let the nurse come in and change her IV bag without comment. I tried to think about next year, imagining a conversation with Martha about how far we'd come, how much better she was than a year ago, when, on her birthday, she was lying unconscious in a bed at Johns Hopkins.

Then Dr. Kennedy, the head of the transplant program, walked in. He remembered, I thought, or someone must have noticed on the chart and told him. I greeted him warmly, and he moved to the end of her bed, standing silently and watching her for several minutes. He was not tall, but serious and intense, a quiet man with the beginnings of grey hair, whose professional demeanor took over the room whenever he arrived. Several nurses and residents always tagged along behind him, standing near the door like a gaggle of geese in anticipation of a question or an order. I had spoken to him only once or twice in the first week, and we'd had one bad conversation a few days before. Impulsively, I had challenged him in the hallway, just outside of Martha's room.

"Why is she thrashing so much? Why can't you make her more comfortable?" I demanded. I'd read an article the night before about ARDS patients dying by "drowning in their own lung fluid," and I could not get that image out of my mind. "Can't you do something more?"

His response was reserved and disciplined, and as I watched the nurses surreptitiously glance our way, I was embarrassed.

Stop this. You're being a fool.

"We could add high-dose morphine," he answered softly, "but there's a cost to that. It will suppress her lung function. We're trying to give the lungs a chance to heal, to rebuild. I know it's hard to watch."

"I'm sorry," I said quickly, and walked away.

If she can endure this, so can you.

....

But on this day, her birthday, I had no energy for anger. She was quiet, and he stood for a long moment at the end of her bed, his hand on his chin, obviously in thought. Then he came over to my chair. He leaned down and spoke softly, so the others could not hear.

"I just want you to know that we've heard from the insurance company. They're taking the position that this hospitalization is not covered as part of the original treatment contract." I looked at him blankly. "Their argument is that we discharged her, and that this is a new illness, not connected to the transplant." I could not speak, so I just let him continue. "I don't want you to worry about this," he went on. "The hospital's lawyers will fight it. We will take care of it. Just leave it to us."

I nodded. "Her birthday" were the words in my head. I don't think I said them aloud, but maybe I did. He looked confused, then left the room.

Liamarie and I flew back to Maine the next day. It was becoming clear that whatever the outcome of Martha's situation, we would not know it right away. The doctors had moved from life-saving to treatment mode. They continued bombarding her system with drugs to clear her lungs and to give them a chance to heal. Antibacterial, antiviral, antifungal, a new one every few days. Martha was holding her own and, except when they tried to lighten her sedation, her vital signs were relatively stable. No one was saying much, just taking every day as it came, checking off one more drug, reporting on one more test that came back without giving us an answer. But the message was clear. At best, this was going to be a very long recovery. Herb needed to be with his wife and support her treatment, but it made sense for me to take Liamarie back to Maine.

Those few days back in Maine were a respite for Liamarie. She fell quickly into the routine of school, and though I had to tell the day care staff that her mother's situation was critical now, Liamarie's behavior was not decidedly different. I think she welcomed the rewind, the shift back in time to when her vacation in Maine was going to have a happy ending. At my house there were no floor games about death, no playing-out of what was lurking. She wore a wide smile most days, and the staff told me she had a favorite costume now, one she consistently chose from the dress up box at school—Belle's bright yellow gown from *Beauty and the Beast*.

For me it was harder. Hard not to feel guilty returning to my routine life, seeing people in my office, being with my family, while Martha was lying in that hospital bed. One afternoon I called the nurses' station, on the pretext of inquiring about her care. But I called for me, and the nurse sensed that instantly.

"Oh, you are her sister, the one with the pretty white hair," she said, and I dissolved.

"Yes, and I feel so guilty being here. I should be with her; I want to be with her." I tried to hide my tears, but she knew I was crying.

"It's all right, it's all right," she comforted me. "You are doing what you have to do. You are taking care of her little girl, and you have to believe she knows that.

"And besides," she added, "Sisters . . . sisters are never really apart."

We were back in Maine less than a week. I'd canceled my Monday appointments but worked every other day that week, making up for the time I was away. I tried to let the routine of work reassure me, convince me that this might have a better ending than the one I feared. I called no one, explained what was happening to no one. Maybe that would keep it from being real.

Thursday afternoon Willo, my secretary and friend, arrived in my office. Years before, when she applied for the job, she told me that she wanted to pick my brain for her own work with troubled teens, court-adjudicated kids, and school dropouts. So, we spend most of the time talking while she files my dictation, organizes my always-messy desk, and balances my checkbook. I don't really need her to do those things. But I do need the effervescent optimism she sprinkles, like holy water, on my dark Irish soul, every time she comes. Most weeks, I get the better part of the deal.

"So what happened?" she began, perching on the edge of my office couch. "She was doing so great. What did she say? How did she look?"

"It's not good, Willo," I began. "She can't speak."

"Well, what did the doctors say? What did they tell you?"

"They don't really know much right now. They can't tell us much."

She would not stop, even when my answers got shorter and darker and more uncertain. I tried to end the conversation, turned to papers on my desk, but it didn't work.

"But what will they do? . . . Are they going to try? . . . They must . . . ," she went on, daring me to admit I must be exaggerating, must be ignoring some hopeful sign, there if I would just see it. Finally, she exploded at me. "Well, what do you think is going to happen? Do you think she is just going to die?"

I wanted to be angry at her brashness, angry that she was pushing me to the edge of my fear. But I knew what she was doing. I knew she was pushing me as far out as she could, hoping I would reach back, and she could catch me, offer me a handhold.

But I couldn't say a word.

I could only nod.

The next day, Herb called again. "She's worse. I need you to come back. They're telling me she might not survive the weekend. I need you to come now." I was alone, frantic, racing around the house trying to decide what to do when the phone rang, a friend checking up on me.

"Oh Anna, it's so bad, so bad. I'm heading to the airport right now," I said. "I don't know if I can get on a flight today, but I need to talk to a real person, I need to tell them this can't wait." I needed to move, to run, to do anything at that moment besides sitting still with my own panic.

I called Bill on the way to the airport.

"Just go," he said calmly. "I've got it covered." *Bless him, bless him.*

Liamarie and I flew back to Herndon the next morning.

Chapter 17

Maybe

>>>>>>>>>>>>>>

Martha had stabilized some by the time our plane landed, but something else had changed for me. I knew that I could not just respond to Liamarie's play. I needed to shape it. And this was not going to be easy.

For very young children, the world is a complicated mix of truths and untruths, facts and fantasies. The boundaries between them are confusing. Is it real or pretend? Will it happen, or will it not? First attempts at organizing that world are definitive, yes or no categories. "Is it red, or is it not red?" begins the sorting of colors. Is it a circle or is it not a circle? Subtlety, ambiguity, and uncertainty are not part of the earliest schemas. For a young child, the world is a place of primary colors that do not mix or blend or bleed.

So, when I thought about the story that was taking place in Martha's room, I knew the challenge I was facing. It was not only the concept of death that Liamarie could not grasp. It was the concept of maybe.

Herb and I agreed that, even though Liamarie could not understand the facts of her mother's illness, she needed to trust that we would tell her the truth. It was important that she know not only that we would take care of her, but also that we would do our best to explain what was happening in her world. And to do that we needed to begin telling her that her mother might die.

"Sometimes, when someone is very sick, the doctors cannot fix them," I began as we sat on the living room carpet.

"Can the doctors fix Mama?"

"They don't know, Liamarie. They are trying very hard, but they don't know if they can fix her."

"The doctors will fix her."

"We really hope they will, but maybe they cannot."

"Why they cannot?"

"I don't know, Liamarie, sometimes all the medicines will not work, and sometimes people die."

"Mama will die?"

"Maybe, Liamarie, the doctors do not know. Maybe Mama will die. The doctors are trying really, really hard to fix her."

"Mama will die."

I knew this was only her way of trying to make sense of her world, to find some solid ground to stand on, but I cringed every time she said it. My own magical thinking got triggered then. *Don't say that out loud,* I stifled, as though the words alone could make it happen.

"Maybe," I repeated again and again, foolishly, "*maybe* Mama will die," but I knew that did not help.

I wondered if it helped her to speak the worst, knowing we would always respond by pulling her back from that thought, but as I watched her play with the words over and over again, alone with her toys, and as a greeting to startled friends who came to the door (Hi George, My Mama will die.), it was clear that it was not reassurance she was seeking. It was certainty. Yes or no, is it true or not true? Mama will die or Mama will not die? Only adults can languish long in the maybe.

Meanwhile Herb and I were holding on to ambiguity and uncertainty for dear life. It was all we had left some days to keep us from despair. For us, maybe was the only safe place. And so I tried to move the play along, to ask the question we needed to ask again. I went back to the dollhouse, this time using the small playschool family figures of two parents and two children.

"Sometimes, when people are really sick and might die, people come to the hospital to visit. To say good-bye in case they die." I took the family and started moving them toward the door.

Quickly, she picked up the children and moved them back.

"Grown-ups can go. It's too scary for children. They need to stay home."

Her answer never wavered. No matter how many times we played out this scene.

....

Herb and I talked about the decision. But our concerns fell on different sides of the issue. He worried that she would have regrets in years to come and blame him for not letting her have a last visit with her mother. I feared the opposite, that a last visit might be so traumatizing for her that it would indelibly imprint the horror of her mother's death in her memory. She would have so few memories of her mother if she died. I wanted all of them to be good ones, ones she could return to when she needed to feel safe and loved. The picture in Martha's room could devastate that.

And besides she cannot be dying, we told ourselves whenever we could. No one was saying that out loud, at least not to me. And though I knew better, I wanted desperately to believe that meant they were not thinking it. Tomorrow her oxygen levels will be lower. Tomorrow they will find a drug that will kill the infection. Tomorrow she will begin to turn this thing around. It simply cannot be true that she will not beat this as well.

On one of Herb's hospital days that week, a nurse approached him and pressed him to force Liamarie to see her mother. "You have to make her come in," she insisted.

That night he repeated their conversation. "She says Liamarie will never resolve the loss if she does not see her mother. She'll never accept that she is gone and not just disappeared somewhere unless she sees her dying." Herb was obviously upset by the idea. "I'm not sure what to do."

I found the nurse's concerns simplistic and out of sync with our experience of Liamarie and how she was negotiating her mother's illness. We talked about it late into the night.

"I don't see that, Herb. I don't think she's confused about where Martha is. I think she's just trying to tell us how she feels. And really, it's not her choice. It's ours."

The next day, the same nurse made an attempt with me. "If

I were like this, I would want all my family and children around me all the time." *Ah yes, but that is different.*

"I'm sure that's true," I replied, and my demeanor let her know that I did not appreciate her lobbying. "But we are making our decision for a different reason," I offered, just a little more gently. She left the room.

Her disapproval was unsettling for me as well, in spite of my feelings, and I found myself approaching another nurse later.

"Do most families bring their little ones when . . . ?" I nodded toward Martha, unable to find the words to finish my question. She stopped. I could see her hesitating, deciding whether she should answer.

"Please," I said, "it's OK; I want you to tell me."

"No," she said, simply and reassuringly. "No."

I am grateful that I never doubted what Martha would have wanted. If she could have communicated with her daughter, she would have chosen to see her, I believe, despite all the tubes and lines. She would have wanted not just to say good-bye, but also to offer her courage to Liamarie. She would have wanted to tell her that she would be looking out for her always, as close as a whisper, as near as her thoughts. Her words, her smile, her strength would have softened the effects of the surroundings and soothed Liamarie's distress.

But she could not communicate. She could offer no reassurance. And she never would have wanted to frighten Liamarie and embed in her memory a picture of her mother so different from the one she holds in her heart.

I hope I am right.

Chapter 18

March

>>>>>>>>>>>>

Monday, March 2nd, was the hospital's first team meeting of the month. I was nervous all day at home and anxious to hear how it had gone. As soon as Herb got back we sat at the dining room table. "What can I tell you?" Herb began. "They give me no hope, but I am hopeful."

I knew he needed to be the one attending these meetings, but I always wished I could hear for myself, read the inflections, and get my own sense of the feelings in that room. *But maybe his optimism, his energy is what really belongs there*, I thought, as he began.

"There were all the new doctors on rotation, but a bunch of the February staff came back on their own time to attend," he offered. "They really care about her. The conference room was packed."

"So what did they say?"

"They're going to try something new. A course of steroids. They're hoping it might jump-start the healing in her lungs."

"What about the infection?"

"There was lots of discussion about that. The antibiotics are really not helping, and they're putting a lot of stress on her system. And it's really the lungs that matter. They've got to start healing."

"So they're dropping the antibiotics and antivirals?"

"Yes, and adding high-dose steroids to lower the inflammation around the lungs. They hope that will encourage healing. We won't see any results for at least three days, but they'll keep trying for seven before deciding it isn't working."

Three days! Seven days! No wonder he was excited. This

seemed like a lifetime compared to last Friday's report that brought me flying back to Herndon with Liamarie. "Bring her now," he had said. "If there's no change, Martha could be dead by Monday." Now they were talking about a week, a treatment that might reverse the damage. If they wanted to try seven days, surely that meant she would be here at least that long. It was as though the prescription alone could ensure her survival, as though all those good minds, all those new ideas, just had to win. We rode a wave of enthusiasm that night.

They give me no hope, but I am hopeful.

So I thought nothing of it next morning when Lisa, the young blond social worker, approached me as I walked toward Martha's room. We'd met in passing a few weeks earlier, and I remembered thinking she looked not much older than Justin's college friends.

"Have you got a minute? I've got some materials for you to bring to Herb."

"Sure," I said, and followed her into the conference room. She took the seat at the far end and laid a yellow manila folder on the table. I pulled out the chair diagonally next to her and smiled.

"I'd like to go over these with you."

She began sliding papers over to me. "A list of practical things that need to be done after death: death certificate, Social Security notification, deed and title changes," it began. A worksheet for Liamarie that read: "The people who will love me and take care of me now that Mom is gone." Lisa slid the papers across the table, describing what each contained, and barely pausing between them. Materials from a grieving group for older children that she thought we could adapt for Liamarie, instructions on how to create a memory box. "Oh, and by the way, do you know what funeral home we should call? The morgue needs that information on file?"

I didn't move. I was aware of my hips against the chair, the solid feeling of my body against the metal. Lisa continued, and I sat quietly, hiding behind our professional alliance. But the split had begun.

One part of me was addressing each sheet. "That looks good. Oh yes, that will be helpful." I spoke of my role now, transferring Liamarie back to her dad, supporting their alliance, and of the work he and I had both done with her already, explaining that Mama might die. And no, I didn't know the name of the local funeral parlor, but I would find out.

Over my left shoulder and behind me, another part was floating, *Oh, my God, she's telling you it's over. There is no steroid miracle happening. She's going to die, and everyone here knows it.* A steady panic started to rumble like an engine revving up inside. *It's all over but the ending.*

You know this, I thought, *you know how this works.* Words are rationed; truth is parsed and fed to you in small bites until there is no more truth except what no one wants to say. *You have done this.* You have sat with parents telling them the "good news" that their child was cooperative or motivated, as you led them down the path to the devastation of mental retardation, brain damage, or mental illness. You know it well, this game of hope and omission.

"Herb tells me they are going to try steroids."

Lisa nodded and, for a second, said nothing. *You know this too—the treatment that has no real hope but a very real purpose.* Sitting there silently, I suddenly knew, in that part of me that had left my body, *the steroids are for us, to give us time to accept that she will die.*

I nodded knowingly as Lisa said she thought Herb had finally heard what they had been telling him more gently for a while. There was no hope except the hope of a miracle.

The racing inside got stronger. The split was apparent. *This must be what my patients feel when they dissociate.* Off to my left a part of me floated, frozen and numb, while my professional head was engaged with Lisa, continuing our discussion of how to process the death and dying of my little sister.

Martha Ann. The sister Ed and I had named, standing together between the beds.

Chapter 19

Returning Home

The next few days were a blur. We kept up our pattern of alternating days at the hospital and with Liamarie. She and I continued our floor play, acting out whatever question seemed most on her mind that day. And when the floor play had tired us both out, we went back to watching videos. *Bambi* was still her favorite, and it was taking on new meaning for me, as I watched her get deeper into the story. "Where Bambi's mother go?" she asked.

"I think the hunter shot her."

"Is she coming back?"

"I don't think so, Liamarie."

"Can Faline take care of Bambi?"

"Maybe they can take care of each other, Liamarie."

And so we talk about how fast animals grow up, not like people.

"Animals can take care of themselves after only a little time of being children."

"But not people?" she asks.

"No, Liamarie, people need a much longer time to grow up. That's why children have mothers and fathers and aunts and uncles and lots of grown-ups who love them and take care of them."

She looked at me quietly. And though she did not ask, I could not stop myself from getting down to her level and looking in her eyes. "There will always be someone to take care of you too, love, I promise."

I did not mind the days at home. They were quiet, focused on Lia-marie, and soothing in their routine. I could think. But as soon as Herb arrived, the house was full of people. Friends came as soon as he was home, and if no one was there, Herb would soon be on the phone inviting them over.

"Come eat with us. I will cook." Having a group around his table was familiar and comforting. It gave him something to do, and the affection of his friends was just what he needed. They were loud; they laughed, prodded, and cajoled him in ways that might have seemed raucous in another family dealing with grief. But it was easy to see how grounding and reassuring it was for him to feel his friends surrounding him, willing to walk this path by his side.

But these dinners that were so soothing for Herb could not have been more wearing for me. I craved only silence after leaving the hospital room, only the freedom to sort my thoughts and put some order to the feelings inside. I wanted no one, just the solitude to think and reflect, to look inside for the strength I would need for what was ahead.

And besides, these people came from a part of Martha's life I barely knew. They seemed like friends from another world who knew and loved a woman I could not touch. They spoke about the years she and Herb had lived in Germany, and the work they had done with political organizations there, the volunteer lobbying, and the legal research that had occupied so much of her life in her twenties and thirties. They talked about her disagreements with the national leaders of labor groups here in recent years, the battles that ensued over strategy and politics, and her leadership in resolving them.

Funny, I thought I'd be hungry for stories. *Fill me up,* I thought I'd say, *with all the details of her life, so I can believe she saw enough, did enough, lived enough, if she is going to die.* But I wasn't interested. My mind wandered while they shared their memories of her. It was not just that they were strangers to me. It was that they were mourning someone else.

Wednesday night the phone interrupted our dinner group. "It's for you," Herb said, and I left the table and took the call in the kitchen.

"Hi there, it's Sue. How are you doing?"

Sue, my children's pediatrician, was a colleague who shared cases with me at times, and I thought of her as a friend.

"It's so good to hear your voice," I said.

"I ran into Bill, and he told me things are not good, so I asked for the number."

"Oh, Sue, it's bad, really bad. And she's got so many friends, and they're all here and telling me stories but . . . but . . . "

"I know," she said, "but it's your sister."

"Yes, oh, yes," was all I could say. "I just don't care about all the rest." Those around the table were losing a friend, an advocate, a mentor, a strategist. I was losing a sister, and that was all I could feel. That was the only thing that mattered.

....

That week more people were coming to the hospital, friends who had heard how critically ill she was. There were no limits on visitation, and I found myself protective of her privacy. "She wouldn't like this parade of gawkers," I snapped at Herb one afternoon. He looked startled, and tried to tell me who they were, how they all knew her. "They are paying homage," he said, and I cringed. But I knew he was right. It was my own privacy I was protecting, my own feeling of invasion as these strangers came to share a piece of my grief. The next afternoon, Herb came home and said, "I asked them to turban her head when visitors come. I think she'd want that."

So I stopped in the gift shop to get her one last gift, something a little nicer than the standard terrycloth hospital-issued turban. I walked past the balloons quickly, and looked thoroughly up and down the aisles of the store, but I found none. Reluctantly, I asked the clerk "Do you have any turbans?"

"Oh yes, right up here," she said and led me to the register, where she reached underneath the counter and pulled out a cardboard box filled with brightly colored head wraps. "We keep them under here," she added quietly. I did not respond, just chose one, paid, and walked away, heading for the elevator and wondering at this incongruous bit of discretion in this place so comfortable with dying.

Herb was stronger each day, more confident about his decisions with Liamarie, more deliberate in his parenting. Liamarie was also shifting. She wanted her papa, and that was increasing daily. She was happy with me as a substitute, but Papa was clearly number one. "I think it's time for me to back out, at least for a few days," I said, and he didn't argue.

Truth was, I was exhausted and needed my own nest. And the people, the constant parade of people was too much for me. Finally, Herb and I talked about this. The easiest way to express it was with a question I knew he could answer. "What do you think Martha would be doing if the situation were reversed, and you were in Johns Hopkins?"

He got it instantly. "No one would be here. She'd have you, and maybe one other friend, occasionally, and she'd shoo everyone else away."

In that way Martha and I were alike. She was more extroverted than I, enjoyed entertaining and being with friends, but in moments of stress she would want to be alone. He knew as soon as he said it that this was my way as well. I need to know that people are there, that they care and understand, but I cannot think when they're around. Wisdom and serenity emerge from silence, watered by the thoughts of others, but blossoming in solitude.

So, Thursday we talked about my leaving. I was hesitant, uncertain about leaving, but I knew I needed a break. That night, in the midst of dinner with four friends, he looked across at my glazed expression, left the table suddenly, and made the arrangements with the travel agent.

I don't remember the flight, except that I kept thinking I had been wrong when I flew Liamarie back to Virginia last week, believing Martha might not live until we got there. It was little solace, but I clung to it anyway. I was on a plane again, and she was still alive.

Chapter 20

The Ending

>>>>>>>>>>>>

When I came home to Maine on Friday, March 6th, Martha was stable . . . not getting better, but holding her own for several days on the new regimen of steroid treatment. I held onto that, wanted to believe it gave me permission to step back, to breathe deeply and take stock. It felt good to be home again, to hug my children and have Bill's strong silent support to lean on. He had been alone now for weeks, keeping our children's lives in order, and I was very grateful. That night I slept well for the first time in weeks. I was exhausted.

The truth that Martha's death was around the next corner was beginning to live in me. I could not fend it off very often, could not escape into hope. I had to settle for believing that we had more time, maybe only a little, but some. I felt time slow, unwind itself so that minutes were extended, hours endless. Only this moment exists when the next portends disaster.

On Saturday Herb called. "They're going to go for fourteen days on the steroids. They figure why give up at seven if she's not getting worse?" Once again, the strand of time extended. "But there's no improvement yet."

Sunday morning. "She's failing . . . cardiac arrhythmia, blood pressure dropping. They want me back there right away." Herb's call was hurried, no time for me to respond. I stood holding the phone in my hand, the dial tone still blaring. For a moment I panicked. *I need to go back, to be there. But what if she dies while I am on the plane?*

Suddenly the panic subsided, and a dead calm replaced it. My place was here: to tell my mother her baby girl had died, to mother my own children as they heard the news. It was not where I wanted to be. I'd have given anything to be in that hospital room, touching her skin, stroking her face, or just breathing with her, each breath until the end. But my place was here.

I took a walk Sunday afternoon when I could no longer stand the wait for the phone to ring. I walked all the way down to Winslow Park, picking up my usual slow pace. It was a Maine March day, cold and windy, and I bundled myself in a wool coat and scarf. The sun hid behind the clouds mostly, but when the clouds parted, its warmth startled me and cut through the bitterness. I walked and cried and tried to be with her in my mind, imagining her face, her arms and legs, giving up the fight to be with us. When I got to the entrance of the park, I froze, unable to enter. *Go back,* I thought, *go back. You love this place. You cannot be here when this happens.*

I ran, feeling the weight of my coat and heavy boots, all the way back to the house.

That evening Herb called again. He was exhausted. I could hear it in his voice. She would stabilize, and then her heart would begin to falter. The staff was working hard to keep her blood pressure up, but they were losing. He stayed at the hospital till midnight, when they sent him home. I went to bed waiting for the phone to ring. I slept better than I expected to but woke exhausted. No call.

On Monday, March 9th, I only had one appointment, late in the day. After the kids went to school, I canceled that and began my vigil in front of the cold woodstove. "Do you want me to stay?" Bill asked. I shook my head no. That is hard to explain, perhaps impossible for others to understand. But if Martha was going to die that day, I needed to face it alone. It feels strange to write this now, to admit it out loud. I did not want my husband with me. I did not want to be with my mother. I did not need words, or comfort, or company. I needed to be alone. Blessedly, Bill understood.

Herb called when he got to the hospital. "They called me at 7:00 A.M." he said. "They said they'd try to hold her together until I got here, but come fast."

All day she fought. The nurses began calling her "the fighting Irish," because she wouldn't give up. Herb sat with her, telling her she could go, that he and Liamarie would be OK. But Liamarie's name would bring a spike in her blood pressure, a push for life when she heard the name. She wanted so much to live, and each time she heard her daughter's name she fought back her own death.

And through her battle, I sat. I could not read or write. I could not find the energy to make a fire in the woodstove. I just sat huddled in front of its cold, black presence. I was transfixed. My eyes were closed most of the time, my mind and body in two different places. I hated the not knowing and not being there to ease her way. But that day, I did not feel we were apart, not for a moment. Each time I closed my eyes, I was transported back to that room, and I too was saying, *It's OK, you can go. I love you.*

I called again at 4:00 P.M. Her breathing was slowing, but she would not stop. Her limbs were cold; all her energy was needed for survival. There was none left for warmth.

Herb called at 5:05. "She's gone," he said quietly. "Her eyes rolled back, and her heart stopped." He was silent.

"Thank God," I said, "Oh, thank God."

A few hours later, Bill and I went to Park Danforth, the elderly high-rise apartment where my mother lived. She was downstairs in the dining room, so we waited outside the elevator on the fifth floor, sitting quietly, listening for the noise to signal the elevator's arrival. When it opened, she saw us standing silently. I watched her spontaneous smile dissolve. She grabbed the railing and backed into the corner whispering, "No, please, no."

"She is with Daddy now," was all I could manage to say.

At almost exactly the same time, Herb arrived home and went upstairs to tell Liamarie that her Mama was dead. Fifteen years later he would tell me that the sound she made, the single long wail, still lives in his bones.

Section III

Grieving

No one ever told me that grief felt so much like fear.
—C.S. Lewis

Chapter 21

Denial

⋙⋙⋙⋙⋙⋙

Weather played a strange accompaniment to the events of 1998. The January ice storm matched the craziness of our lives, and I almost welcomed it. I imagined it as a dramatic backdrop in years to come, when we told Liamarie about these difficult months. We would spin a grand Irish story of Martha's bravery and courage and successful treatment. And in the telling, the ice storm would play its unprecedented part. So it was not paranoia I felt, but mild amusement when the weather amplified the chaos in January.

But in March, faced with the rituals of a wake and funeral in Virginia, I needed the weather to cooperate. I had no patience for a world that fought me, adding drama to my chore. I wanted only easy passage as I planned to fly down, alone with my mother.

I dreaded the trip, and not only for the obvious reasons.

In the years after my father died, my mother traveled extensively, living frugally so that she could enjoy two or three big trips a year. Giving up this pleasure as her health declined had come hard, and she often fought it. I knew this trip, any trip on an airplane, would trigger this ambivalence, this loss as well.

I convinced my mother to accept a wheelchair at the airport to preserve her strength. Standing behind her, I felt like a nurse, accompanying her on her journey. A ticket agent questioned us with a smile. "So, where are you ladies going?"

I tried to be discreet, answering quietly, "A funeral."

"Your father's?"

"No, my sister's."

All eyes moved to my mother. "She's going to her daughter's funeral," the agents whispered and guided us toward the front of the line. I felt invisible and ignored. Like a selfish child, I wanted to say, "But my mother will die soon. I am the one who will live a lifetime without my sister," but I was too ashamed to say anything.

It was a fourteen-seat commuter plane, an older one, and I began to regret making reservations from Portland the moment we boarded. The ceiling was so low I could not stand up, and there was no separation between the passenger area and the pilots' seats.

I saw pelting rain freezing on the windshield just above the flashing control lights on the dashboard. *Oh why did I do this?* The two-hour drive to Manchester or Boston would have been a fair trade for the comfort of a full-size aircraft.

The heater was defective, a crew member confirmed, as we tried to get comfortable. The co-pilot turned and, seeing my mother shivering, offered his coat, a heavy navy blue wool overcoat with airline insignia on the sleeve. She wore it draped over her like a blanket throughout the flight. The engine noise was deafening, precluding any reasonable conversation, and, incredibly, the plane had no restroom.

How is this possible? I raged to myself. Was it even legal for a commercial flight to be so poorly equipped? I was paralyzed by the stunning reality of the flight, unable to challenge or complain. *This must be a dream. No need to complain. I will just wake up any moment and laugh.* Then my mother spoke.

"If I can do this, maybe I could do one more trip to Ireland."

"I can't hear you," I mouthed.

We landed at LaGuardia to refuel. Two crewmembers and I walked my mother across the runway in the dark to find a restroom. The wind blew the rain sideways, and it took three of us to keep her from falling as she stepped slowly, effortfully, across a long piece of tarmac, past two other parked planes, following the flashlight path to a restroom meant for the maintenance crew. We were soaked by the time we got there. The bathroom hadn't seen much maintenance itself recently, but, thank God, it was functional. *This can't be happening,* I kept thinking. *I can't be going to my sister's funeral. I certainly can't be inching my way through the darkness across the tarmac on a howling night, taking an eighty-five-year-old woman to the bathroom.*

So often I hear people rebuke themselves about silence in the face of trauma. "Why didn't I speak up? Why didn't I demand to know more?" they will ask as they process events later in my office. We can only handle so much, I try to explain, and when our coping mechanisms are overwhelmed we retreat—to shock, to silent disbelief, to robotic dissociation if necessary. And so I did as well, retreating into fantasies of a dream state, unable to advocate or question. *This can't be happening,* my mind kept repeating. *Maybe Martha's death did not happen either.*

When we landed at Dulles, I picked up a rental car and headed for the Summerfield Suites. I was grateful to see we had a living area and a separate bedroom off to the side. I knew my mother needed her own space, and time to rest away from the crowds that would come later. "You stay here," I suggested. "I'll go over to Herb's and find out the schedule for the next few days."

She nodded and took her rosary from her bag.

"I'd like to bring Liamarie back here, if that's OK." I wanted to soften that first meeting for my mother, perhaps for both of them. Maybe it would be a little easier in a neutral space. It would be the first time they would see each other without the living link of my sister between them.

"Yes," she said, lying down on the bed. "Yes, I think that would be good."

I drove the short distance to Herb's in silence. I took the long way.

Herb's house was full. Two family groups, one with children just a little older than Liamarie, were in the living room, and Liamarie was deep into playing with the big kids. She looked over and waved but did not run to greet me.

"How is she doing?" I asked Herb.

"OK, I guess. She cries with me sometimes, but she doesn't talk about it much. I think she cries because I'm upset. And she's still stuck on the age thing."

Since Martha's death Herb and I had talked about this several times. Despite his explanations about illness, disease, and doctors' failed efforts, Liamarie came back to one story, the only story that made sense in her understanding of the universe. Birth, childhood, adulthood, old age, and death. The sequence was not flexible, not subject to change or interference in her mind. So the only version of her mother's death she could accept was that Mama had gone to the hospital and gotten "very, very old very, very fast" and then died.

We were interrupted, then, by more friends arriving to pay condolences. I slipped away. The house was full of her absence. I wanted something. I opened the hall closet, looking for her long black wool coat. I wanted to touch it, to smell her fragrance in its deep fur-collared hood. Maybe there was a glove in its pocket. But only Herb's topcoat and a few of his jackets were there alongside the guests' coats.

"Herb, where's her black coat?" I asked as he walked past me toward the kitchen.

"Gone. I got rid of it all. I called the women's shelter and they came yesterday and took all of her things. Why, did you want it?"

I was stunned. "No, it's just . . . Everything? Did you let them take everything?"

"Yes, they got some great stuff, I know. They were pretty happy. But I just had to get it out of here. I couldn't stand it."

The doorbell rang, and he left to greet an older couple from his church. I stood frozen, empty, trying to gather myself around this new loss. Not a scarf, not a handkerchief. Nothing of her remained in the house. I held onto the inside of the closet door for a few long moments. I heard a piece of a greeting to Liamarie, the phrase "happy in heaven now," and Herb's quick interruption. "We think even God is sad, and that Mama is very, very sad not to be here right now. You are so kind to come," he added as he whisked them into the kitchen.

I found him a few minutes later. "Can I take her?" I asked. "I want to bring her over so my mother has a bit of time with her alone."

"Of course, and I'm sorry. If I'd thought you wanted some of her things . . ."

"It's OK, Herb, it's OK."

....

Liamarie burst through the door of the hotel as soon as I unlocked it. "Wait, Grandma might be sleeping," I cautioned, but she was in before I could stop her. She stood, arms outstretched, announcing her arrival with a broad grin and a master of ceremonies voice.

"Grandma, I'm here!" She paused, turning to see my mother getting up from the bed, her rosary still in her hands. "My Mama died, you know."

The moment took us both by surprise. Liamarie's full energy, not a hint of sadness in her voice or expression. My mother stood quietly beside the bed. Her response was measured, and I could see her struggling to say the right thing. "Yes, love, I know. And I am so sorry that she died."

"We have her in our minds and our hearts," was Liamarie's quick response. She recited this little memorized phrase like a rhyme she'd learned at school, quickly and without emotion, as though the substitution was a fair trade. My mother turned away briefly so I could not see her face.

Liamarie was clearly in shock and denial. I knew how brief this would be, and my heart ached for what was to come. My mother stood silently, not sure how to react. Before I could say anything, Liamarie continued. "She went to the hospital and got very, very old, and then she died."

My mother glanced at me, startled, but before I could explain, Liamarie added, "Grandma, you are very old; when are you going to die?"

This was not the meeting I had imagined. While I struggled to find words, my mother said, "I don't know Liamarie, whenever the Lord calls me."

Instantly I cringed. In a phrase, she had introduced an idea I knew Herb would oppose and we could not explain. A loving, all-powerful God calling your mother home to heaven when you are three and still need her here on earth? No child could make sense of that, nor be expected to accept it. "I do not want her growing up hating God for taking her mother," Herb had said to me earlier that week.

"Liamarie," I said quickly. "Come here, and see what I brought for you."

It would be weeks before Liamarie's denial shifted enough for that stored piece of information to trigger the questions I knew it would. For now, it had a more immediate use. Liamarie knelt beside the coffee table, playing with the small pullback car I had stuffed in my suitcase. She looked up, trying to get my attention, so she could show me how fast she could make it go. But my mother was talking to me, unaware and unwilling to be interrupted by the tug on her arm.

After a few attempts Liamarie fell back, sat on the floor and dropped her head. I heard her mutter under her breath. "Grandma, I think you better stop talking and listen. I think God is calling you." Fortunately, my mother's hearing was not as good as mine.

Chapter 22

Ritual

⊱⊱⊱⊱⊱⊱⊱⊱⊱⊱⊱

I grew up around wakes. My father's oldest brother was a funeral director. He and his wife, my godmother, lived upstairs in the large white house whose first floor was a funeral parlor. On Sunday afternoon visits, while the grown-ups talked, I snuck downstairs to see the caskets and the stands for burial flowers. I remember the clean white satin and the vague smell of lilies.

When my father died, people lined up outside, standing in a cold January wind, waiting to pay their respects. I did not know many of them, business associates and colleagues, but I remember the line, which stretched out the door to the sidewalk, left thirty feet or so to the corner, then again fifty feet or more down the adjacent side street. "The line has never been this long," my uncle said, and I felt proud. So when Herb wanted to have a wake, I understood.

The funeral home was not unlike the one my family owned: an early 1900s expansive home, decorated in formal damasks and dark wood. There was an open front hall with straight chairs lining the sides, a few of them already taken by waiting mourners when I arrived. The viewing room was off to the right and its doors were closed.

Bill and I came in together, having delayed to get Liamarie settled with a friend of Martha's who had agreed to babysit. As I entered, I saw my mother and brother sitting together at the far end. Herb cut me off at the door.

"I want you to come in with me to decide . . ." he began. I was confused for just a moment. "Open casket or closed. Just us," he added, answering my expression. Bill took my coat.

Herb and I walked into the viewing room silently, side by side. Metal folding chairs in neat rows lined both sides of a center aisle. The casket looked vaguely like a centerpiece, framed by floral displays at the front of the room, and, as we approached, I saw the simple white basket of purple irises I had ordered.

We walked quickly, and as soon as I could see Martha's face, I stopped and looked over at Herb in horror. The embalming work was terrible. Her skin was a sickening brown and her face dwarfed by a double chin she never had in life. This was not my sister. This was some caricature, some ghoulish replacement I did not recognize. I was angry, and for an instant considered telling the funeral director what a poor job he had done. But the moment passed.

Closed. There was no question.

I thought I was protecting my mother when I told her that we had decided the casket was to be closed, but I regret that now. "But I . . ." she began, and I interrupted, "It's a good decision," and she quieted. I wish I had been less sure and let her decide for herself whether to take one last look at her baby daughter. I could not stand that anyone, not even her mother, see Martha that way. And I could not imagine my mother carrying that image of Martha to her grave. Better, I thought, that they both be protected from that unnecessary pain.

But who is to say what pain is necessary for another's grief? I will never know if she regretted that we decided for her. I know I do.

My mother stood calmly that night, greeting stranger after stranger who told her their stories—of Martha's courage, her intelligence, her friendship. So much was new to her, I thought. So much of Martha's life had been lived outside the family circle. I watched her endurance with wonder and pride. My mother would have said it was her faith that kept her strong, her belief that Martha's

goodness ensured her place in eternity and that all those affirming stories only reinforced that certainty. She did not ask again to
open the casket, but when the line of mourners receded, she sat,
looking at the framed photo beside it, her face a study in serenity
and pain.

I knew it was not going to be that simple for me. Faith has
never been simple for me. I knew early on that I could not believe
as my mother did, with a certainty and conviction that had no
need for doubt. But watching my parents live their faith gave me
the bedrock I could believe in: the values of integrity and compassion, and our obligation to care for those around us.

And I believe in believing. I believe that spirituality, that
part of us that reaches for something beyond the rational world, is
what makes us human. Refusing to open the doors to that mystery
is like owning a mansion and living in only three rooms. I cannot
be sure, but I do not need to be. I believe that searching for the
sacred in the universe leads us to find the sacred in ourselves.

I too was learning at Martha's wake. Strange faces appeared
before me, extending their hands and their stories in greeting. I
listened intently. Some were new, pieces of her life I had missed.
Others seemed new until a word or phrase suddenly brought her
voice, finishing the sentence in my head. "Oh yes, I remember
her telling me about you!" I interrupted excitedly, bouncing in
place, suddenly able to add another face, another person, to the
fragments of her life that now felt fragile and precious.

The crowd continued to grow and surrounded Herb, who
did his best to introduce me to each new arrival. Once the receiving line was complete, I slipped silently to the back of the room
and found a quiet place to sit alone. It was a strange feeling to be
with these people grieving, holding each other, all of us in pain. I
was sharing tears with strangers, grieving the same loss. Their tes-
timonies rang true: "She was there for me . . . She was fearless . . ."

There is power in the solace of strangers. And another in the
comfort of my friends who did not know her at all but knew only
my pain at her loss. We need all of these layers of solace, each offering another view of the loss, another way through the grieving.

The funeral the next morning was simple, brief, and, in Catholic tradition of that time, no eulogies were permitted. Just the simple funeral Mass, the celebration of life. I know the priest spoke briefly, but I have no memory of what he said; I was focused on Liamarie sitting between her father and me, quiet but not tearful, wiggling, and looking behind her to see familiar faces in the crowd.

Liamarie's mood had not changed at all in the past few days. It was classic for children in denial. She treated all the activity like a big party, delighting in everyone's attention. She recruited playmates as soon as we returned to the house and whisked them upstairs to her room, away from any expressions of grieving, to focus on her toys and games. When adults spoke of her mother, she rarely replied, and when she did, it was with little emotion and often a comment to distract. In the light of day, her denial held fast.

One thing was changing, however. She was holding onto her dad, letting me know he was in charge. "Papa will do it for me," became a frequent answer when I offered to help. *Of course,* I thought. *One parent gone, only one left. Of course you need to hold on tight. And more than that, going with me had led to disaster. Letting me care for you was an adventure that turned into a tragedy.* In Liamarie's mind, causation and correlation are not separate. I am, for the moment, the face associated with the loss of her mother, and no explanation of cause and effect will change that. Only time will, and so I wait.

The night of the funeral, sitting alone in the living room, I heard Herb upstairs putting Liamarie to bed. Her denial was beginning to break. As her body unwound, her defenses dissolved. "No, Papa, no, not that way!" I heard her rage over some shift, some imagined tragedy in her bedtime routine. "That's not right, Papa." Then the sobbing began. I held my arms and rocked to the sound.

My mother and I had planned to fly back to Portland alone. Bill and the children would come later, on a different flight. But as we walked into the ticketing area, we were greeted by an airline representative. "No flights will be going to Portland today," he began. "It's snowing there, and a jet slid off the end of the runway as it landed earlier today. It was not one of ours," he added, as though it mattered. After a delay, we were flown to Boston, where we landed in the midst of a major snowstorm and were herded into vans for the two-hour drive north to Portland.

Once again, I was caught between reality and fantasy. *The two worst flights of my life . . . could this really be happening?* My mother's age allowed her the front seat where she talked with the driver, cheering him on as he crawled carefully up the snow-filled highway. I was in the back, squeezed between two women who chatted amiably with a young couple in the middle seat, traveling with an infant asleep in a car seat. "Can't you just drop them off in Scarborough, the women began to lobby, so they won't have to retrace their steps from the airport? We wouldn't mind," they insisted. I sat stonily, relieved when the driver said he could not change his route. I was not feeling generous.

Four and a half hours later, we arrived at a deserted Portland airport. All flights had been canceled. The ticketing booths were empty, only a skeleton crew remained. It was pitch black outside, the plow had not begun to tackle the parking lots, and my car was buried in two feet of snow. The van unloaded just outside the terminal door, stacking our luggage before pulling away. A restroom stop was essential, and, as I took my mother's arm to lead her in, she protested, "But you can't leave the luggage here."

I exploded, "Mom, it's either you or the luggage, and there's no one here to steal it in the middle of a snowstorm anyway!" I could have sat on the floor of the deserted terminal and cried. *Why, after all that, did it have to be such a struggle to get to the saddest event of my life? Why is the universe taunting me, sending me cruel, unkind, even devilish reminders that the world is against me now? And why, why,* I thought suddenly, *am I going to be alone in caring for my mother?*

"It's OK, dear, It's OK," she said quietly. "It will be all right, I think." Her gentleness at that moment chastened me. *Where did this patience come from?* I wondered guiltily. She had not complained through all the hours of delay, through the tedious van ride in the snowstorm. And now, as I am yelling at her, she is kind.

My mother had many virtues, but patience was not at the top of the list. She could frustrate us all at times, spouting her irritation at mundane events that complicated her life. The new clock radio she couldn't operate brought a tirade about the world deliberately trying to make things harder for older people. Being put on hold on the phone infuriated her, insulted her, and somehow seemed confirmation that she was no longer important. Aging had certainly made this worse, but it had not created it. One of my earliest memories is of her standing, fists clenched, eyes raised to heaven, saying, "God give me patience," through gritted teeth. It never sounded like a prayer to me.

Yet here, in the midst of this snowstorm, she was serene. Perhaps, like many family systems, ours was no different. I walked with her silently toward the restroom. I was the one feeling desolate and helpless, wounded beyond my reserves. No doubt she knew and rose to compensate. *Remember this*, I thought quietly, *remember this when you feel hopeless in the face of family roles rigidly assigned.* More is possible in all of us, and crisis, instead of reinforcing the roles, is often the catalyst that shifts them.

There was one final event in the rituals for Martha. A week after the Virginia funeral, we drove to Lowell, Massachusetts, where Martha would be buried with my father and grandparents. Herb did not hesitate when this gravesite was offered. He remembered her firm statement, long before she became ill, "If I die, don't you ever leave me in Virginia. I could never rest in peace in this place." She considered the state government backward and corrupt and felt no loyalty to Virginia.

The burial service was set in a small chapel in St. Patrick's Cemetery. As the car drove through the gates, I remembered childhood visits here with my parents, walking from stone to stone as they explained who was buried in each spot. Martha and I skipped on the lawn, racing each other surreptitiously, to avoid the "Stop running, girls, it's disrespectful," from Mom.

The cold stone shell of a chapel was unheated, and there was no sun, just bitter wind. An elevated lectern stood alone inside, with only a few metal folding chairs for mourners. Most people had to stand. My brother had written a piece, images and memories of his little sister, which he shared with me at the wake. It stimulated me to write as well, not about images, but about words, the words that had echoed in my head all through that week. I faxed both pieces to my cousin Jack, Martha's godfather, who was also the funeral director. He had them in his hands when he greeted me. His eyes were glazed, and I could see the grief there, and in the eyes of his children, teenagers and young adults now, who had known Martha all of their lives. It felt good that there was no one there who was not part of this loss, even those whose job it was to bury her.

"Young Jack will read Ed's piece," he began, referring to his oldest son, "and Anne will read yours."

"No," I replied. "I will read my own." He looked doubtful, but my expression was firm. I wanted the chance to speak one last time about my sister. In this group were people who had known her as an infant and toddler, her babysitters, friends of my parents who had watched her grow up. And in the back, a few powerfully loyal friends from Virginia stood silently together.

I could see Liamarie from the raised pulpit where I spoke. She was wearing a red wool dressy coat I gave her a year ago. She swung gently from side to side, letting the full skirt twirl around her knees, and looking up occasionally to see these strange faces, who met her gaze with such pain.

When I finished speaking and returned to my seat next to her, she grabbed my hand excitedly, "You talked about me, Mary Beth, I heard my name!"

"Yes, love, I talked about you," At three and a half that was all she would remember about what was said here . . I heard my name.

I began this way. "Ed has given you some lovely images that capture Martha's spirit. I would like to add some words. Martha and I talked often, sometimes twice a day during the last year as she went through her treatments. In all of these conversations, three phrases stand out, and echo for me now."

"It is what it is," I went on, quoting her words when she was diagnosed and whenever she faced dark news. "She wasted little time feeling sorry for herself or wondering 'why', but focused on the 'how' of moving forward."

"'I need twenty years, not five,'" I continued, explaining this was her reasoning for taking the risk of the transplant. "I need twenty years to raise my daughter."

"And finally," I went on, "I remember something she said a few years ago now, when Liamarie was still an infant. We were playing on the grass on a summer afternoon. Martha was staring at her daughter, fascinated and entranced. She looked over at me and said 'I never knew how much you could love until I had a child.' Martha's love for Liamarie is, for me, the centerpiece of all of this. I will try, and I invite you all, when we think of Martha, not to think of breast cancer, or of bone marrow transplants, or of the ARDS that took her life. Think rather, of the love she had, and the risk she took for someone else, because of that love." The crowd was silent.

"Most of you know that I had the pleasure of caring for Liamarie during Martha's hospitalization. I would like to end with words from this wonderfully resilient and wise child, who has clearly inherited her mother's spirit."

It was a story that took me back two months, and a lifetime ago.

"You know what, Mary Beth? I'm the happiest girl in the whole world!" Liamarie was kneeling on a kitchen chair and made her announcement with a big smile and a side swing of her arms.

I swept her up and we spun a celebration around my kitchen. "The happiest girl in the world . . . The happiest girl in the world!" I sang, and she giggled. "You know what, Liamarie? I know someone who would love to hear that." She stood on the chair and waited while I dialed the direct line to Martha's hospital room.

"I've got someone here who wants to tell you something very important," I announced when I heard Martha's soft voice. Liamarie took the receiver in both hands.

"Hi, Mama, I'm the happiest girl in the whole world," she repeated on cue.

I could hear Martha's voice, stronger now with the enthusiasm of her response.

"Are you almost done Mama?" Liamarie asked.

"Almost. I'm almost done. I'll be home soon. I love you, and I miss you."

"Me too, Mama. I love you, and I miss you too."

An hour later, I took Liamarie's hand, and we climbed the stairs slowly to begin her bedtime ritual. "I love my mama, and I miss her, but I'm still happy," she said quietly, stretching her leg to take one big step. "Mama loves me, and she misses me, but she's still happy." Another step and a little balance check. She paused and turned her face to me. "You can love someone and miss them and still be happy."

When all had left the chapel, and we were heading toward the cars, Herb called to me. "Liamarie wants to go down to see the grave." Jack led us, a short walk down the hill from the chapel, to the site itself, an open hole dug in the cold March ground. We stood around the grave, wooden adults and this tiny child, staring silently at the gaping earth that was about to swallow her mother.

I can only hope that Liamarie is right.

Chapter 23

Condolences

The night I returned home from the funeral, my house was filled with flowers. Vases, baskets, and plants occupied every table and covered the long, cobalt-tiled window ledge that extends the length of my living room. It took every ounce of energy to restrain myself. I wanted to throw, smash, destroy every bud, every blossom. I stood in the middle of the kitchen, frozen, visualizing myself flinging glass vases against the brick hearth, heaving potted plants across the room to transform every shred of these efforts to console me into the chaos and disaster and rage I felt inside.

How dare you take my sister and give me flowers in her place!

I stifled the scream, buried my face in Bill's chest and whispered, "Get me out of here."

It was the first of many lessons for me about condolences. My reactions were powerful, illogical, guttural. I did not will or want them. They simply were. That moment passed, but the rage did not. It went underground, laid a minefield waiting to be triggered.

Anyone who tried to soothe me could trip a wire without knowing, and I would stiffen before them, my face blank. Outside I looked frozen, shocked into silence, stunned by sadness or grief. But that is too simple, and too kind. Inside something had gone off. Somewhere deep in the soft space beneath my left ribcage, an explosion had happened. *Be silent, be silent, be silent,* began the mantra in my head. *Collect your arms and legs, pull the string tight inside, gather your limbs so you do not fall. Move away, mumble something, if you must, but move away.*

Simple words, meant to be kind, set off a torrent, and I needed all my reserves to weather its passing, not to let it spill out and fragment us both. These are the words I remember:

"This too shall pass."

No, it won't. Death does not pass. It is permanent. I shall never again have my sister. What are you trying to tell me? That I'll feel better later, that the pain of this will pass? I don't care. I'm not grieving the pain, I'm grieving the fact, and that will never pass. I don't want the pain to go. I can't imagine being "over it," thinking of it without the pain. Right now that seems sacrilegious, disrespectful of what has happened. No, this will not pass. Do not tell me this will pass.

It is now, and ever shall be. Amen.

"She is at peace."

At peace? At peace?? Six months ago, when my ninety year old mother-in-law died, I believed you. Her ten years of fighting cancer were over. Her six months of dying from it were mercifully complete. "At peace" surely fit, and I was comforted.

But do not tell me Martha is at peace. I want to rail at you, *What kind of peace? The peace of a mother who has been taken from her only child? The peace of a woman who loved life so deeply she fought at every juncture to stay?* Peace? I can't imagine it. I can only imagine her screaming at God, *How dare you give me a taste and then take it away? I am not finished; I am not ready to be at peace!*

She is at peace, you say, so I should go on with my life and be at peace with this as well. But I am at war with this, and I cannot believe that the heavens themselves are not shaking with her rage.

"They were so lucky to have you."

Lucky. You want me to think of her as lucky? I want to tell you all how unlucky she has been, how many times she lost the toss of the dice. Whatever I have done cancels none of that, so do not focus on me; that does not matter. What I did was insignificant compared to what she endured, what she sacrificed, and what she has lost. I was the one lucky to bear such close witness to the process.

Besides, I want to scream, *it did no good. I believed that she and I could beat this. I did my best, and it failed miserably.* So do not talk of luck, and hand me no awards. There is nothing to celebrate.

"It's worse for those left behind."

Worse? We who have lost a sister, a mother, a wife deserve pity and compassion. But this seems so small compared to what she has lost. Who grieves for that? . . . all the days she will not have, all the moments she will not share. I'm confused when I'm told it's worse for us. For all our pain, we have each other, our lives, our futures. She has none of that. So much of my sorrow is for her loss, not mine. How do I grieve for that?

Am I supposed to believe that eternal peace is a good substitute, so fulfilling that one never looks back, never misses what was left unfinished on this earth? I cannot fathom that at this moment. *And even so, if it's eternal*, I want to challenge God, *couldn't it have waited a few more years?*

"She will give you her strength."

I want this to be true. I want to take her courage, her forthrightness, her comfort with herself into all the corners of my psyche where fear, hesitation, and self-doubt reside. I want to live for both of us, richer for the gifts she has willed to me.

But each time I try, I feel guilt. Why should my life be better when hers is over? It's not a fair trade, and, even in my most narcissistic moments, I cannot accept gifts bequeathed at such a price. Perhaps it is denial. I refuse her spirit as if that could will her back to life. Perhaps survivor guilt. If I must live longer, then leave me my weaknesses and failings. Let her strengths die with her so no one will credit me with them.

"She will give you her strength," you tell me. But I cannot take it. I have no right to it.

....

I am not proud of these primitive responses to the kindnesses of friends and strangers alike. I am only grateful that they were, for the most part, unexpressed. They might have mistaken my struggle, my wordlessness, as sadness alone. But this was not true. I was a walking minefield. I did not know where and how and what would set me off.

I was learning at a cellular level what "trigger" meant. "Where did you go?" I often said in my office when someone's face suddenly went blank, or black with rage, or collapsed into despair. "Were you reminded of something?" But "remind" is not correct. I understood that, as simple words—peace, rest, lucky, strength—catapulted me in the same way. I was gone, unable to ground myself, floating somewhere, trying not to look like a fool. The kindness of others was no match for the distorted lens I wore.

And I was learning something else as well: the worst response was silence.

"And how is _____ doing?"

Fill in the blank with anyone but me. Ask about my mother, Martha's husband, her daughter, anyone but the real flesh and blood person in front of you. Arms reaching out toward me suddenly jerked 90 degrees to the left like some rubber cartoon character. Oops, sorry, gotta sidestep here to avoid connection. Too much pain in the real relationship in front of us. Let's talk about someone else. And I collude, going wherever their question takes me, so I do not have to feel my own pain. I abandon myself.

"I saw you, but I wasn't going to say anything."

This came from kindness, a sense that gentle avoidance would save me pain. It was familiar, and I thought guiltily of how many times I had chosen it. Don't mention it. It will only upset them. Don't meet their glance if you're in a hurry; pretend you haven't seen one another.

But I am already translucent. I already feel like a ghost, a body with no substance inside, walking through the grocery store as if it mattered whether there was food in my cupboard. I am a shadow, a see-through film of myself. When you ignore me, I become invisible altogether. The disappearance is complete. I have no place in this world.

No, see my shadow, name my pain, even if I cry, or bring you sadness. It makes me feel I still exist. I am alive, and my pain must be part of this. It's my pain that grounds me. Without it, I am a film, a translucent specter floating up the aisles. Help me be real again.

See me. Speak to me. Listen to me.

....

In those first few weeks after Martha's death, there was a drumbeat inside my head. One word, over and over: *sister, sister, sister.* Why was I in so much pain? Why did this death and only this death, cut so deep?

Death was certainly no stranger. Before I was out of my teens, I had lost both grandfathers, a twenty-one-year-old cousin, and several dear aunts and uncles in my extended family. Then, at nineteen, my father's sudden and unexpected death came. I had grieved them all. But this was different, and that word, *sister, sister, sister*, kept hammering away at me.

When people spoke of their own grief experiences, I pulled away. Each effort to connect made me feel more alone. And so I began to write. When the house was quiet I snuck downstairs, wrapped myself in a quilt, and wrote across the top of the page:

SISTERLOSS

It is not the same, this loss of a sister. Why do others compare it with their loss? They try to console me with their stories. "I know how hard this is for you. I lost my father last year," or, "My cousin died suddenly, and I'm still not over it," but the words slide off me like water.

Don't tell me your story; don't even suggest that your loss is somehow the same. *These are the words I stifle as I move quickly away. I understand the intent, the reaching out to the universality of loss, but right now that is no consolation. It just makes me angry. I want only to revel in the specialness, the uniqueness of what I have lost. I need to know it deeply to cleanse the wound if it is ever going to heal.*

A sister is someone who shares your roots, yet stands in a different place in seeing the world. She knows the assumptions, the family rules, the templates from which you were formed. Yet, despite all of this, she is different.

Much does not need to be said between sisters. A core of truth exists without words. That makes explanations different, not justifications but offerings. "Look, this can be different in spite of what we know is true . . . Look, you can put the pieces together this way" . . . same pieces, different arrangement. Sistering is a funny blend of alliance and hope, of understanding and enlightenment, of support and challenge.

Even a spouse, a devastating loss to imagine, does not come from your own genes. He is other, a completion of self but separate from self. To a spouse you can always say, "You do not understand. You do not know what it was like. You have not learned the truths as I have learned them."

Not so a sister. She is self in all the ways that genes and shaping matter. She shared your room when you woke with a nightmare. She shared whatever nightmares were outside the room as well. As close as anyone can come to living your life, she has been. In all the important relationships of nurturance, she was witness and participant.

And yet . . . and yet, she took the raw material of my childhood and changed it into something so different from my life I marvel in amazement. How could such similarity breed such uniqueness?

In the similarity I find comfort, solace, and understanding. No one else understands the layers of meaning in

an Irish Catholic mother's simple denial—"It's fine, dear.
I don't mind."—except a sister. All the rules of gender, of
religion, of mother-martyrdom are known without saying.
Our poor mother, even in her noblest of moments, striving
to overcome them, was no match for what we knew without
words, even in spite of words, to be true.

I am alone now in my history. I have lost the closest
companion to my life, the one who knows the shapes, the
patterns, the meanings that inhabit my deepest realms.
The emptiness of that loss is enormous. The futility of
replacement is devastating.

I have also lost a big piece of my hope for the future.
For, as we shared a past, as if with one pair of eyes, we
saw a future with two very different pairs. As we knew so
well what was true, we could challenge where that truth
must inevitably lead us. Watching her be things that were
impossible for me was cataclysmic. Not because I wanted to
mirror her life. Not because I admired everything she was
that was different. No, it was the possibilities . . . the raw
material turned to a different creation that fascinated and
gave my future hope. If this could be, then more too was
possible for me. More than I am now, more than I believe
my limits will allow, may be possible.

I cherished how different we were. It gave me hope.
Now I shall never know how she would have been at fifty
or sixty, or how she would have faced so many things ahead
of me. And in the not knowing, I feel trapped in my own
possibilities. I see again through only one set of eyes, and
they are clouded with tears.

The writing let me start to breathe again. When I found the
word I wanted, the phrase that fit, something fell into place inside.
Nothing put the pain at rest, but words gave it a place to sit quietly
for a while. Words gave it my reality, only mine, and in those early
days after Martha's death, that was the only one that mattered.

It would be years before I would understand the complexity of adult sibling loss. Years before the world began to pay much attention to this subject. Ten years after Martha's death, I came across the phrase "disenfranchised loss," and a familiar ring went off in my head.

Losing a brother or sister in childhood is understood to be a trauma, a tragedy worthy of the deepest pain. But when that sibling is an adult, the assumptions are different. And the questions I was asked after Martha's death: "Did she live nearby? Did you see her often?" betrayed the world's belief that, because we were adults now, separate and distinct, this would hurt less. That unless our lives were woven into the same neighborhoods and the same school systems, we had let go of one another. But I did not know that then. I only knew that the questions seemed odd and irrelevant.

I only knew that I could not stop hurting.

Chapter 24

Las Vegas

It was only three weeks after her death, and everything was different for me. I was back in Maine, trying to reclaim the routine of my life. Liamarie was gone; the solace of holding her seemed so much further away now that Herb had taken her with him to Las Vegas. I had no picture of that place in my head, no way to conjure up their space and her presence when we talked. They might as well have been in Africa.

We did talk, Herb and I, almost every night.

"She has to wear a uniform at this day care, a little white blouse and cotton jumper. It makes it easy for me to get her ready," he said.

"Does she mind? That seems odd to me."

"No, I tell her it's just the rule here, and she accepts that. What's hard for her to accept is that I can't be with her every moment. And she's asking questions, the same ones over and over."

I could hear the tension in his voice.

"Can you come?" He asked suddenly. "Can you come for April vacation? Bring the kids, I'll buy the tickets. As a thank you for all you have done. Please. We need you to come." I said yes instantly. The undertone of desperation in his voice matched my own. The newness of being apart as we grieved was palpable for me, and I was grateful.

On the plane to Las Vegas, as Matt and Margaret played a game to keep occupied, I lay my head on Bill's shoulder and gathered my thoughts. I knew that Herb's personality would be an asset to Liamarie in the months ahead. He would be positive, upbeat, willing to do anything to ease her pain. He would not isolate or retreat or refuse to address her fears. Herb would tackle parenting head on, and I believed that would easily overcome any attachment issues caused by his being away so much in the past year.

But I did worry about one thing. Liamarie was a preschooler, and her manner of grieving was pretty easy to predict. Toddlers and preschoolers manage stress behaviorally. They do not have the words to articulate their distress or to soothe it. So their bodies express it by regressing back in time. Bottles are reclaimed, diapers reappear, and newfound skills are abandoned as the child's message is made clear: I need to be a baby again; I need you to be with me, hold me, take care of me, and help me feel safe.

Herb was handling his loss in a different way—moving out into the world, surrounding himself with friends and family, limiting his time alone, and avoiding silence. He needed to do something—at times anything—to assuage his grief. Liamarie needed just the opposite. She needed security, stability, familiar rituals, and comforting routines. She needed to be held and read to, to have her questions answered a hundred times over. She needed nothing more than sitting still, and this would be excruciating for Herb.

When he called me each evening, the tension between his need to move and her need to sit still was always in the background. One night she refused to go out to dinner and instructed him firmly, "You are the dad. You need to stay home and cook dinner for me!" We laughed at her forcefulness, but I sympathized with their struggle. It is not easy for parents to balance their own grieving path with that of a young child. And the widowed parent has no spaces, no breaks from the child's need to connect. Others can step in to give you a bit of time, but they cannot take your place. It is the singular presence of the surviving parent that children crave. The task of recreating safety and security out of the pieces of a shattered family ultimately falls to them, and only them.

"Just be with her," I counseled.

"But it's the same thing over and over," he challenged. "What is it doing?"

"Being is doing, Herb, and right now, it's the only thing that matters."

I hoped that Herb's early grieving would slow in time. Hoped he would stop running, not just for Liamarie, for himself. But there is no "right way" to grieve in the early days after an unexpected death. Some of us are on the floor, screaming our pain; others cannot sit still, cannot face the silence. Until the shock passes, there is no right way. There is simply the only way we can manage to keep breathing and to face the next moment, the next hour, the next day.

This was not the trip to Las Vegas we had planned. Instead of coming to enjoy the sun, sit by the pool, and help Martha recuperate, we had come to share the emptiness. Herb's job was still here, and until he could leave gracefully and settle his bill with Johns Hopkins, he needed to remain with this company. A matter of weeks, he hoped, not months, and then he must decide what was next.

Liamarie was gleeful when we arrived. *How much can this child bear?* I wondered, as she hugged us all and showed us around the condo. Another new day care, another new home. I just wanted to hold her.

The first day was the worst for me. I kept thinking of the trip Martha wanted, and how much we would have enjoyed celebrating the end of her treatment here. Tears welled up with every familiar piece I saw: the pool, the tile, the bathroom shower curtain. They all brought back her words of excited description. She had spent only a few weeks here, interspersed with chemotherapy, and the decorating was incomplete. I saw her touches and, in the empty spaces, imagined what she would have chosen.

Herb had two pictures of her in the living room. He warned me that they would be here so I would be prepared. I could not bear to have a single picture of her displayed at home yet. It was too dangerous. Like a sudden knife in my chest, her face caught me off guard and left me breathless, grabbing something, anything to fend off the feeling of falling over. It punctured my denial, and I needed that to function.

Here, the pictures were oddly reassuring. I wanted her to be a part of our visit, and the pictures helped. I imagined her watching us, saying, "See, don't you love the fireplace, and look at that refrigerator! I told you Herb picked one that was big enough for us to live in if things went bad."

I sat in the recliner, alone for a few moments while the kids played outside. The chair had the squeaky softness of new leather, and I looked to the side to be sure there was not a price tag still pinned there. I remembered Martha laughing on the phone, telling me how extravagant she felt finding it, and announcing to Herb, "I have to have that chair to recuperate in. Yup, that's the one." But sitting in it, I felt like an interloper, a sibling who stole her favorite sweater when she wasn't home. I closed my eyes really tight. *When I open them, she'll be here,* I thought. She'll pop out of the bedroom, yelling, "Surprise!" *Please,* I pleaded. I'll even forgive her the cruelty. I opened my eyes. But there was no magic.

My days in Las Vegas were divided into layers. Early morning was Liamarie time, when my two children were asleep. She and I played, watched her favorite videos, and talked about her mom. Mostly we snuggled. Touching was important for both of us, and we lay on the floor amid giant pillows that let us roll into one another as we read. "Read this story and this one again," she asked. There were very few "why questions," very little talk of what just happened and what it meant for her. She simply drank in the presence of family and the comfort of my physical presence and its familiar mothering.

In the middle of the day, Bill and I took the children, headed out to some attraction and became Las Vegas tourists. We did not last long on the casino strip. Its gaudy displays seemed hideous, and we were horrified at the people we saw. Not the glamorous well-dressed elite like the TV images in my head. Instead, casino after casino was filled with middle aged, overweight women in polyester pantsuits, some with walkers parked beside their slot machines, sitting for hours and hoping to hit the jackpot. Matt was incensed and refused to buy even a cold drink in the casinos. "This is horrible, Mom. I will not give them a penny," he insisted, and I admired his fervor. I could hear Martha's word—*faux, faux, faux*—echoing in my head.

One afternoon when Herb was free to join us, we took a ride out to Red Rock Canyon. The last time Martha was there, she sent a picture of the three of them on a bench, the deep umber hills of the canyon in the background. I wondered if Liamarie remembered being here. Just then her behavior answered. She got itchy and agitated, and, from a few feet away, I heard her suddenly screaming to leave, angry with her father at some imagined slight. "I want to leave. I want to go home right now!" she yelled. *Oh yes*, I thought, *she remembers.*

Late in the evenings, as Bill watched our kids in the pool, Herb and I sat at the dining room table and talked. One night he brought out a shoe box labeled "Martha." It contained unopened condolence cards, her wallet, and her leather-bound appointment calendar. Tucked inside was a small white envelope marked "Hair Pictures." Herb opened it cautiously. Four pictures: front, back, and two side views of her close-cropped hair for the stylist who made her a wig. He handed them to me. Her expression was flat, hollow, disembodied. So stark, with no attempt at emotion. I had never seen that look on her face before. Was she imagining us seeing them as we are today? Was that the hollow empty look of someone looking back from beyond her own death?

The rest of the box was more emotional for Herb than for me. Notes, cards, and words of sadness from people I'd never met. He opened each slowly, and it seemed to soften his pain to tell me who they were, how they knew Martha, and what their special memories of her meant to him. When we were done, we threw away nothing. Everything went back in the box as it was, but we had at least walked through it together and survived.

Another night Herb showed me the applications he was reviewing for an au pair to come when he is able to leave Las Vegas. One was an accomplished athlete from Sweden who seemed worldly and sophisticated, but her questions were, "How many movie the-atres are nearby?" and "What kind of car will I be driving?"

"I am leaning toward this one," he said, handing me another folder. She is twenty-three years old and from a small mining town in central Poland. "She is quieter," Herb said, "harder to interview on the phone." But her questions were about Liamarie, and how she is dealing with her mother's death, and what the au pair's role will be in the family.

We talked about a job offer in Seattle. It is a big job, a chance to head up the security for a wealthy computer executive for whom he has done previous international travel and security work. He interviewed for it while Martha was doing the trans-plant, and I remembered her excitement. "Never mind me," she had said, "just go and get the job and we'll have something to look forward to." If Martha had lived, there is no doubt that they would have taken it.

"We would be set financially, no question about that. Maybe it would be good to start over, to move completely away from all of this." I can see the runner in him, tempted to keep going.

"But," he went on, "no friends, nothing familiar. I don't know if that's good for either of us."

Each night we talked into the wee hours. About Martha, about Liamarie, about the future.

Tentatively, he told me that that women were already approaching him—a teacher who worked in day care, a friend of a friend.

"So soon?" I was startled. "Is this what you want?"

He shook his head. But his tears took us deeper.

"One night, Martha was angry I know, but she yelled at me—she said, 'If anything happens to me, you better find some-one else really quick, because you cannot do this by yourself.' Maybe, maybe . . ."

I could picture her, in a rage against this cancer, aiming her worst fears at him.

For a moment I was angry. *Damn those words.*

"You cannot believe that, Herb. And I will not believe she

meant those words. You are not alone. You have wonderful friends, and I will do everything I can. We will all help you. I will come on weekends whenever I can. And you can come to us when I can't. You can do this." I was pleading.

But there was truth in Martha's fear, and we both knew it. Herb's expansive personality made him the fun parent, the adoring Papa, but it was Martha who knew child development, Martha who countered his exuberance with practical limits. His tears that night were about self-doubt and fear. Mine went deeper. I needed him to believe his love for her could be enough, at least for a while. I wanted him to trust himself, and know he could learn the rest.

Listening to Herb face fears about the future, I was coming face to face with another truth about the past. A truth that suddenly seemed stunningly arrogant. I believed that Martha and I together could do anything. She had the physical stamina, the courage, and the endurance. I added emotional support, encouragement, and substitute mothering for Liamarie. It never occurred to me that we would not win. And sitting across from Herb in this hollow, empty place, I still cannot stop the voice inside my head that keeps interrupting: *What happened? What did we miss? How could we have failed?*

Chapter 25

Solo

>>>>>>>>>>>>

I have always preferred to be alone. As a child, I retreated to the living room for hours after school, scouring my parents' collection of vinyl records until I found what matched my mood. I rocked back and forth on the upholstered couch, lost in the music. My mother chided me to go easy on the furniture but always with a smile. An accomplished pianist who could play anything by ear, she understood this draw to music. She'd entertained herself for hours as a child, playing for her own pleasure. She even protected me when friends came to play. She'd peek around the living room arch, whispering, "Carol's here?" I'd shake my head, and she would nod. Then I would hear her at the door. "Can she come and get you in a little while? She's busy right now."

But the rest of my temperament was a mystery to her: my arranging a shopping trip with a friend, then canceling an hour later when four more girls had been added to the plans; my love of books over board games; solo conversation over group events. I never thought of myself as an introvert. Ed was far more solitary than I, and I felt average by comparison. The word I used to describe my discomfort then was "meaning." "I don't want to do it, it has no meaning . . . No, it's stupid; it doesn't *mean* anything." It was obnoxious, and it drove my mother crazy.

"What are you talking about? It's not supposed to have meaning; it's just for fun!" she would argue. "Go and be a good sport. You'll have a good time." The look on her face made me feel there was something really odd about me. When that argument didn't work, she tried another. "Do you know how lucky you are to be invited? You're going to hurt people's feelings if you refuse." I certainly didn't want to do that, so I often complied. And usually she was right, I did have fun. I was not shy or lacking in self-confidence, and I could find a way to be accepted in any group. I just didn't want to join one and have my life complicated by social expectations. I was always aware of a seriousness in my temperament, a desire to play less and think more, that was odd for a child.

Not until I had my own children did I really understand. When Justin asked, "Is it OK that my friends like to be with me more than I want to be with them?" it felt so familiar. His assessment of summer camp at age eight—"Well, it's OK, but after a couple of days it's pretty obvious they're just trying to keep you busy"—had that same drive to purpose that had seemed so odd to my mother.

I have long since made peace with my temperament. But I knew, in the face of this grief, that it could be dangerous. I do not reach out easily, do not seek the consoling words and arms of others. It felt hypocritical. I know the right advice to give others in grief, and yet I would resist it myself. But it is who I am, and I needed to find my own path. Grief, for me, would be a solo; a solitary journey.

....

I was afraid to have too much space. I craved it but feared the darkness of it. My practice was a good excuse. People can only wait so long for a therapist. Others can cover for emergencies, but no one really takes your place. I was out so long watching Martha die that I could not afford another leave for grieving, I told myself.

I decided I would take days, grieving days. I drew a long diagonal slash across the day in my appointment calendar and planned nothing. Grieving days filled themselves with odd mixes of things I had to do, wanted to do, and dreaded doing. I never knew what would come next. They were driven by an emotional logic that did not tolerate planning. I just got in the car and drove.

First day out, I killed a squirrel. Not a minute from my driveway. He swerved, I swerved, and we both guessed wrong. The thud left no doubt. As I turned the corner out of Spar Cove, I imagined baby squirrels waiting for a mother who wouldn't return. Tears welled up and spilled over. *Shit, did it have to start this way?*

Suddenly, I knew I needed to do three things: send pictures of the wake to my brother, send an Easter package to Liamarie, and write to Johns Hopkins. Sending the pictures was an easy chore, so I picked up a mailer and stuffed them in with a brief note. The pictures had arrived a few days after the funeral. There were two copies of each, for myself and for Ed, the photographer's note explained. I'd found it odd at the time—snapping pictures of mourners, and Martha's casket, and her smiling photo surrounded by floral displays.

"They are for Liamarie someday," he'd explained, "so she will know how much her mother was loved. I will send you copies." When they came, I found them oddly reassuring. *Yes, this did happen. She really is dead.* The pictures framed the facts gently, held the truth as though it could be contained in a 4x6 inch piece of reality. Not like my mind when it shocked me, stabbed me, flooded me with the truth. So I kept the photos in my bag, took them out periodically, titrating my awareness, opening and closing the small photo book. *She is dead, you know,* it whispered.

I wrote a letter to Dr. Kennedy. I needed to tell him two things: that I appreciated his directness, his compassion, his intellectual strength, and his human concern; and that I needed to know whatever he knew about what happened. "We were a team in this," I wrote, "and I have to continue to do what she would have done—learn, listen, and understand." So I asked for whatever he had: the autopsy report and the post-mortem team discussion notes, called M&Ms (morbidity and mortality) in most hospitals. I didn't know what he would release, but I worded the letter carefully, hoping he would understand I was not looking to blame or criticize. Taking it to the mailbox felt like one more thing I had accomplished, one more piece of our plan I had executed.

I sat in the car for a long time after I mailed it. I flashed back to the day Margaret was born, experienced again the rush of adrenaline I had felt when the phone rang, and the pediatrician's urgent voice told me they were immediately taking her from me. "She has A/O blood incompatibility. We need to put her under the lights. You can have her for ten or fifteen minutes for nursing but no longer than that. Call the nurses if they don't come to get her. We don't want her out longer than that."

"Tell me what will happen if I refuse," I said.

She stammered, startled. "There's no need to worry . . ."

"Just tell me," I repeated.

"Well, if the toxins are allowed to build, there could be brain damage, but that's not going to happen if we . . ."

"OK, that's what I needed to know." By then the nurse was hurrying into the room, and I handed Margaret to her without a word. Brain damage versus having my last baby with me in my hospital room? No contest. I agreed without hesitation or grief.

I was hoping that this would be the same. That some piece of knowledge Dr. Kennedy shared would make it OK, would make the insanity, unfairness, and sadness of this recede. I wanted some fact, some truth to make me feel better about losing her. But what if it made things worse? What if they told me it was a simple bacteria Martha got because she left the hospital walking by the flu-filled emergency room? Or the takeout food she ate the night Herb came home? What if they told me it was some foolish, mundane, preventable choice that took her life? There was no doubt that would make it worse. But I had to know anyway. I could not soothe myself with ignorance, could not leave the facts alone. And for a few moments, sitting alone in the car, I could not stop shaking.

I headed to Wilbur's candy shop and bought a small basket filled with candy and wrapped securely with plastic. I worried how to pack it and then settled on buying a large stuffed bunny to cushion it. At home I stuffed them both in a box, then took colored markers and sat at the kitchen table, trying to draw bunnies and eggs around the side, hoping that Liamarie would know when it arrived that it was from me. The drawing was awful, and the task seemed grotesque. A voice inside mocked me, taunting, *Here is a big Easter bunny instead of a mother.*

The clock rescued me. It was time to pick Matt up and take him out to the USM Music School in Gorham for his piano lesson. As I drove to Cheverus High School, I reset my thoughts. *Be ready to listen, to be in the present.*

I willed myself to think about now. Matt was ambivalent about this new USM teacher, uncertain that he wanted to take his piano studies in the direction she suggested, so as I pulled up to the high school, I took a deep breath. *Let his enthusiasm and energy for music be his guide,* I repeated to myself. *It has led him well.*

A flashback of the day he auditioned for an older woman, a gifted jazz musician who took only students who passed her screening. "I will work with you," she said grandly at the end of their time together. Matt was just ten and sat silently on the piano bench until we left. "She is not the right teacher for me," he said simply when we got in the car.

"Why?" I asked.

"I don't know if I can explain it," he said, "but it's like her world is filled with blacks and grays, and I am filled with colors."

But as he bounded out the front door of the high school that day, I could see he was in a good mood. He jumped into the front seat with the news that that he had gotten the lead in the school's production of *Into the Woods*. "I'm going to be the baker; it's not official, but it will be tomorrow!" he said.

"Tell me, tell me!" I said, grateful to have only good news to discuss as we drove.

....

I waited for an hour in the lobby of the Music school at USM, devouring half of a new book, while he had his lesson upstairs.

"Heavens, don't you want some light?" A faculty member flipped on the wall switch, and I realized I had been sitting in the darkness, straining to make out the words on the page.

Companion through the Darkness: Inner Dialogues on Grief (Ericcson, Stephanie, 1993) was the title, and it was the first good one I had seen, written by someone in the pain, not outside describing it. Her words were real, visceral, the uncensored wailing that felt so familiar. The author was a young woman, pregnant with her first child when her husband died of a heart attack. I felt guilty. *It's "only" my sister*, I thought. *What right do I have to hurt so much?*

A woman's voice interrupted me. "Can I offer you three dimes for a quarter?"

"What?"

"The meter. I need it for the meter outside," she explained as I tried to orient to her face.

"Oh, of course," I said, fumbling for my wallet.

Back to the book. "Do you know how many comforters it takes to replace a husband's warmth?" the author asked, and something cracked inside me.

Do you know how many joys it will take to make up for the ones she will never have? I answered, closing the book quietly and heading for the car.

Sit for a moment before Matt arrives, get back into now.

And the ticket on the windshield with its harsh note— "Expired meter"—helped.

All the way home I was grateful. I listened to Matt enthuse and complain and think out loud. He was a teenager, absorbing this loss as teenagers often do, by diving headlong into his own life. Blessedly, that life was blossoming and expanding around him, a heady antidote to death. Athletics, and, increasingly, music and theatre cushioned his adolescence, giving him an easier ride than most. He jumped out of the car most days, dashing into the rehearsal hall, and I was grateful for his life force, for the channeling of grief, and for the promise it held for all of us.

Months later, I would watch him in a blackened theater. He was alone, a single spotlight haloing him at the end of a long narrow extension that reached twenty feet into the audience.

"No more feelings," he sang,

"Time to shut the door . . .

Just no more." Tears filled his eyes slowly, until they spilled over and coursed down his face as he sang.

"How do you ignore . . .

All the witches
All the curses
All the wolves, all the lies,
The false hopes, the good-byes,
The reverses . . .
All the wondering what even worse is
Still in store."
His face glistened as his voice fell to pleading.
"All the children . . .
All the giants . . .
Please . . . no more"
"How can you do that?" his friends asked him. "How can you make yourself cry every time?"

I did not need to ask.

....

Work was my salvation in those first weeks after her death. The rhythm of the hour-by-hour sessions soothed me. I walked across my garage and up the stairs into another world. I felt no need to share my story and was grateful that the boundaries of my work meant most people did not know what pain my life was holding. It was enough to bond over their stories, over the effort we shared in trying to resolve them. The focused attention of the clinical hour was hypnotic, and I entered it with gratitude.

Other things were not so easy. No one tells you that grief is so exhausting. That the weight of an anvil sits squarely on your chest and walking with your hands by your sides is an endurance test. Your arms fight to pull themselves up, cross, and cradle the pain under your chin.

Some days the fatigue was so compelling that simple things seemed overwhelming; driving to a meeting seemed too much to ask. The day I went to the Board of Examiners meeting was one of those. My responsibility was ethical complaints, reviewing the facts and circumstances that charged one of my colleagues with improper behavior. Blessedly, my caseload that spring had been light, but one afternoon in late April, I needed to attend, to report on a complaint for review. I did not want to go. I dreaded the small talk, the exchange of condolences I knew would be ahead of me.

I drove the hour-long trip to Augusta in silence, without even the radio for company. In my bag was Martha's check. It was dated December 12, 1997, almost five months earlier.

That day Martha sat across from me at the dining room table with a pad of lists and notes in front of her. I was making my own list and was focused on covering everything I should ask. What did she give Liamarie for allergies? Did she use aspirin or Tylenol for pain? What brand of children's cough syrup did she prefer? Did she ever need a humidifier at night? All the small, practical things I would need to know when Martha was in the hospital and I was caring for Liamarie.

Martha was efficient, businesslike. There was no surplus emotion as she pulled the check out of her handbag and handed it to me matter-of-factly. "Here, this is for expenses." When I started to protest, she interrupted wryly, "Take it. It may be all you'll get." I knew the disease was hindering them financially. She had joked about having her own account with the airlines, who by then knew her family and medical history, as she commuted back and forth to Baltimore from Maine weekly before the transplant began. I'd offered her money once or twice, but she dismissed it with a wave. "Oh, we'll be fine. It's only money." Somehow she trusted they would pay their bills eventually. I'd thought about cashing the check. Was it insulting not to do so, depriving them of feeling they were paying their daughter's way? And yet, I didn't like the notion of being paid. I'd offered to help. I wanted that to stand on its own, not to be fettered with account sheets of what they owed or how much of their money had been spent.

So, I put off cashing it. I stuck it in the envelope with Liamarie's medical release form, and I forgot it was there. Herb came across it one day in February when I was in Herndon, and he argued with me, insisting I cash it. Still, I couldn't bring myself to do it. After she was intubated and lay so close to death, I would look at it and wonder. *Will it cover the rest of Liamarie's childhood . . . a down payment on a job that will last a lifetime?*

After her death I put it in a drawer, but then I got nervous, afraid it would get misplaced or damaged. It was on my mind a lot, and I moved it to a pocket in my appointment calendar. I wanted it with me wherever I went. Like a talisman, I fingered it, smoothing its wrinkles. Periodically I'd pull it out just to see her handwriting and the simple notation "expenses" in the left-hand corner.

I was distracted at the board meeting, unable to sit still as we went through the paperwork for the licensure candidates. *I should not have come*, I thought. *I am not ready for this.* Finally, I presented my review of the complaint. Discussion, questions. I am not following this. I am irritated and annoyed. A colleague leans in, asks if I am OK. "Things will be better in time," he offers. The clot of rage stops just behind my throat.

"I'm sorry, I think I need to go," I answered. "There's something I need to do."

I headed straight for the small office supply store where I had seen the laminating ad two days before. The clerk, a young girl, looked at me strangely as I handed her the check. I held my breath as she put it through the machine and trimmed the edges. Sealed in heavy plastic, it felt much better. I'm not afraid of it or doubtful. I took it with confidence, put it back in my calendar, and paid the clerk, ignoring her questioning look.

Someday, I thought, when Liamarie is eighteen and going off to college, or perhaps at some moment of tension between us when she is resisting my attempts to mother, I will pull it out. "Listen, young lady," I'll say. "Your mother paid me to take care of you. And this check can't be cashed till the job is done." I like to think we'll laugh. And maybe, in that moment, she will know how much I am truly on her side.

Chapter 26

Turning Four

May 10, 1998, was Liamarie's fourth birthday. It was also Mother's Day.

That year, it seemed even calendars could be cruel.

Planning for this began two months before, in the last week of Martha's life. I was in her kitchen, cleaning up after breakfast and absentmindedly watching Liamarie play with a set of plastic family figures. Fathers and daughters were sitting around a small yellow Lego table. I noticed that there were no mothers, but I did not comment. I wondered if she was working through her concerns about having only a father, trying on a scene in which fathers and daughters sat alone. But an hour later, she approached me and asked squarely, "Can I have my birthday party at your house?" and I realized I had missed the point. This was about her birthday, only two months away, and anticipated by the recent parties of her friends, all turning four.

We forget how central and significant birthdays are. For most children they are huge markers of growth and progress in the world. "Now I am four" or "six" or "eight," is a phrase spoken with enormous pride of accomplishment up until the mid teens, when the pride is masked but not diminished. Her play was asking a simple question, "Who will do this for me? Who will make the cake, sing the songs, and collect the presents?" In her mind, that role belonged to a mom, not a dad.

Young children incorporate grief in a very self-focused way. How will this change my life? Who will be there for this event?

The younger the child, the more literal and concrete that question is. Who will braid my hair? Who will drive me to school? Who will fix my bicycle? This startles parents who are reeling from the much larger changes they see on the horizon when a family is faced with divorce or death. It can seem selfish or narcissistic to parents who do not understand. "Dear God, doesn't he get what we have lost?" one mother ranted at me, "Why does he care about getting to soccer practice?"

But this is not selfishness or narcissism in any pathological sense. It is simply the child's way of asking, "Am I safe? Is my world still secure?" In the language of ritual and routine, habit and schedule, young children are asking the same question we are all asking in our fancy adult words about loss and grief and desperation. Will I be OK? Will my life go on? And if so, please tell me how?

"Of course, Liamarie," I said quickly, not even waiting to ask her dad. I grabbed her in an excited hug that hid my face. "Of course you can have your party at my house!"

....

The long dining room table in my house was set before they arrived. Cinderella plates and cups and napkins. And as a centerpiece, her gift, a fifteen-inch-high Cinderella doll in a flowing blue gown. Liamarie shrieked with delight when she came in through the kitchen and saw the display. "Cinderella, Cinderella, Cinderella!" It was just the reaction I'd hoped for, to break the tension in the house.

"Party first, eat later." I announced, and even Matt and Margaret put on their party hats without complaint. We all wanted to connect again, to reassure ourselves that we were there for Liamarie and that she had a family that went beyond herself and her dad. But "celebrate" is a strange word for the mix of feelings that floated through the house all weekend. It was Herb and Liamarie's first time back in Maine since Martha's death. The first time they would sleep on the futon they had shared with her, the first time we would sit around my dining room table where her face had always been part of the vacation photo.

"And presents!" she yelled again, seeing the small pile of wrapped gifts on the coffee table.

"Yup. But not until we sing and you blow out your candles. Then you are *really* four years old."

I smiled, grateful for her energy and her pure pleasure.

For adults it is so complicated. We are consciously aware of our loss, even as we compartmentalize our feelings and refuse to give in to sadness. It is always there, like a dark spirit lurking behind our laughter, agreeing to stay out of reach if we will play the role with conviction.

But children live in the present. Feelings contaminate each other less. There is the pure joy of celebration, the delight at her doll, the "I can't wait" wigglyness of her glances toward the presents as we went through the cake-and-ice-cream ritual. At those moments, Liamarie's happiness was everything it could be on this day. Joy exists as intensely as ever in the mind of a child.

So too, does the blackness. It does not dull the joy, but comes on like a typhoon, turning her laughter into a defiant scream when Herb suggests it is bedtime. "*No, no, no,* I won't go downstairs!" she screams, and we are helpless to stop it. There are no words for the expression of sadness on her face. Sobs overtake her, and she flails against the arms that try to contain it. The purity of her loss takes my breath away.

I envy her the separation. It seems cleaner than wondering if every moment of joy will be muffled by loss, and every moment of grief subdued by what is still joyful. I know it is more integrated, more mature to blend them, but as I watch her on her birthday catapult from the heights to the depths, I am jealous and grateful.

At the visit's end, I walked them to the security line at the airport gate, trying not to be emotional. I waved off Herb's "thank yous" when I saw his face straining as well. He took Liamarie's hand, and I turned to go. "Mary Beth!" she yelled.

Wordlessly, she dissolved us both as she ran back to give me one more hug, and planted gently on my cheek the "butterfly kiss" she had always reserved for Mom.

Chapter 27

Spring

Two months had passed since her death, three since she was conscious and with us. It seemed a marker, a line on a ruler of sadness and adjustment, grief and repair. I was not crying every day. I could bring myself to tears easily, but they came less unbidden, like a wave I could not resist. I knew when they were apt to steal in.

I could talk about her death as a fact without losing control. Not always, but sometimes, when an acquaintance asked innocently, "How's your sister doing?" I could relay the facts calmly. It was treacherous water I entered, though, and I could not stay long. Too many details, too much sympathy, and I started to sink into the sadness again. I felt like a water rider, an insect skating on the surface. I must stay light and move quickly to stay afloat.

I was not always aware of her absence. I could sing again with energy. Sometimes her face was there, but not to dampen my song, rather to encourage me to sing stronger, fuller, with less hesitation in my voice. My voice lesson was my therapy, I thought, as I was drawn again and again to sing the same song:

> How could I know I would have to leave you
> How could I know I would hurt you so . . .
> You are the one I was born to love
> Oh how could I ever know.

> Forgive me, can you forgive me, and hold me in your heart
> And find some new way to love me,
> Now that we're apart

How could I know I would never hold you
Never again in this world, but oh . . .
Sure as you breathe I am there beside you.
How could I ever know.
How . . . could I ever know.

"I don't know how you can get through it," my teacher said as the last chord faded on the piano. I didn't know either, but somehow it felt fitting to wail her pain with all the voice that was in me. I think it was more satisfying than tears.

I could feel happiness. Part of me was grateful. Another part of me felt guilty and sad. It was so early to let go of someone, to let the mundane facts of my own life creep in and become important again. Certainly those around me want that for me . . . to be Mom . . . wife . . . therapist again. To be strong . . . confident . . . happy. But did I want it? What was I afraid of?

I was only nineteen when my father died. I knew him only as a child knows a father. And in the years after his death, it became harder and harder to imagine him in my life, to feel him relating to me as a woman and not a child. He was part of an old version of me, not a current one, and that made memories of him difficult to access, less useful to recall when I needed them. Was I afraid Martha would recede that way, would fade in my memory? I knew that did not make sense.

Suddenly I realized. This was not about me. My father is as unconnected to my adulthood as Martha will be to Liamarie's childhood in time. The pain of that stung, but I knew it was true. I cannot change it. No amount of holding on to memories will keep Liamarie's life from moving forward. And every step into her own future takes her further away from the life she and her mother shared.

Every loss takes you back down, I tell people processing grief in my office. Down into the well of sadness that you carry from past losses. It is not that they are unresolved, not that you did something wrong in grieving. But each return has something to teach, some level of understanding to offer to this moment. There is a richness in those waters, and when we dip ourselves in them again, the blending of past and present, old grief and new, rarely disappoints. It offers a connection, a consolation, a fragment of understanding. A little piece of awareness to stand on when the whole world feels like the fun house floor, rolling beneath your feet.

And then there are the moments when, just to keep me humble, the universe slaps me hard. Two weeks after Liamarie's birthday, Justin defended his senior philosophy thesis and passed the oral presentation with an A+. Jumping with excitement, I grabbed the phone to tell Martha of her godchild's accomplishment. *Gotcha!* my denial snapped. And I sat down, stunned for a moment, holding the receiver in my hand.

Chapter 28

July

>>>>>>>>>>>

Herb and I established a rhythm in those early months. Every second or third weekend, one of us would travel. I wore a path to the Manchester, New Hampshire, airport and hopped the thirty-nine-dollar shuttle to Virginia as often as I could. When that was not possible, he brought Liamarie here, and we tried to immerse her in the activities of our family. She loved these trips.

In early July, here in Freeport, I did her bath, then wrapped her in a huge towel and carried her to my bed to snuggle. She smelled wonderful; her hair was still wet, lying flat against her head. It made her features stand out. Her large brown eyes were two inches from mine as we cuddled and dried her off.

"Mary Beth, why you live in Maine and not Virginia?"

I knew where this was going. A month before, she stood on the second floor balcony, looking through the long row of living room skylights at the tall hemlocks in the front yard.

"I am sorry about your trees," she began then, "but we have to kill them. That's where Papa and I are going to build our new house."

Now she tried another tack. I should move to Virginia and live next door to them.

"We could visit every day for breakfast, invite each other over for lunch, and come over after school." Her eyes are serious, her expression earnest. Why, she is asking, do we have to be apart?

I took a deep breath.

All the practical answers about jobs and money and houses felt as empty as the look on her face when I offered them. She didn't understand. And at that moment, neither did I. What could be more important than being together now? Dropping my life seemed eminently reasonable as I looked into those big brown eyes trusting me to have an answer.

But I will not move, and gently I tried to help her understand why people who love each other cannot always be together. Why lives and careers are more important than hugs and kisses. She listened attentively, but none of it made sense to either of us.

I had watched Herb, quietly scanning the want ads in our paper. I could see the wheels turning. *Could I make a life here? Could I transplant myself again?* I admired his openness. But Maine was not his world. I feared he would be stifled here, without the energy of the city and the international community of friendships he had at home. There were no job listings that matched his skills. He closed the paper silently.

I talked less about her mother that visit. She asked fewer questions, and my occasional mention of her mom's name made her quiet, seemed to take the energy out of her for a moment. The tide was shifting, and it was hard for me to watch. Since last November, while she was dealing with separation and the initial phases of loss, conversation about her mother had been healing. It helped her understand and make sense of the sadness. It helped to remember.

Another part of healing was emerging now. It is the ability to forget.

Few of us have memories before age four. If we do, they are sensate memories, kinesthetic experiences stored before we have complex language to secure them. The precarious bounce of riding on a parent's shoulders, the smell of a favorite cookie wafting down from a too-high countertop. These are the images that begin memory.

These earliest memories are tracks set down to be written over again and again in childhood. Daddy's voice as he swings you over his head and says, "You're getting too heavy for this." Grandma's hands reaching for the cookies and setting the table to share the treat. These happen over and over until they become blended elaborated memories that span years. Years that Liamarie has not yet lived.

She has only the bare melody of mother-daughter love recorded. It is a sweet melody, a healthy one, ready to be elaborated. But someone else will have to do that elaboration now. Liamarie must be open to mothering from others. And some forgetting may help that. This is as hard for me to write as it is to know. But I do know it.

"I don't want her to forget her mother," Herb says. "It upsets me when she can't remember."

I am not sure how to respond.

We, who lived a lifetime with Martha, cherish our stories and memories. They keep her presence in our lives. We can never forget. Later, when Liamarie is older and wants to reconnect with her mother, we need to share the stories that will bring Martha alive for her daughter.

But Liamarie will live most of her life without her mother, and now we must allow that space of forgetting to be, so she can open her heart and fill it with more than memories.

Chapter 29

The Box

>>>>>>>>>>>

I began to collect things: the check safely sealed in its hard plastic shell, some notes from our phone calls, a Cinderella napkin from Liamarie's birthday party. And the death certificate. Herb gave me a copy in June, and like some macabre secret, I'd been carrying in my pocketbook for weeks. I looked down at it, sticking out of my bag, and wondered if the words would change. I pulled it out, worried a bit about the wrinkling, and then peeked at her name typed across the top left hand corner, not opening the paper fully. Just checking . . . are you really gone, dear sweet sister?

You need a box, I told myself one hot summer afternoon, and a flash of memory appeared. A dark carved mahogany box I gave Herb and Martha on their tenth anniversary. It was a beautiful keepsake, and I wrote a verse to go inside: "A box to put your dreams in . . ." it began.

I shook the memory off as I pulled in to T. J. Maxx and walked to the housewares section. It took me only a few minutes to select one. It was shoebox-sized, made of decorated cardboard, cheap but sturdy. It is a little bit ugly, with a decoupage of pink flowers and metal handles on the ends. I do not love it, and this is good. *I need a safe place to hold my sadness if I can ever let myself be happy again.*

At home I gathered my things and put them inside. At the very bottom of the box, I put the autopsy reports: a preliminary one in April and a final one dated May 27. They came in response to my letter to Dr. Kennedy, and I'd read them one afternoon sitting alone on the couch in my office.

I scanned the narrative quickly. "Diffuse ... extreme ... marked ... severe," all attached to some descriptor of lung damage. I thought it would help to see those words. The end of the autopsy summarized: "probably little potential for recovery of pulmonary function."

I wanted this to soothe me, to reassure me that death was her only option, that no quality of life was possible. Instead, what I could not take my eyes from was the cause of death. Three were listed:

ARDS

High-dose chemotherapy with peripheral stem cell transplant

Breast cancer

I sat looking at the list for minutes in silence. I felt like I had been slapped across the face. All the conversations we had about bone marrow transplants came flooding back. The doubts, the delays, the signs her body gave that we might have seen as signals to stop. Our tentative questions, her angry rebuttals. My relief when she held firm.

Holding that autopsy in my hands I asked myself, *Were we so enamored by her strength that we cheered her on into death's arms? So sure of her survival we refused to let the signals of her body be heard?* There they were, the words "high-dose chemotherapy with peripheral stem cell transplant" under *Cause of Death*. I was appalled. She chose this, we encouraged her, and it killed her.

The danger was not only in the treatment. The danger was in being swept up in the glamour of the fight, blinded by the brilliance of courage. I wanted to believe Martha could do anything, and God help her, she tried to live up to that belief.

I remembered someone sitting on this same couch years ago, explaining how her experience with cancer in the 1960s was colored by the times. "It was Vietnam, and the movie *Love Story* had just come out," she said. "It was almost glamorous to be dying young." Are we so infused with media that we looked unconsciously to fit our experience into a story, and if so, is it more soap opera than life, more glamorous than real? Are we tempted to let tragedy be defined around images of superhuman courage, of mythic endurance? And then . . . do we expect a happy ending?

And what role has technology played in this drama? I wondered, as I held the autopsy report in my hands. The sophistication of our machines and our treatments is seductive. Complexity equals wisdom; science equals certainly. But it is not true.

I remembered the February night I took Herb's mother's call while Martha was at the hospital. In her heavy Spanish accent, she tried to counter the darkness in my voice. "I know she will recover," she assured me. "I am praying so hard to my mother, and my mother cannot refuse me." I was envious of her simple faith. I wondered how she could be so sure, and how she would accept her mother's "no" when it came.

Maybe we, of this generation, have exchanged a simple faith in prayer for faith in science and technology. Was I any less sure at the beginning of this procedure that, because she was at Johns Hopkins, she had to be all right?

In my family, medicine has always equaled mystery. It irked me, but there was no avoiding the fact that my relatives, otherwise competent and curious college-educated professionals, wanted medicine to stay beyond their reach. They could not remember diagnoses, preferred simple explanations to technical ones, and chose vagueness, imprecision, and a willing comfort with ignorance that frustrated me enormously. As a child I thought they were just acting stupid. Later, in college, I wanted to shake them. *Come on, you can get this if you just try,* I imagined myself saying, though I never did. Perhaps they knew something even then. Perhaps they wanted to keep all of this in the realm of faith, because it is safer there. "Trust the doctors," my father said. "That's all we can do."

My trust is different. I do not believe in ignorance. It frightens me and makes me feel vulnerable. I believe in facts. Send me the book, the article, the journal review. Explain to me the science of

medicine, and I will rub it on my fear like balm, soothing and comforting. There is much more science now, more facts, numbers, and
protocols than my parents had. It's a heady balm. But does it dull
our intuition? Is the brilliance science offers blinding us, and the
balm anesthetizing not only our fear but also our internal wisdom?

If we'd listened to her body in that month it resisted, she'd
be alive today. If we'd said, "This wasn't meant to be, your body
is telling us to stop here," I would not be writing this. But I cannot kid myself, either. We'd have traded one set of problems for
another. We would have fear, doubt, failure, and disappointment
as constant companions. We would not have believed faith in the
body's wisdom to be a higher voice, one guiding us to health. No,
we would have called ourselves cowards and lived in fear that, if
the cancer returned, it was our lack of courage that was to blame.

I wanted to think there was lesson in all of this. Something
that would protect me. Something that would push back the fear
and helplessness, and find some distance from the cruel reality of
randomness. I wanted a place to put my faith.

But I could only fold the autopsy carefully and put it back in
the bottom of the box.

Chapter 30

August

>>>>>>>>>>>>>

Liamarie was not doing well. Herb's voice sounded strained. "She keeps saying she wants to go to heaven to be with her mother." He was exhausted, and I could feel it over the phone lines as he repeated her words:

"If Mama can't come back, why can't I go to be with her? Why can't I go to heaven and see her there? I want to go to heaven and be with Mama. Why won't you let me go?"

"It's the same thing over and over," he said, "and I don't know what else to tell her. We go around in circles. And this week she started asking me to take her to the train station in Reston."

"Please, Papa, can we go down to the train station where we picked Mama up? Maybe she will still get off the train. Please, Papa, can't we just try? She *always* got off the train, she did . . . she did! Why won't you try, Papa?"

"Do you think I should?" His voice broke. "I don't think I can do it."

"No, Herb, no, it is just cruel to both of you."

As Liamarie's denial receded, she was trying to understand. But at four years old, the concepts of time, and permanence, and cause and effect are fragile at best, just beginning to be formed, so she cannot make sense of what death means. This is torture for parents. No matter how well you explain at one moment in time, a few days later a new version of the question is there. And the loss is rediscovered, the wound reopened over and over again, as young children grow and understand.

"There are no new answers, Herb. Just the ones you have given before. She can't really understand now, and we'll all have to give those answers over and over again for a while."

"But it's like going back to the beginning all over again. I am really worried about her. She is still not sleeping through the night, and she is down to twenty-eight pounds. Can you come this weekend?"

"Of course."

Margaret and I flew into Dulles Friday afternoon just before dinnertime. At the gate Liamarie ignored Margaret and ran into my arms, leaping up and clinging for dear life. Travelers smiled at the scene, but I was trying to control my expression. She looked awful; anxious and strained. Her slight frame seemed to have stretched upward without adding an ounce of flesh. I was shocked, and I held her as tightly as she held me for those first few moments. I didn't want her to see my face.

Twice on the drive home she wanted to stop. "I'm going to throw up, Papa." I distracted her, showing her something out the car door window. I signaled Margaret, who jumped in to tell her a story.

"Three times on the way to get you," Herb whispered. "She's not eating much, and she says she gets stomach aches when she does."

"Look, Liamarie, we are almost home," I offered.

Herb's stew was simmering on the stove when we came in, filling the house with its comforting aroma. We sat around the small kitchen table, Liamarie on her knees so that she could easily touch both her dad and me. Initially she resisted eating anything, then insisted Herb cut up the stew in ever-tinier pieces, a few of which she took when he fed them to her gently. After a few bites, she held her stomach and complained, "No more, Papa, it hurts me." She crawled over into my lap. I got her to eat a few more bites with coaxing, but my heart wasn't in it. I didn't want my presence to be associated with a struggle over food. She needed whatever moments of mothering I could offer, and, as she sank into my body, it was clear that was what she was craving. She cleaved to me as dinner ended, pulling her arms tighter around my neck as

I stood and carried her to the living room. We snuggled on the couch silently until she fell asleep in my arms. Her weight on my chest was comforting, somehow . . . the shared weight of exhaustion and despair.

The next day we went over to Reston Town Center. Herb took Margaret to do a few errands so I could spend some time alone with Liamarie. I headed for Barnes and Noble, and she seemed to recognize the entrance. "Maybe your mom took you here before," I suggested as we walked in.

"No," she said quickly, "I came here with my dad. My mom was already dead then." Her statement was loud and harsh, and two startled customers looked back as they passed us in the doorway. After some roaming in the children's section, Liamarie picked a chapter book from the *Magic Tree House* series. The cover illustration was a large aggressive crocodile threatening two children in a boat on the Amazon.

"Are you sure this is the one you want?" I asked. She nodded, and we headed for the reading section. I was still hesitant about her choice so, as we made ourselves comfortable on the bean bag cushions, I said, "We can try this book, but you might not like it. It's really a book for first or second graders who can read it with a grown-up, or even by themselves."

Quietly she replied, "Maybe when I'm in the first or second grade, I'll have a new mommy and a baby sister I can read to."

"Tell me about the new mommy." I asked gently.

"It has to be Mama's friend. Papa says if we ever get a new mommy, she will have to be someone who loves him, loves me, and loves my mom."

It was a lovely thought, and I shifted it only slightly. "I think that's right, Liamarie, and you know what else? I think even someone who didn't know your mom when she was alive could learn to love her though the memories that you and your dad would share."

Then, with a directness that cut through all the possibilities, she asked, "Why can't you marry my dad and move here and be my mom?"

"Well, remember love, I'm already married to Bill."

"When Bill dies," she said, "then you could marry Papa?"

"It's possible," I said, "but I don't think that's what will happen."

"What will happen?"

"Well," I began slowly, "I think that you and your dad will be alone together for a while, and then maybe, after a time, you will meet someone you both want for a new mommy. Sometimes it takes time," I said foolishly, helplessly, to those big brown eyes.

"I need a mommy now," she answered.

Walking the streets of Reston was hard for me. It felt eerie and sad to be visiting shops I'd heard Martha talk about, walking beside her daughter in her place. We met up with Herb and Margaret, then after some lunch, decided to go to an early movie. "*Air-Bud II*, it's a G-rated comedy about a dog who plays football," Herb offered. "It should be fun."

The theater was packed, and, as the movie unfolded, I began to get nervous. The script begins with a single mom whose husband was killed in an accident, leaving her alone with a young son. She meets a new man, but her son is not happy about this, and, under pressure, the man retreats. As the story unfolds, the tension builds. In a climactic scene, the dog saves the day, retrieving the man and leading him back to a tumultuous welcome in a football stadium.

Liamarie had not said a word throughout the film, her eyes locked on the screen. But as soon as the man's face appeared, and the stadium crowd's roar filled the theatre, she burst into tears and wailed, "I want my mama; I want her back. I want my mama back right now!"

Herb began quickly gathering her things. "Let's go." But this only made her scream louder.

"No, I don't want to leave. I'm not leaving! I just want my mama back right now, right now, I said!"

The crowd around us was shocked, but no one spoke, and the movie ended a few moments later, Liamarie still sobbing in her seat.

We left the theatre as soon as the credits began, and I sat on the sidewalk curb, holding Liamarie on my lap and ignoring the people stepping over and around us. Herb and Margaret went to get a drink a few feet away. Liamarie was still crying, tears streaming down her face, and as we sat there holding each other, I let her see my own. I could not have stopped them anyway.

"You are crying too," she said.

"Yes, Liamarie, it's OK. It's good to cry sometimes when you are sad. Even grown-ups cry. And I am so sad right now, because I miss your mom so much."

She seemed relieved to see my tears, and as we sat on the sidewalk together, knees and legs spun past, but I only saw her face. We talked about crying and trying not to cry and trying to be happy sometimes, and how hard it all was. She had stopped sobbing, but her expression was flat, her voice constrained. Then she looked up at my tears and asked softly, "Mary Beth, why you not cry all the time?"

I stood her up then, and crouched at eye level to answer. "Because, Liamarie, your mom was a happy person. She would want us to try to be happy too, even though we miss her so much. She would not want us to be sad all the time."

Again, that flat stare and measured tone. "But I am sad in my heart all the time."

Both Saturday and Sunday mornings, Liamarie bounced into the room Margaret and I were sharing, delighted to wake us up with her proud announcement, "I slept all night in my own bed, and didn't call my papa!" I knew how rare this was, and Margaret and I welcomed her in to snuggle with cheers. It was too soon to expect her sleep to be undisturbed. Herb knew that and was patient with her bad dreams and nighttime waking to reassure herself that he was still there. But it was exhausting for him, and I was glad to see that just our presence in the house for a weekend was helping her relax and feel safe enough to sleep.

But on the last night just after midnight, she cried out for me. "Mary Beth, Mary Beth, are you still here?" I rushed to her room. "I'm here, and I'll stay with you until you go back to sleep," I said, not wanting to move her. I sat on the dark rug next to her bed, leaning my head on the comforter. A soft light from the streetlamp bled in around the window shade so that I could see her face in the dark. For almost two hours she lay quietly, not speaking. She did not want to be held or stroked, just to close and open her eyes and see me there, sitting on the floor beside her bed. I had never seen her so still. And in her eyes—desolation, emptiness, despair. I could only witness.

....

On the flight back to Maine, I cannot shake Liamarie's expression. Something has changed in me since Martha's death, and I have not wanted to face it. I saw it in Liamarie's eyes last night, and the image will not go away. It is not what I am doing that I question. I continue to work, to console my children, to reclaim my life. But behind that action, something deeper has shifted.

As long as I can remember in adulthood, I looked to the future with optimism. In the eyes of my children, I saw hope and confidence and unlimited potential. A sense of being able to tackle whatever was ahead of me was unspoken but solid. That is not to say that I do not worry. I can fret and imagine disaster and obsess about what might occur with the best of them. But in my heart, I never really believed it. Deep in that solid place inside, there was a mantra: *We are good. We are strong. We can dodge bullets.*

That's what has changed. Now there are moments and hours, and sometimes even days when the future has no form but fear, when I cannot think about what might happen without an overwhelming sense of dread or foreboding. What if Justin cannot find a balance between his introverted intensity and his need to make a difference in the world? What if Matt's talents do not take him where he wants to go? What if Margaret's sensitivities persist, and she never recovers from this trauma?

Before, these thoughts would enter and be quelled easily. The mantra would soothe me. Now there is a hole, a hollow, empty place where strength used to be. I am flooded with uncertainty and have to fight to quiet the fear. I feel unsure of myself in ways unfamiliar. Am I really strong? Am I really good? Perhaps it has been an illusion, a run of luck that has come to an end.

I looked over at Margaret, asleep in the seat beside me. Her grief is still a very silent one. She avoids those who offer to talk, and at school they find her sitting quietly alone at recess. Last week she told her teacher that bad things will just keep happening now that they have started.

"Why do you think that?" her teacher asked.

"Because, first, we had a long good time. Now it is the bad time, and it will be long too."

At eleven, she has no illusion of control. The world simply proceeds on its own path. But I have always had the illusion of control. More than that, I believe in having one. I believe we need that illusion to propel ourselves forward. Just as we choose faith to face the darkness of unknowing, we choose the illusion of control to manage the chaos.

Outside, the wind is making this a bumpy flight. I am glad Margaret is asleep. But inside, the chaos is much closer for me. I feel it like a fractured windstorm, surrounding me with bursts and gusts, blinding me to anything beyond this moment and the task of standing upright. I fight now for the answers that used to be so automatic, the certainty that I will prevail.

I should feel stronger, having survived all of this, but I do not. I feel like a windshield still in place but shattered and broken. Push one piece and it might collapse. Add one strain and I might not rise to respond. It's faith in me that I have lost. I don't know how to get it back.

Chapter 31

Healing Voices

≫≫≫≫≫≫≫≫≫

The idea began last January, one afternoon when I was struggling to keep Liamarie entertained in a tiny studio waiting room while Margaret took a piano lesson. I swept a brochure off the side table so we could draw, and its title caught my eye. The Berkshire Choral Festival: a summer week held on a prep school campus nestled in the Massachusetts Berkshire Hills. Two hundred and fifty amateur choristers, professional soloists, and an internationally known conductor. Rehearsals seven hours a day, preparing for performance of a single piece of classical choral work on Saturday night. The list of conductors and choral works for the coming summer was impressive. *Music camp for grown-ups,* I thought. *What a wonderful idea!* I stuffed the brochure in my pocket.

Music has always been healing for me. On those afternoons after school when I retreated to the living room to sing, I rocked back and forth on the couch, eyes closed, completely transported by the sound of the orchestra and the power of the music. I learned all the familiar musicals and sang unrestrained with sopranos and baritones alike. But some days the record I chose had no words. I let the harmonies of the orchestra flow and my voice followed, singing themes from concertos, runs from a Chopin etude, counterpoint from a Bach fugue. Long before I could name any of these, I could feel them. And when I dissolved myself in them, I felt most alive. I lost all sense of my body. I was not ten, and chubby and self-conscious. I was absorbed and transformed into something extraordinary, something beautiful and complete.

These memories made me smile as I pocketed the application and imagined rewarding myself with a week alone, immersed in music, after all this was over. It would be my treat for helping Martha through her ordeal.

I completed the application apprehensively. I had done very little choral singing recently, but I included the amateur solo opera work I'd done a year before and hedged the time factor a bit when listing the choral works performed "in the past five years." I chose the week carefully, selecting Bach's St. John Passion, a piece I'd never sung before but whose power and discipline seemed a fitting end for what we were going through. I asked one friend who might be interested, but when her schedule didn't match, I did not look for anyone else to join me. This looked so right to do alone: soothing, healing, celebrating. I crossed my fingers and sent it off.

The response to my application came by way of a phone call, a decidedly British voice on my answering machine midafternoon on Monday, February 9. "I'm calling about your application to sing the St. John Passion at the Berkshire Choral Festival. There's no problem with the application," she went on, "but the conductor has decided to sing the Passion in English, not in German, and we wanted to be sure that is not a problem for you. Please call if this is not acceptable; otherwise we will presume you will join us to sing." I laughed briefly to myself.

Oh, God, I'd sing it in Japanese if they wanted; no, it's not a "problem." What was a problem was the message just before it on the machine.

"Hi, Mary Beth, it's Herb. Call me as soon as you can. I need to fill you in."

I'd spoken to him at seven that morning, so I knew she was scheduled for a 4:00 P.M. lavage of her lungs. The doctors warned they might intubate her then. "Incubate," he had said to me on the phone, and I jumped when he said it, ignoring the mistake. I knew things were serious if intubation, even temporarily, was being considered. "It is a possibility," he repeated, "just a possibility." Her readmission to Johns Hopkins the day before sat in me like a weight . . . equal parts relief and terror. All day I wished I could dispense with work, and whenever the machine answered a call, I jolted a bit from my chair. It was after four when we spoke.

Herb spoke with an intense, driven calm. Since early that morning, he had sat by her bed watching her struggle to breathe with an oxygen mask, too weak to carry on a conversation. "I love you," she had signed, pointing to herself, clutching her hands over her heart, then pointing to him. But at 2:00 P.M. she suddenly stopped breathing. He saw it happen and was rising from the chair to get help when the team descended. This was ARDS. This was, in Dr. Kennedy's words, "total organ failure of the lungs." It was that afternoon that I had first heard the words that terrified me: "Please be ready to come right away. If I need to make a decision about life support, I cannot do that alone. I need your help."

Now, six months later, I looked out the window of my sparse prep school dormitory room at a glorious watercolor image of rolling green hills and wondered, *Will this idyllic place always be juxtaposed with tragedy? Will the ecstasy of two hundred and fifty voices raised in song ever stop reminding me of what else happened the day I was accepted?*

I arrived late and tired on registration day. The drive through western Massachusetts took longer than I expected, and I sang with the practice tape all the way down. By the time I got there, my voice was worn, and I was regretting not practicing more at home. Though I'd agreed to share a room, I was grateful when the registration person asked, "Do you mind being alone? We have no one to match you with."

"Not at all," I replied. *Thank you, God.* I walked over to the dorm and found my room, a small stark cubicle outfitted with two cot-sized beds with thin mattresses. Within a few minutes of unpacking I fell asleep.

My days were full. Morning, afternoon, and evening rehearsals are the focus of everyone's attention, and the choristers, though amateurs, are not dilettantes. Many are music teachers or members of professional choruses at home. They take their singing seriously, and part of almost every introduction in the cafeteria includes, "So, where do you sing?"

It felt good to be surrounded by musicians, to be able to sit alone on the grass with the score in my hands and not feel odd or strange. Others are doing the same, the internal music driving the lift of an arm, or the silent sway of a head carrying a phrase to completion. Being back in this world brings its own set of memories, ones I have long packed away.

I am nineteen, a sophomore vocal performance major at college, struggling to prepare a principal role in Benjamin Britten's opera, The Rape of Lucretia. I'm nervous, and for a while my teacher and I excuse my vocal glitches, ascribing them to tension and insecurity about being the only underclassman selected to perform in the music department's big spring production. But I watch her concern grow, and increasingly she asks questions about the treatment I have had for problems with my cervical spine. I'm becoming wary as well, beginning to dread rather than welcome this opportunity to perform. Something is wrong, and we both know it.

While I am home on Christmas break, my teacher attends a medical meeting of otolaryngologists. She goes every year, she has told me, and always learns something useful about the mechanics of voice production. When I return to school in early January, she is gentle but the news is devastating. The glitches are structural, probably unlikely to change, attributable to the muscular connections between the vocal chords, the hyoid bone and my spinal curvature. The implications of this go far beyond the spring production. My dreams of singing professionally are over.

I called my parents that night to tell them the news. There would be no opera performance in the spring, and I had some decisions to make. I tried not to cry, but they knew this was life-altering news. The music department offered to let me become a piano major, but I knew that was just kindness. I had neither the talent nor the interest in piano, and I would not make that choice.

"Just take some time and think about it," my father had said gently. "You don't have to decide right now." I can still hear his voice, solid and steady. "You know we will support whatever decision you make." I wanted to say, "I love you" at that moment but stifled the impulse. I would cry if I did, and I did not want to end the call that way. I swallowed hard. "Thanks, I know."

Music is woven into tragedy for me as well, I thought, as the sun fell behind the hills and turned them black before my eyes. My father never got to know what I decided. Two days later, in the middle of a meeting at the local parish rectory, he suffered a cerebral hemorrhage. Later that evening, in the small Catholic hospital just across the street, he died.

It would be years before I sang again. And it would be the pull of my own children's voices that drew me back. First, Matt, who pleaded for piano lessons at five, then at twelve sang the role of Amahl in *Amahl and the Night Visitors*. Later, Margaret, who sang herself to sleep before she could talk, and pleaded as she watched her brother perform, "When is it my turn, Mumma?" Slowly, gradually, music was woven into two new lives, and I could not resist rejoining the song.

....

For all the memories of tragedy, the festival is healing. The hills, the sun, and most of all, the music. Bach at his magnificent, exhausting best. I was frightened when I first opened the practice tape to learn the soprano part. High, fast, vocal gymnastics was the best description I could think of, and my voice was out of shape. But after two rehearsals, I felt confident and relaxed. Though my voice does not have the flexibility I want, I am not too far off the mark in my mastery of the score, and that is a relief. This will be great fun and good healing. I only wish it could also have been celebratory.

Past and present, memories long forgotten seep back into consciousness, weaving together the deepest stories of my life. It is the music that summons them, and as I sit with them, hold them, I understand anniversary reactions better. These echoes of past triggered by nothing more than a date on a calendar, the sound of a chord, or the smell of a season. They take you on a journey unhampered by time and space. A journey guided only by the emotional refrains of your life. Like a bell deep in the unconscious, a soft clanging summons images, sensations, and emotions to merge and coalesce. Like a great church bell in the distance it calls to remind you, and you remember.

························

I have told no one why I am here. Not yet. I have hinted. Whenever I have to admit I'm not singing in a choral group at home, I add some reference to family illness, deliberately vague, discouraging questions that might elicit details. Here I am not identified by my grief. At home everyone knows, and when I pass, I can see their faces change. Here I can choose my identity. Strangely, I resist letting my grief be a part of it. It stands just outside the circle, ever ready to be summoned. Though I am tempted, I leave it there.

I am toying with moving on . . . pretending there will be a future where Martha's death will not be the centerpiece. That there will be a time when I will say, "My sister died when I was fifty," the way I say, "My father died when I was nineteen." A fact, but not emotionally connected to this moment in time in obvious and excruciating ways.

It's a strange dissociative game I'm playing with myself and the world. Sometimes I believe it. I am lost in the music and the mountains, and I am not aware that part of me is forever changed. Then the music recedes, and I remember. I am here. Martha is dead. I am here because she is dead and because of what that has done to me. Why is everyone singing?

The soloists arrive midweek, and on Wednesday morning, as I walk back from breakfast, the haunting sound of a mezzo-soprano voice wafts over the hills. The voice is full and rich, and it moves slowly up the scale as though each note were a devotion, an offering to the sky and the sun. Carefully, deliberately it moves from one note to the next, resting for seconds in each, letting the breath explore the sound on the vowel. Each note becomes its own aria, dynamics and timbre shifting to take it through a range of colors on its unhurried way forward. The simple vocalize captures me, and I freeze, standing silently until it is over.

Immediately I decide to attend the soloists' rehearsal that afternoon, wanting to put a face and form to the haunting power of that voice. There is one in my imaginings: a large, statuesque woman, her head raised with confidence, the resonance flowing in one unbroken line from the soles of her feet through her expanded core of breath support, and echoing through the bones in her face and skull. I smile as I remember the few times I had that feeling long ago. The body like a tuning fork, possessed by the tone, every muscle relaxed and open as the note expands inside and radiates out, filling space like light expanding into darkness. "Sing to the last row of the balcony," was the way my childhood voice teachers tried to convey the experience. The tuning fork was the only way to get there.

But when I enter the shed, my illusion is shattered. A small, soft pincushion of a man stands on stage, preparing to sing. His face is contorted in the familiar grimaces of the green room . . . eyebrows elevated, chin tucked as he pulls his soft palate up inside his mouth, opening the space for the head voice to resonate. He emits a few warm-up hoots into that space, and I have no doubt. It is a countertenor voice, not a mezzo. It is that rare male voice that sits in the same range as a female contralto or mezzo-soprano, an artifact from the Baroque era of music, when women were rarely allowed a performance career, and male voices had to be altered to sing the female musical lines. I have never heard one in person before, and I am fascinated by his technique and the extraordinary tone his small frame produces.

He is there with another man, a tall muscular complement to him, who nods reassuringly and offers encouragement to his questioning glances after each phrase. They both look over and smile at me, the only other person in the audience.

After rehearsal I walk over to offer my astonished praise.

"Your voice is stunning; I have never heard anything like it."

He seemed delighted. "I had a career as a tenor," he said, but my high range was limited, so that restricted the roles I could perform. My teacher encouraged me to forget those notes and explore a bell range above them."

"What did you do?"

"I took a year off, did no performing, and just worked on my voice. Once my countertenor emerged, my career took off."

I left the shed with a sense of amazement, humbled and excited at the same time. The unexpected is here for me, prodding me to stop leaning on what I think I know and be open to what is new.

....

So much about my own behavior here is unexpected as well. So much I would not have anticipated. It's a bit humbling for a psychologist who thinks she knows herself pretty well. I did not expect to play this game of silence with the universe. And I certainly didn't expect the universe to play back.

Yesterday I met a nurse. I liked her instantly. She was quiet, thoughtful and reflective. She sensed my boundaries and was comfortable respecting them. As we chatted, she told me that she worked in Baltimore serving the inner city families who live in and around Johns Hopkins. The universe plays a card.

I shared my profession but little else, and ignored her mention of the hospital. Later in the day we came across one another heading for the nearby town of Sheffield. She invited me to join her. I begged off, saying I needed to return early for a nap before evening rehearsal.

Today we sat together on the bus coming from the group tour to the Norman Rockwell Museum. I took the lead this time, asking about her work and telling her I had been at Johns Hopkins earlier this year. She did not ask why, only whether I drove from Maine. "No," I replied, "I commuted from Herndon, Virginia, where my sister and brother-in-law lived." I'm bluffing here, not sure I'll answer if she asks the obvious question. But I keep my poker face. The universe backs down.

Tonight, after 10:00 P.M., I walked the campus alone. It feels isolated, but in a safe and protected way, as if I could walk anytime and not worry about danger. I took myself down to the main road, pausing beneath the canopy of huge old trees that line the driveway and join overhead to create a tunnel as the driveway extends a quarter-mile down to the road.

This is like Kübler-Ross's work on the stages of dying, I suddenly thought, as I retraced my steps back up the long hill to my room. The dying bargain for time (if only I can live till Christmas, my son's wedding), or mode (if only I have no pain or loss of dignity). Something they can trade with death, whose gift to them, unwelcome and unbidden, is impossible to refuse. A trade offers a sense of participation and control of the process.

Is it the stages of grieving that I'm negotiating? It seems I am bargaining with life. I will live if . . . I will let go of my sadness if . . . I will reclaim the centerpiece of my life if . . . If what? What choice do I have? It's a bit of a charade. I am far from suicidal; not going forward is inconceivable. If what, then? What am I willing to trade? I am playing a funny little game of chicken with the universe. It taunts me, and I back off. I step forward gingerly, then pull away. Why does my silence feel so powerful?

Thursday afternoon was our first rehearsal in the performance shed. It is huge, with risers for the chorus and a wide stage for the orchestra and soloists. It has an open air feel and a sense of spaciousness that makes me feel tiny as I stand embedded in the middle of the soprano section. Rehearsal was exciting and a bit frightening. The chorus is very good, but we can be lazy and careless—a fault of amateurs. I am guilty, too. There are still parts of the music I do not know as well as I should. I found the singing a bit harder tonight. I can still "muscle" the tone rather than trust myself to sing softly in my head voice.

Trust is what I came to learn: to trust my voice, my intuition and skill, and let anxiety and fear of failure recede. I have made some progress here. My voice is stronger, and I am looking forward to the weekend's performance.

I came to learn something else as well. I need to decide how to live the rest of my life. I cannot be the way I was before Martha's death. I cannot go ahead with the same energy, single-mindedness, and assurance. I don't have answers yet, but I'm beginning to understand the question. It is not *whether* to live that I am negotiating. It is *how*. The rest of my life has to be deliberate, and chosen. I must be responsible for it in a way I never have been. I don't know what I will choose, but I know it must be more conscious and constructed. Like the counterpoint of a Bach fugue, the threads must be woven precisely. No random harmonies will do.

But like the countertenor, I will need to go beyond what I have known. Perhaps that is what the silence is about. To open the space above the notes I know. To find my own hidden range.

Chapter 32

Fall

❯❯❯❯❯❯❯❯❯❯❯❯

Fall has always been my favorite time of year. I welcome the heat of summer lifting, the cool crisp breezes in Maine air, and the need for a sweater on August nights. The first smell of the wood-stove is delicious, and I look forward to evenings in front of my Jøtul, relaxing and letting my feet burn. But the fall of 1998 crept up on me. September was six months since Martha's death, a fact that startled me when I turned the calendar and counted. *Can it be six months?* I thought. *Not possible.*

Fall colors are Martha's colors. Her burnished copper hair highlighted with reds, her eyes soft blue with flecks of gold. Everywhere I looked, fall was throwing her colors at me like tiny arrows. A simple flash of foliage blurred and morphed behind my eyes—the rust color of her favorite sweater in the deep magenta hills, the float of her Irish shawl in the shifting greens at dusk, the pattern of a familiar scarf in an orange/gold branch waving in the wind.

My mother and I took our annual trip into the mountains, a quiet stay in ski country before the snow falls. We missed it last year as Peggy was dying, but this year it seems essential. It's a chance to go at a slower pace together, and to give my mother the undivided attention she so seldom gets from me. The weather was clear and bright, but the mountain foliage was not. It was muted, a disappointment to the tourists. The vibrant yellow of the birch trees was missing, meteorologists explained, because the January ice storm had killed so many. I believed it was nature in mourning.

My own mourning was finding its path, and my children

were my primary healers. In a scene that repeated more times than I could count in the months after Martha's death, Matt found me sitting alone at the woodstove and walked quietly to the piano.

"Do you want me to play for a while?"

"I would love that."

And, for an hour or more, he sat and improvised, playing his own pieces, fragments of jazz classics, chord progressions that rose and fell, creating tension and resolution. He shifted smoothly, never lifting his hands from the keyboard. Pathways flowed, subtle shifts finding their way from one piece to another, winding through gentle key changes, like a path through the forest, bringing each scene into focus, each emotion into expression. The language of music filled the space between us, and when he was done, I offered only a simple "thank you," and he smiled.

Margaret was almost twelve, and on the ninth of September, Martha's six-month anniversary, we headed off on a shopping trip after school. "I think Martha would have liked being remembered with a trip to T. J. Maxx and a few bargains," I suggested.

She looked hesitant, as always, when I mentioned Martha's name, and peered over at my eyes. "Are you crying?" she asked, scanning my face.

"No, I'm OK," I said, used to this dialogue with her. "Come on, let's go."

As I walked through the photo frame aisle, I could feel myself surreptitiously scanning. I do not have any pictures out yet, but I am beginning to want one. I am not sure I could see it every day without too much pain, but I can feel the tide turning. I know the photo I want. It was taken on Martha's first Christmas with Liamarie. They are dressed in matching holiday dresses I splurged on as an early Christmas gift, and Herb took wonderful photos. The dresses frame matching ear-to-ear smiles. *The definition of happiness*, I thought when I first saw the picture.

"Mom, can I try these on?" Margaret interrupted, coming up behind me, and I was glad to move away.

....

The six-month anniversary week had its own markers in my life. Justin turned twenty-two on September 12, and he called that afternoon. He was in D.C., frantic to get to another apartment near the Capitol before it was rented. "It's impossible. Everything is gone by the time I get there," he complained.

We talked for more than an hour about his new job as a congressional aide, about the hypocrisy of politics, seen at its worst that week when the Ken Starr report on Bill Clinton hit the news-stands, about his decision to defer law school. In the shade of dis-couragement, he was second-guessing everything. "I don't know if I really want this. It is so different from the world of ideas and philosophy. But I think I want to be in the world, not in an ivory tower." From Plato's Republic to the morality play being staged in Congress, our conversation covered the gamut.

I did not have answers for him. Just a willing ear, a little per-spective, and some encouragement to take it day by day. Housing would help enormously. He'd been staying at Herb's for just a week, but I could hear the agitation in his voice. Like his mother, he needs his own quiet nest. Mostly I think how lucky I am that he calls and shares his struggles and listens to my inadequate offerings.

Across the kitchen table, Matt sat patiently. The call had inter-rupted our conversation, a frustrated tirade about a talented musi-cian friend doing drugs. He was concerned, but also annoyed. "He's a lousy drummer when he's stoned, Mom, and he just doesn't get it."

He sat while I talked to Justin, curious to hear how his life was going, and after the call, he was waiting for me at the piano, ready to pick up another part of our conversation, one we had begun to have more and more.

"I know I have to go to college, Mom, but I know what I want to do with my life. I can't imagine spending four more years doing what others tell me I have to do. I don't care about a campus and a football team and all that. I feel like I just want to start my life and take courses."

His artistic drive is so strong, so clear, even at this young age. He wants to trust it but struggles with choosing a path so different from his brother's. "You are not Justin," I remind him for the thousandth time. "It's OK not to want what he wanted." We have had this conversation before, and this time it traverses some delicate terrain, trying to find a balance between trusting his inner voice and preparing himself for a world that will make demands on his dreams that he cannot yet imagine.

And Margaret, who three times that week pulled me to the bathroom mirror to stand beside her. "I'm taller, Mumma, I really am," she insisted, stretching her neck to show off that extra half inch. She could not be more proud. But Friday, she got her period for the first time, and she was devastated. "This is the worst thing that's ever happened to me in my life," she sobbed in my arms. "I'm not ready for this; I'm not." I was startled, but I should not have been. Abandoned by her own body, abandoned by childhood, she was finally able to cry it out.

And that six-month anniversary week offered one more marker of time moving forward. Mirka, the nanny Herb has chosen, arrived from Poland and began her stay with Liamarie. I met her first on the phone, and she was warm and curious.

"Hi, Mary Beth, can I call you that?"

"Of course, and can you help me pronounce your name?"

"Well, call me Mirka, it is a nickname, but easier to pronounce than Miroslawa."

"Oh yes," I said, and I could hear Liamarie giggling in the background.

"Herb says I can call you anytime if I have questions. She is so tiny, and she does not eat much," she says tentatively. "I was afraid to pick her up when I first saw her. Afraid she might break."

We laughed, and I felt close to her already.

Herb's nightly calls end with putting Mirka on the phone.

"He talks to her like a grown up," she says hesitantly one night, and I am impressed with her insight. "Even I don't know what he means sometimes."

"Good," I said and laughed. "Just say that and help him keep it simple. Remind him."

"But my daughter is a genius!" I can hear Herb teasing in the background.

"Of course, Herb, of course, but sentences, please, not paragraphs . . . she's still just four."

Mirka is from a small mining town in the Silesian area of Poland, and though she speaks three languages, her world had been small before coming to America. The Subaru wagon is twice the size of any car she drove in Poland, and suburban D.C. traffic is initially overwhelming. But Herb is a patient teacher, and small moments of terror lead to laughter and help cut through her reservations about speaking her mind. One night Herb tossed a ham in the trash, dissatisfied with its taste. Mirka gasped behind him. "That would feed my family for a month!"

And Sunday after church, he treated her to a buffet at a local restaurant, but she could not relax. "Too much food," she told me that night, "and people leave it half-eaten on their plates. In my country fruit is so rare. I did not taste an orange until I was fifteen."

Most of our conversation is about Liamarie. Mirka is observant and thoughtful, not afraid to set limits, but willing to play games and spend time doing the simple things that give Liamarie pleasure. And she wants to know about Martha.

"What was she like? Was she like Herb?"

"Oh no," I said, "not so excitable, and a bit more comfortable sitting still." I want to reinforce her gentle way with Liamarie. "More like you are, Mirka."

And as we talk night after night, her growing protectiveness is apparent. One evening she began our conversation carefully. "Herb is so busy. He does not like to stay home." I can hear the question she is not sure she can ask, and I answered it instantly.

"He still needs to run, Mirka, I know. That's why it's so good you are here."

"But I am not her papa. Sometimes she just needs her papa."

"I know. Give it time, Mirka, just give it time."

My words are soothing, comforting, affirming her quiet intuitions about Liamarie as we get to know one another. I cannot wait to meet her, and in my heart I keep saying "thank you" to whatever guardian angels are responsible for her arrival.

Chapter 33

Holidays

❯❯❯❯❯❯❯❯❯❯❯

Markers of time. Repositories of memory. Celebrations of accomplishments. Simple stop signs to make us look back and forward with intention. I thought I knew about holidays, but in the year after Martha's death, they became a mystery again. I was only beginning to understand what I have pretended to know all these years.

My birthday came in mid-October. I did not dread it, more aware than ever of age as a gift, not a curse. Complaining about turning fifty-one seemed self-indulgent and shallow. Anyway, I didn't feel it. It was to be a neutral day: appointments in the office, dinner at a nearby restaurant with my family, then home to open a few presents . . . small, thoughtful things from the kids and something special, probably jewelry this year, from Bill.

I wasn't prepared for the onslaught. It began building as I left the office, walking across the garage and heading inside. The house was empty. I felt a surge of resistance: *No, no, no,* it began to chant. *You will not do this; you will not leave this year behind.*

Blessedly, I was alone. *Cry it out,* I thought, *then shower and change and go to dinner.*

But the tears would not stop. They came in waves, each one bigger than the last. This was not sadness; no, nothing so benign. This was angry resistance, rage-filled refusal to accept that my life was going to go even one day past the year in which my sister lived in my life.

No, no, no, I will not do this, I cannot leave this year behind, it chanted louder and louder. In the shower I flailed, pounding the tile and howling my despair. I could not stop it. Like no other time I cried, this grief seemed to have no bottom, only an endless pouring up and out. *Don't make me go on, God, don't make me, don't make me!*

I managed to dress and leave for the Yarmouth seaside restaurant where my family waited. They were sitting at a table near the door when I came in. I was grateful for that, still feeling I might have to get up and leave at any moment. But in good old Irish Catholic tradition, I began to coach myself. *You can do this, just relax and be here in this moment, the feelings will pass.* I did not want to disappoint, to upset this moment for my mother or my children. *No, not here, not now,* that voice was coaching. *Let it go and just be here.*

But inside, the battle raged. I tried to answer a simple question and found I could not speak. My throat closed as waves met the wall behind my eyes. I dropped my eyes and pretended to eat, but I could not swallow. Something was pushing back deep in my throat, and every bite of food hurt getting past it. I looked down at my plate.

"I'm sorry . . ." I began, and pulled my coat from the back of the chair.

"Is your dinner all right?" my mother asked.

"Fine. I just don't feel well. I need to go," I said quickly. "Will you take Grandma home?" I said directly to Bill, who knew what that meant. I could not endure the ritual opening of presents around the living room coffee table. I heard the kids come in quietly an hour later and lay some gifts on the glass coffee table without comment. No one challenged my breaking the rules.

The next morning I came downstairs early, determined to salvage some celebration.

"I'll open them now, I think," I said.

"No kids?" Bill asked.

I shook my head. Then I looked at the table. There, hidden among the multicolored packages, was a small silver foil wrapped box with a tiny dime-sized bow.

When I saw it, I stopped breathing.

One look at his expectant face told me he had no idea. Smiling, he waited for me to open it. *First you have to breathe,* I thought, *just breathe.*

Memories flooded back. A visit Martha and I had made to two favorite Freeport jewelry stores last August. In one she was tempted by an amethyst ring, set in a halo wire that matched a pendant I had given her years before. She resisted, but I made note. In the second shop, while she bought some inexpensive piece, I admired a set of garnet studs and pendant, uniquely cut stones that looked almost like rubies in the light. That October 15, my fiftieth birthday, the set arrived, a gift from her.

A few weeks later, I bought the amethyst ring, and they wrapped it in silver foil with a tiny green bow. "Is it for someone special?" the jeweler asked. "It's for my sister, and if she opens this on Christmas Eve, it will mean she has successfully completed a bone marrow transplant." I replied.

I held Bill's gift in my hand for a long time before I said anything. The same box, the same tiny bow. *Be here, be here, be here.*

"I think you will like them," Bill coaxed gently, not sure what was stopping me.

He was right. Beautiful blue-green Maine tourmaline studs. I held the box open for a long time, letting the light catch their deep, rich color. "They're beautiful, just beautiful," I said quietly, and he smiled. But the words I could not speak pulled past and future together in a swirl of emotion too complicated to express. Lasts and losses, losses and lasts.

"I wanted you to have something special this year," he said.

And she would have been the first person I called.

....

Thanksgiving Day I woke before 5:00 A.M., lying quietly until 6:00 so as not to disturb Bill. It would be just our family around the table this Thanksgiving. Herb was taking Liamarie to New York City to spend the holiday with his parents. This time, Mirka would be with them. I smiled when I thought of her meeting Heriberto and Lia for the first time, remembering how overwhelming it had been for Martha. ("Everyone talks at once in Spanish and English;

time has no meaning; no topic is off limits, and emotion rules," she had told me in amazement).

I kept looking over at the clock, hoping to avoid the alarm, rise quietly, and keep the house in silence for a few more hours. The turkey was stuffed and in the oven by 6:40 and the first round of dishes done. I went back to bed, sliding in beside Bill as he slept. *What will this holiday bring?* I wondered. I felt calm, quiet, as I lay there waiting for turkey fragrance to fill the house, but I did not trust myself. My birthday had taught me a lesson. Be prepared. Be watchful. You cannot know what color of mourning will be reflected in the rituals of celebration.

Funny, I always thought it was about memories: the empty chair at the table, the picture she should be in and is not this year. But it is so much more than that. It is as much about the beginning of the future as it is about the end of the past.

Where is it going? Why do I get to go, and must I leave her behind if I do?

Chapter 34

December 1998

In early December I flew to Herndon for a weekend. Christmas was approaching, and I could feel the tension building in me. I needed to see lights and decorations away from home first, a sort of trial run for the real thing in a few weeks, when we would all be in Maine together.

It still hurt to go to Martha's home. Walking up from the driveway, I closed my eyes and saw her swagger, her long legs covering the distance in several steps fewer than my own. It was a relief that I no longer expected her to appear in the doorway, but I wondered if the other feeling would ever go—the one that said I was an intruder, breaking in and taking something that did not belong to me—a thief stealing pieces of the life she should have had.

Herb's redecorating was complete. A new dining room set and updated living room furniture transformed the first floor. Clean contemporary lines with a Spanish flair replaced the "Goodwill eclectic" of the past. A large mirror with colorful inlays embedded in a wide wooden frame hung over the dining table. Strong colors and sharp angles startled me a bit as my eyes got used to them. He needed to make it different and new, and he had accomplished that handsomely.

A few familiar pieces showed up in unfamiliar places. The glass-doored cabinet from the kitchen was now a bookcase in Herb's bedroom. Next to it sat the glider, the one where we had both rocked Liamarie as an infant. I stood quietly looking at its soft, plaid cushion, barely worn.

I remembered the afternoon she sat in that chair, recuperating from her mastectomy. We had pulled it up as close as we could get to the couch, where Liamarie and I sat with a big book in our laps. Martha could not lift Liamarie or even hold her in her lap until her scars were healed, and Liamarie didn't like that. We pulled it up close so Martha could lean in and join us, playing with figurine cutouts that fit into slots in an oversized Nutcracker ballet book.

"See, the ballerina goes here," Martha explained. "And where does this one go?" After handing Liamarie the piece, she leaned back and winced as her torso stretched. I distracted Liamarie.

"Look, it slides right in here. Let me show you how." I took her tiny fingers and guided them to slide the nutcracker in place.

When I looked up again, Martha was staring at us as if at a tableau. Her face was drained of color, her eyes filled with dread. I knew instantly what was going through her mind. *Is this the future? Am I to leave my child in your care?* I could not stand the question and rose quickly on some pretend errand in the kitchen. I let my hand rest on her shoulder briefly as I passed. There were no words between us, but her head shifted slightly in response. It was the only time I saw her afraid.

....

Liamarie was full of energy and enthusiasm on this pre-Christmas visit, and showed me around the newly decorated house with the skill of a docent. Mirka's presence had made a huge difference, and Liamarie seemed calmer and more relaxed. Her body was thriving again.

"Guess what, I weigh thirty-five pounds!" she bragged, and I cheered. At four and a half that's still tiny, but it's five pounds more than the weight she has held for the past year. It is a good sign.

"Will you come to see my ballet class? You can watch from outside."

"I would *love* to do that!"

"I get to wear a tutu, and it's pink!"

Later that afternoon, Herb dropped us both off at the ballet studio. I was the only "visiting parent," watching from behind a one way mirror. A row of six four-year-old girls tried diligently to produce the precise moves the teacher demonstrated. First position. Second position. A quick balance check; one stumbles, and they all giggle in response.

Liamarie stands out, not in her ability to control her movements, but in her natural grace. Her arms, noticeably longer than those of her peers, curve into an arc, fingertips touching gently in front of her waist. "Now wave to the music; feel it in your arms," the teacher commands.

Liamarie's long arms float to the music, the wrists bending unconsciously, her fingers fluttering softly down to her sides as the music ends.

....

"Sit in the back, sit next to me," she insisted when Herb came to retrieve us.

"OK, but you need to tell me what you want Santa to bring," I replied, buckling us up and signaling our "chauffeur" with an imperious, "On, James."

"He's not James," she said, and Herb guffawed.

"OK, on Herb," I corrected myself. "Now what about Santa. What do you want him to bring?"

"Maybe a new baby dollhouse for my new baby."

"What new baby?" I asked, thinking she had a new doll.

"The new baby my dad's going to have with his new wife. I want him to get a new wife and have a baby, and I want to be the flower girl." In one mouthful she has accomplished the meeting, the wedding, and the new sibling.

Herb's face in the rear view mirror looked stunned, but he laughed and managed a response, "Whoa, Liamarie, that might take a little time."

We talk a bit more about time, and about waiting for the right person, but I am strangely grateful for her wish. It means that she is moving on. No fantasies of Santa bringing Mama back; she is beyond that now. She is looking toward the future, wishing only that it would hurry itself along so that her family could be whole again.

The last night, a few hours after the house was dark, Liamarie knocked on my door.

"Mary Beth, I'm scared."

"Scared of what?" I asked, getting up immediately.

"Of the darkness in my room," she said, climbing into my arms.

I took her out to the living room, and we settled in the leather recliner. She tucked her head underneath my chin like an infant and fell asleep almost instantly. Later she shifted, resting her head over my heart, and I could feel my heartbeat vibrate through her skull. Finally, she lay on her back, her head cradled in the hollow of my arm, her face pointing straight up at me as she slept. We stayed that way for hours. She was not deeply asleep; she hit my elbow with her knee once and whispered, "I'm sorry," though her eyes were closed. When she finally started to stir, sunlight was beginning to fill the room. She grabbed me tightly, as if afraid I would leave, and said quickly, "I'm still afraid."

"I know, love, I know," I replied, holding her close. "But look, Liamarie, the sun is up. I think we scared away the darkness together."

Three weeks later, just a few days before Christmas, I sat at the Manchester, New Hampshire, airport and watched Herb, Liamarie, and Mirka walk toward me. Mirka is tall and slender, with a long athletic look and an ease of movement that is strikingly reminiscent. Change the hair color, squint a bit, and you might believe it was Martha coming toward you.

Mirka was excited about coming to Maine for the first time, and I was looking forward to introducing her to my family. Here she will be my guest, and on vacation from her studies at George Mason University where she is taking courses. I hoped that would mean we could have more casual time together, getting to know each other and sharing Liamarie. When I am in Herndon, I can see her deferring to my presence, giving me time alone with Liamarie and taking some break or study time as well.

"Mary Beth, can I ask . . ?" she begins tentatively on her first day.

"Mirka, you can ask anything . . . anything you like," I interrupted. "I am so grateful you are here, and whatever will help you, I will try to do."

She smiled. "Can you tell me what Martha was like? Do you have pictures? Does Liamarie look like her? I want to know so much, but I don't want it to be hard for you."

"Oh, Mirka." I shook my head trying to find the words. "So much about this is hard, but you . . . you are such a gift, and if I believed in angels, I'd think you were one. And if you are, Martha certainly had a hand in picking you out, so ask away, please ask away."

There were tears in my eyes by then, but we were both laughing.

Our Christmas Eve ritual of opening family gifts went better than I had expected. Oddly, the fact that they were a threesome helped. "To Herb, Liamarie, and Mirka," seemed OK to write on a tag or two, and by the end of the evening, we were spontaneously adding her name as we presented family gifts. She had slipped effortlessly into their little family, providing much-needed help but, more importantly, a calm and serenity we all needed.

I might have expected Mirka's presence to be difficult, a constant reminder of who should be there, but it was not. I might have anticipated her physical likeness, and even her name, to invoke my sister in a painful and caricatured way, but it did not. I sat in the corner of the family room as we opened gifts together, thinking how little I understood.

"Mama . . . I mean Mirka," Liamarie's voice and laugh brought me back. She stopped, then said, "Mirka's my mama now," deciding to go with the error.

"No, Liamarie, I am not your mama," Mirka replied gently, "I am just your nanny," and the moment passed.

But my internal response was instant and strong.

Good for you kid, try it out, open your heart to others who will mother you. Let us all know how much you need and want that in your life. Don't let us slide comfortably into our denial and wishful thinking that you are fine, adjusting well, and resolving your loss. Go for it, Liamarie!

All of this was humbling. I thought I knew a lot about grief. But every day I was learning something new. After they left, I sat for a long time alone. Maybe there are no rules for this journey.

Maybe there are only guideposts. Be on the lookout for us, they caution as you pass. Some of us will be in neon, stopping you in your tracks. Others so subtly written you may miss us. But we do not tell you where your path will lead. No easy trail markers with instructions. Go left for resolution—three months. Straight on for spiritual peace—one year.

They can only tell you that others have walked this way before you, felt what you are feeling, and have survived. This last part is seldom written. But it is the most important. Others have experienced this, and their lives continued. The experience was powerful, devastating, transformational, and survivable. This last, the most humanizing piece of information, is omitted. And it is this simple fact that we are seeking. Tell me that this is survivable. If I can believe that, I can find my own path through the darkness.

There are a few other things I need to remember, things that will forever change the way I offer help or condolences to others in grief.

Time does not heal. Do not look for distance from the event to provide relief. Often it provides the opposite. Others acclimate to the fact of your loss and expect you to do the same. Instead, the pain deepens and spreads out. It is not as sharp or cutting, but pervasive and broad, seeping in at a cellular level, becoming part of your being. No, time alone does not heal. It merely gives you a chance to absorb the loss, to breathe it in and store it in a way that is not paralyzing. But this is not healing, repairing, filling in the wound. Nothing can do that.

If there is anything about time that does heal, it is experience. Living with the loss, creating a life around it, inclusive of it, does heal. In that way, this Christmas was healing. The ritual of the tree, the gifts, the familiar decorations—all proceeding as they have in the past—was strangely soothing. When Martha's absence threatened to spoil the moment, I imagined her watching, disapproving of our break from the festive atmosphere she loved so much.

Do it right, I imagined her saying sternly, *as if I were there.*

And when we did, she was.

No one's loss is like yours. Respect for that uniqueness is essential. I shall never again be so quick to offer my loss as a balm to others. There is no antidote to another person's pain. Respect that, acknowledge their loss, and let it exist in its uniqueness. There will be a time for conversation, for community, for sharing the universal experience of loss. This, the early phase of grief, is a time when no one's story matters but your own.

And what is my grief? It is not a well of sadness. It is more like an internal earthquake, shifting tectonic plates. There are crevasses now where I can fall, disappearing into a place with no bottom. I look whole on the outside, but the terrain within is broken. I must be cautious of aftershocks. Her handwriting on a shopping list in my kitchen junk drawer is enough to rock the fragile ground and threaten to break my hold.

Grief is not a broken heart for me. Grief is a fractured soul.

Chapter 35

The Hospital

In January 1999, I became the patient. When I woke after surgery, I was annoyed. I was lying on my back in a hospital bed, a catheter draining on my left and a morphine pump attached to the IV in my right arm. I was trapped, unable to roll to either side without tugging uncomfortably at something, and I wondered at the nursing plan. *Whose bright idea was this?* I could not move, so I slept sporadically, flat on my back with my arms outstretched as if on a crucifix.

A medical student arrived to take my vital signs. With the stethoscope resting on my chest, he jumped suddenly and, before I could stop him, ran out of the room. A few minutes later, the resident was by his side, listening to my heartbeat. "Has anyone ever told you that you have an irregular heartbeat?" she asked, and I nodded, trying not to embarrass him. "Connected to respiration?" I nodded again, and she took a few moments to explain this to him. He looked chastened. "But you can help me with this," I offered, and together we reset the lines.

I was on Maine Medical Center's cancer floor. Around me, next to me, walking in the halls were others there for surgery, or chemotherapy and, yes, even bone marrow transplants. I saw a few walk by with masks over their faces, IV poles in their hands as they trudged through the halls, valiantly trying to exercise.

The unit was brand new, opened only two weeks before. It had the strong smell of new paint and the unmarked glisten of walls not yet fingered or spattered. The floor was designed in a large circle with one additional corridor that jutted off like the straight line on a "b." I was near the end of the corridor, so I didn't see much traffic, just the occasional venturesome soul, pole in hand, or a visitor heading for the one room beyond mine.

My roommate is Hazel. She's probably in her late sixties and from northern Maine, four hours and a culture away from the hospital to which she has been sent for treatment of her cancer. She's feisty. "So there *is* a Dr. Tammara!" she exclaims when he arrives, residents in tow, to examine her. Her meaning is not lost on anyone, especially those of us who have heard her complain that she has not seen him since her surgery. In a few moments he has charmed her, and she is asking whether she might take the young medical student home with her.

I feel guilty, lying in the next bed. He did come to see me, shortly after the surgery, even staying to talk about the impeachment scandal in Washington. He came in again the next day to let me know he would be away on Saturday. I really don't need, or deserve, such attention. And I am not sure why I am getting it. But that is not why I feel guilty.

I don't have cancer. I'm here for a hysterectomy and bladder repair. A severe case of bronchitis coughing tore the muscles around my bladder more than a year before, just before Liamarie moved in. When my doctor suggested surgical repair, I laughed, "I have other things on my agenda the next few months," I told her. "OK," she said, "but you'll be back. Don't lift anything more than ten pounds," she advised. Liamarie weighed about thirty, I guessed.

Months went by, and Martha's illness and death took over my life. Only recently had I let myself pay attention to the pain in my gut and the feeling of pressure whenever I exercised. It was getting worse. When I returned to my doctor in late fall, she didn't even examine me. "I didn't think you'd last this long," was her only comment as she handed me the surgical referral. She was running late that day, so I didn't tell her why I had.

Dr. Tammara is a gentle soul. He speaks in a softly accented voice, and his style is a bit more formal than his American counterparts'. "I pulled some strings," he said grandly, "and got you up here on my new unit. Rank has some privileges." He laughed when he mentioned rank, as if that was silly pretension. But he is the head of OB/GYN oncology and surgery in spite of his humble presentation. I knew him by reputation, one of the advantages of being a therapist, intimately involved in so many people's lives. He thinks we are strangers, and I cannot challenge that without breaking confidences. But the stories I cannot share made me feel he is the surgeon I would want for myself. He is gentle, respectful, and, in his own words, "a man of honor." How lovely to hear this said without embarrassment or arrogance, just simple pride and self-respect.

I do not have cancer. It's my shameful secret up here. It echoes in my head, but I do not speak it aloud. Occasionally, a nurse refers to my being a "general surgical patient," and I cringe a little, thinking Hazel will understand. I am not waiting for the dreaded pathology report that she asks about every day. She leaves the hospital without knowing its contents, with only the doctor's gently ambivalent reassurance, "I don't think it will tell us anything new."

I do not have cancer. And yet fate has brought me here to the cancer floor to lie in this bed and pretend, to imagine what it must have been like for her to lie in a ward just like this, with no reprieve, no alien status like mine.

I do not have cancer. But I cannot be grateful, cannot feel blessed, cannot even feel obligated in some positive way. I can only feel guilty.

The guilt is what I need to face. If I can't beat it, I can't go on with my life. Not with force, with energy, or with passion. I will live in regret that I am experiencing what she cannot. I'll let the unfairness of that stifle my goals and sabotage my successes. I'll live in anger that I must feel happiness when happiness seems a cruel gift wrapped in despair. I'll see my life through a veil and refuse to break its grey hold on the light. I know what guilt does—chronic, persistent, pervasive guilt that seeps in at a cellular level and alters every movement, every feeling, every experience. I can't let that be her legacy.

So I walked the corridor. Just once, an hour before I was discharged. There were no paintings hung yet, no benches or tables to break the smooth flow of white walls. It was silent and had the feeling of a movie set, as though nothing behind the façade was real. Many of the rooms were empty, and I passed them quietly. In one doorway, a woman caught my eye and offered a cheery "Hello," inviting conversation, but I smiled softly and continued.

Around the corner, almost back to where the circle began for me, I came to the rooms. Two large angled rooms with enormous glass windows. Stunning views over the city of Portland and toward the White Mountains beckoning in the distance. A familiar bold-lettered warning sign was on the entryway: Hi-dose chemotherapy. Do not enter.

These are the transplant patients. The beds were occupied but angled so I could only see the backs of their heads and the IV poles next to the beds. They do not know I am there, yet we see the same view through their windows.

I stood for a moment, waiting. There was no movement, no sound. I felt nothing. But I stood expectantly, waiting for absolution.

Section IV

Growing

Let love clasp grief lest both be drowned . . .
—Alfred, Lord Tennyson

Chapter 36

A Child's Anniversary

>>>>>>>>>>>>

How do you remember without words?

Watching Liamarie experience the first anniversary of her mother's death, I was reminded again and again of how childhood memory works. Sensate memory is primary. Recollections are visceral, embedded in the cells and muscles. Words are only a secondary accompaniment, insufficient to convey the depth of recollection.

"She's not sleeping again," Herb reported, "and when she does she wakes with nightmares. Some days she is just agitated, irritable, and ready to fall apart over nothing. It's as though her whole body is remembering."

That is not far from the truth. Like most four-and-a-half-year-olds, Liamarie's language is about the present, about the immediate experience of her life. She has very little vocabulary yet to talk about the past or to express feelings about events far away in time, even in her own life.

"I can hold her, but I don't know if it helps to talk about it. Sometimes it just seems to make her more agitated, and she just can't settle," Herb continued.

"She can feel what happened a year ago, Herb, but she can't really describe it. And she can't use words to soothe herself yet like we can, to explain what she is going through. I think the best thing you can do is tell her that you understand that it's a very hard time, and that she needs extra hugs right now. Too much explanation of why might just overstimulate her."

"Good. It's so hard for me too, to go over and over it."

....

When I was with Liamarie, I could sense her tension and respond with tone and gesture. I felt my body going into play therapy mode, my own visceral return to my child inpatient hospital experience. There is very little language involved in providing a container to hold the anxiety, sadness, and other powerful emotions in a four- or six- or nine-year-old. Words are tools to convey presence, safety, comfort. Their literal meaning, their sequence and syntax barely matter. They are utterances that support what is far more important.

Every muscle in the therapist's body needs to convey two conflicting messages: I am relaxed, in control, able to soothe your pain; and I am with you in that pain, experiencing it with intensity and awareness. Watch me, this posture says. Lean if you can. Trust me to bear this with you. I will show you one step forward, one way to feel better. It is exhausting, and my heart goes out to Herb, trying to do this every day as Liamarie grieves.

It was hardest for me on the phone, when Liamarie's entries into memory were clipped, tangential, and sometimes out of nowhere. "Do you remember when you took me on the plane all by myself?" she asked one night unexpectedly.

I wondered which flight she meant. There were three: the original trip home on the fifteenth, then a week later a disappointing trip back to Maine "for just a short time," we promised. Then finally, the sudden trip a week later, when we did not believe Martha would survive the weekend.

I cannot see her, cannot read her face, the movement of her hands, the telling leg bounce. Without these cues, it is hard to tell what emotion lies behind this simple question.

"What do you remember?" I probed, hoping she would give me more cues.

"Oh, I don't know . . . is Margaret there? Can I talk to her?"

A moment of connection unsatisfied.

Another day in March, when the D.C. area got an unexpected snowstorm, Liamarie called again.

"Do you remember the snow lady we made? Her name was Martha," she reminded me.

I took a snapshot that day through the kitchen window as she and Margaret worked. Margaret was kneeling in the snow, her hair to her waist, and Liamarie was reaching up to put a hat and gloves on their tiny creation.

"I do, and your mama liked her a lot when she saw her," I said.

"But she was melting then."

"Yes, but she still made Mama smile."

I can see Martha laughing at it through the kitchen window. I wonder if Liamarie can see her too.

....

Shortly after the first anniversary of Martha's death, Margaret and I flew to Herndon for an overdue visit. My surgery and recuperation had made my separation from Liamarie longer than usual, and I was looking forward to holding her.

"I miss my mama. I miss my mama. I miss my mama." Herb says it is like exhaling now—a frequent repeated statement, brief but sad, over and over again during the day. Sometimes it has no apparent antecedent. Sometimes it comes in frustration over some small thing gone awry.

"I don't ever want to suppress her sadness or tell her she can't say that," he worried. "But sometimes I think it is manipulative."

"It might be, but I'm worried about something else."

If every four-year-old discomfort, disappointment, or frustration leads to that thought, grieving can be attenuated. If every problem leads to a source with no solution, the loss becomes the centerpiece around which all other emotions are experienced.

"Ask her what else she is feeling," I suggested. "See if you can move her back to the emotion that triggered the sadness. That one may have a solution or at least a separate identity that we can do something about."

"I miss Mary Beth too," she answered one night, and he suggested a call, which seemed to soothe her.

Not all feelings are about Mom, though all may lead to thoughts of Mom. We need to help her separate those she can respond to with energy and action. We need to give her back her power. The feeling that has no solution cannot be allowed to overwhelm her—and us.

....

The first night of the weekend, Margaret and I put her to bed. "I miss my mama," she offered again. "I miss her too," I replied.

"Sometimes I miss her more when people are here," she said quietly.

Of course. The touch of a hand, sitting on my lap, watching me with my daughter—all these are sensory reminders of her own mother. I know our voices are alike, and our way of nestling her, tucking her head against my neck. How painful for her to want and need this so much, yet have it be a reexperience of what she misses every day—the sights, sounds, smells, and tactile experience of mothering. And so I sat on the bed, and we talked about how visits make us remember more, and this is good and bad. It hurts to remember.

"I know, Liamarie. I love to hug you, but then I wish your mom were hugging you too."

"It makes me sad and happy at the same time."

"Me too, Liamarie. Me too."

Margaret's presence is a mixed blessing as well. Liamarie adores her and always wants her to come with me on visits. But I watch the look on her face whenever Margaret and I have some private word or glance between us. It is more than being left out, more than wanting to be included. It is anger, resentment, the look of a child locked out of a candy store, watching others inside selecting treats. Watching us be mother and daughter is another visual memory of what is missing for her now. There is no one to offer her that intimacy, no one to rescue her when Margaret reaches for me.

Liamarie has not asked yet why her mother died, but the question is coming. Causes are beginning to matter as she approaches five, and her cognitive development pushes her more and more toward an understanding of why things happen as they do. Soon the simple concrete answers about illness and failed treatments will not be enough. I sensed it on Saturday evening when I put her to bed. I tucked her in and snuggled next to her on the bed as we arranged her animals.

We spoke softly. "I miss Mama."

"Me too, Liamarie, I miss her all the time." This time I added an opening. "You know, sometimes it makes me very, very angry that she died."

She did not move and was silent for a long moment.

"It's all God's fault, you know," she finally offered.

"Do you think so?"

She nodded solemnly.

How do you explain to a child that the God she is learning about in Sunday school, an all-powerful God who could create the universe, is not to blame for her mother's death? Pray to Him, put your faith in Him, we instruct our children, and He will take care of you. By taking your most important caretaker away?

I could try to explain a God who does not cause evil but permits it along with disease, suffering, and tragedy for reasons that are incomprehensible to many adults, never mind a four-year-old child. But I do not. If God did not make it happen, He certainly let it happen. In the causality of a child, there is no distinction.

And so I could only offer the simple truth. "It is very hard to understand, even for grown-ups, why God would let your mama die. It doesn't seem to make any sense at all."

She gave me a long hug and seemed relieved I had not tried to justify the unjustifiable.

Chapter 37

Sleep

Since Martha's death Herb has struggled, mostly unsuccessfully, with Liamarie's sleep issues. Getting her to fall asleep at a reasonable hour was challenging. Insisting that she stay in her own bed throughout the night was a battle. And finding ways for her to sleep deeply without nightmares seemed impossible. While these were clearly grieving and trauma issues, they were not entirely new concerns. Some had been there long before her mother died.

When Martha first asked me to take Liamarie, it was the thing she apologized for the most. "She just doesn't sleep. It's my fault. I just can't seem to get her to go down early, and she always ends up in my bed. Sometimes she's still wide awake at ten or eleven," she admitted.

It was a sensitive issue. Martha's usually consistent parenting had faltered in the months of her chemotherapy. She was alone, exhausted, and unwilling to engage her daughter in a daily battle over bedtime. I had colluded then, reassuring her that we could fix the problem later. And when Liamarie came to stay with us, we did make progress, gradually moving her bedtime back to a more normal hour. But even then nightmares were a problem, and her need to have me at arms' length all night long was impossible to break.

A year after Martha's death, Herb was still struggling with all of this. Often nothing soothed Liamarie except the physical connection of knowing he was there beside her, her hand or foot against him like an umbilical cord. "She has to be touching me. If I roll over, she wakes," he confided.

She might start the night in her own bed, then wake in a panic and run to his room. Over and over again, he brought her back to her room, only to be awakened an hour later. When his anger and frustration showed, she would panic, shaking all over and sobbing uncontrollably. "Only you can make me not scared, Papa, only you."

What is it about sleep that so triggers the grieving, the loss—especially the fear? All the words we use to describe sleep mirror the neurological process of turning down the body's systems for activity and alertness. Turning these down also turns down our defenses. One has to feel safe to let go.

Sleep is a "letting go" response, I tell my patients. Those with issues of control, fear of dependence, or hypervigilant anxiety can often articulate what an act of trust it requires to "let go," even to one's own body.

And to make things harder, in the transitional states between sleep and wakefulness, we are subject to visual distortions, perceptual hallucinations, and waves of emotion uncensored by logic and unmodulated by cognition. Shadows become monsters, a closet door unrecognizable, a mild toothache unbearable.

Who among us has not awakened in a panic, heart racing, thoughts taken by some imagined terror? "Oh, thank God to be awake!" we exclaim as alertness gives us back our sense of time and place, and the logic of common reality.

How much more difficult for a young child, caught in the same terror, but without clear boundaries between fantasy and reality, without the logic of the real to fend off the imagined, without the experience of the known to quiet the unknown. And more than that, what if the terror is not imagined, not the dreamed-of monster, but the real flesh and blood loss of the arms that held you and kept you safe?

"Only you, Papa, only you."

⸺⸺⸺⸺⸺

That spring I brought a tote bag full of books with me on a weekend visit. Manuals for Herb, parent guidance resources, and my well-worn copy of the Boston Children's Hospital classic, *Solve*

Your Child's Sleep Problem (Ferber, Richard, 1985). Herb and I talked long into the night, trying to balance empathy for her fears with the reality that both of them needed more rest.

For Liamarie, I brought every children's book I could find about sleep, and we spent hours reading them and talking about how she and Papa were going to find a way to help her sleep in her own room all night long. When they came to Maine for Easter, things had begun to improve. She had had three or four successful nights.

Three weeks later, Liamarie called.

"Guess what, Mary Beth, I put myself to sleep and stayed in my own bed all night long!"

"How many nights now?" I asked excitedly.

"Twelve. Papa has a chart, and I've got twelve nights!"

She was so proud, then suddenly silent.

"But I still miss my mama," she said quietly. "I still want her back."

Another letting go, I thought. She was telling me, and herself, that this did not mean anything inside had changed. She had learned to sleep, to disconnect the loss from the letting go, but that was only a surface change.

"I want her back now," she whispered.

"I know, love, I know," was all I could say.

Chapter 38

Turning Five

≫≫≫≫≫≫≫

Flying in to Dulles airport, I kept thinking about time. It was fourteen months since Martha's death, but almost eighteen months since Liamarie had lived with her mother, awakened to her presence, reached for her as a primary caretaker. This weekend was her fifth birthday, and I played with the fractions in my head. Eighteen months divided into sixty months. Can that be right? Had Liamarie lived almost a third of her life without her mother? A third of my life took me back to before Margaret was born, which seemed like a lifetime ago. I wondered about relative time and memory and what it was like for Liamarie.

Last year Mother's Day and Liamarie's birthday fell on the same day, and we deleted Mother's Day from the calendar. It was too painful and too confusing. But this year they are side by side, Mother's Day on May 9, her birthday on the tenth. This year we need to face the pain. Herb had warned me, "It's been a tough week. Everything at school is about Mother's Day, and last night she crawled into my lap and said, 'Papa, I am the only person I know who doesn't have a mother.'"

On the drive back from the airport, Liamarie had me happily ensconced in the back seat next to her car seat. "Tell me Mama stories. I want to hear Mama stories."

"OK, well, when Mama was just a little girl, we lived in a camp in the summertime, near a lake. When Grandma wasn't looking, your Mama would take off all her clothes and push open the screen door very quietly. Then she'd run out of the house down the dirt road toward the water."

"She took *everything* off?" she asked in amazement.

"Yup. She liked to be naked. I guess she liked to feel the air on her butt."

Liamarie giggled, and her eyes were wide. "And what did Grandma do?"

"She ran after her. Over and over again. And after a while the neighbors would yell, 'The little blond girl went that way!'"

"Did she get to the water?"

"Oh no, she never got that far. If Grandma didn't catch her, the neighbors would hear her calling, and one of them would stop her."

"Tell me another one," Liamarie asked.

Liamarie cannot get enough of these stories of her mom as a child. She likes them so much better than stories of her own infancy with her mom. As her identity develops, she incorporates her mom's childhood into her own. She did this ... like me. She thought that ... like I do. These add to the fading memories of her mother as adult, as caretaker and nurturer. I repeat the stories over and over, but she does not mind. I wrack my brain. I wish I had more stories to tell.

Sunday is Mother's Day. A trip to Massachusetts to the gravesite would have been exhausting and would spoil Liamarie's birthday celebration. "Do you think I should do it?" Herb had asked weeks earlier. "No, but how about your garden?" I asked. They had a small patch of flowers along the side of the house. Martha had planted it carefully a few years earlier.

"Good idea. I'll get something to plant while you are here." Herb tried to get lilies of the valley, a favorite of Martha's, but they were unavailable. When I arrived, there was a blue iris plant, a shade lighter than the ones that had filled my funeral basket at her wake. It sat on the steps most of the day.

"So when do you want to plant Mama's flowers, Liamarie?"

"Not now, Papa, maybe later."

It was almost dark when her reluctance finally gave way.

"You get to pick where you want them," Herb offered.

"I want it here, inside our flowers."

"You mean the ones you and Mama planted?" Herb said, startled. She nodded.

Could she possibly remember? I looked over at Herb. There were tiny shoots peeping out in a semicircle shape. We dug a hole and placed the iris gently inside the buds. "Two springs ago." Herb whispered.

"Happy Mother's Day," Liamarie said softly, touching the blue flower with the tips of her fingers, light as a butterfly, but her face was a mask.

....

The following day I visited her day care. She reminded me several times over the weekend, "You are going to school with me on Monday, right?"

She led me, pulling me into the room where her teacher waited alone. The other students had not arrived yet. The teacher walked toward me, warm and welcoming, but I was distracted, confronted suddenly with the eight foot wide *Happy Mother's Day* banner that headlined the wall. Beneath it was a long row of colored drawings, crayoned versions of Mom. Each child had drawn a stick figure version of Mom, some in action with a child. Across the top, the teacher had written, *My mom is special because . . .* Below the drawing, each child's words completed the sentence.

My mom is special because . . . she fixes my computer is one child's entry.

My mom is special because . . . she plays games with me reads another.

As I scanned the long row of portraits, Liamarie's stood out.

My Mary Beth is special because . . . I love her. Pure and simple— it is not what I do, just that I am—a far away, not very real substitute for the mothers who are so present every day in the lives of the children around her.

"Oh, Liamarie, it is beautiful," I managed to say.

....

This year's birthday party theme had been the topic of much discussion, and I came prepared. The rainbow fish idea was easy to create, cutting a layer cake into two fish-shaped cakes which we made together in her kitchen, fitting the pieces together to make two fish.

"Look, look, it was a rectangle, and now it is a fish!" She is delighted.

"This is rainbow fish!" We cover the green frosting with bright multi-colored glitter. I am no artist, but it is as good as I can come to matching the plates and cups on the table.

"And this is rainbow fish's friend. It has to be all green," she says. Then she chooses a single gold scale and places it on his side. "There, that's all. It's the best, isn't it?"

I hesitated.

"It is, you have to say it," she demands, trying to bait me into a fight. But the children are arriving, and I don't have time to explore what this means to her.

The highlight of the day was the noontime trip to meet Papa, who had a special surprise. She could not contain her delight as we drove into the parking lot of the pet store, and he revealed her special birthday present, a green parakeet "that is *alive*," she whispered with wonder. They picked out a cage, and we carried it carefully out to the car.

"He is alive and lives in my house now," she repeated all afternoon, sitting far across the room and speaking softly. "The pet store man says we have to be quiet and give him time to get used to my house," she reminded me.

Liamarie has wanted a pet for months and this seems to be a perfect compromise for their moderate-sized home. It is an opportunity for her to care for something, to nurture and be responsible for another living thing. To nurture is to be nurtured, and for grieving children, pets can be a wonderful tool for healing.

Almost every time I visited, Liamarie pulled me aside to play a game. Her expression was determined, and I was reminded of sitting on the floor with Legos and Barbie dolls when her mother was dying. This time, she told me, the game was called "Second President's Daughter." I was stumped at first, unable to figure out why this particular game had meaning and where it came from. Herb was no wiser. Other than some general discussion of presidents in her classroom, its origin was uncertain to both of us. After a few useless questions, I reminded myself to step aside, let her lead, and start listening.

"You are the second president, John Adams." she began.

"Are you sure?" I asked.

"Yes, I am. He is after George Washington, and his son or grandson—I don't remember which—will be president someday too."

"You mean John Quincy Adams?"

"That's the other one's name, but that's not you. You are John Adams."

"OK, so what do I do?"

"Sit here." She placed me in the rocking chair. "This is your throne. We are living in the White House, and I am your only daughter. I'm six."

"But you are five."

"Not in the game. I'm six. Be quiet. People are coming."

She sat in my lap and began directing my responses as I greeted an array of petitioners, coming to ask for my help. At first they ask for permission to build a bridge or a mansion. Some I helped; some I dismissed when their plans were foolish. She seemed delighted with my power, coaxing me to be firm. But very quickly, the petitioners began to ask for something else.

"They want your daughter's hand in marriage," she whispered.

"But you are only six," I whispered back, and she giggled.

She nodded and confirmed they all want to marry her. It's my job to refuse, to put them off, to hold her to myself, telling them all she is "too young to be taken from me." The tighter I held, the more resistant I was to their pleas, the more delighted she was.

As the game progressed, angry petitioners put her under a spell, hoping they might be able to convince me to let her go. She fell limp in my arms like a baby, popping up *sotto voce* to correct me if I took the story in the wrong direction. Once she was under the spell, princes from far away came to offer solutions—the funnier the better, I discovered. One wants to hit her on the head with a banana peel, another assures me that his outrageous dance will awaken her. She laughed intensely with each suggestion, even in her "spell," eyes closed but with an expression of delight on her face.

As the game neared its end, I was to provide her hand in marriage to the prince who could wake her. But there was a catch. . . He must promise to wait and leave her with me until she is full-grown and ready to be wed.

....

At least three times a day, we retreated to the same glider where she was rocked as an infant, to repeat the story. The wisdom of its soothing message gradually became clear to me as I followed the unconscious language of play.

I am the "second president," as I am the second mother in her life. As a male character, I probably represent some blend of Mother and Father, a universal "parental figure." Our White House mirrors the power of the one just a few miles from her home, where, "the President, the boss of the whole country, lives." This sets the stage for our tableau of bonding, as I hold her and fend off the fools who might hurt our kingdom. I am powerful, and she is delighted as I dismiss and refuse petitioners. I am to keep her safe, her world free from murderers and fools.

Soon, princes want to marry her. Six is still childhood, but about as far into a real future as her five-year-old's imagination can go. My outrage is exciting, and she hugs me close every time I express my shock and refusal. Even when she falls under a deep spell, my bargain for her awakening guarantees that she will stay safely with me until she is ready to transition to the magic of a prince's "happily ever after." Not a bad plan, Liamarie.

Chapter 39

Berkshire Choral Festival II

>>>>>>>>>>>>

Just a few months after Martha's death, I went to the Berkshires to sing Bach's St. John Passion. A year later it would be the Brahms Requiem that I performed in chorus with two hundred other choristers. Last year it was the rolling green of the Berkshire Hills that cradled our campus and provided a backdrop for the music. This year, it was in Santa Fe, New Mexico, and the scenery of the desert was a dry and stark contrast.

The campus is tucked against a hillside that frames the buildings, a mix of classic architecture and southwestern stucco. You can hike up the hill from the parking lot, and in minutes be looking down on the campus valley and across to a broad expanse of open New Mexico desert. Far in the distance, the horizon is drawn by spectacular mountain peaks that pierce magnificent sunsets.

We were at St. John's College, a small, private, liberal arts college with a Great Books curriculum. Browsing the bookstore is like walking through a library of time: stacks of philosophy, theology, history, and literature volumes with ancient but familiar titles. Here, there are no departments, no majors, and no textbooks. Every student takes the same required courses and reads the seminal works of Plato, Ptolemy, and Euclid in their original form, following Western civilization's great books in chronological order from Ancient Greece to modern times. From Aristotle to Einstein, St. Augustine to James Joyce. Here, everyone takes the same journey through the wisdom of the past, trusting that along the way, they will each find keys to their future.

A year ago the music was of the passion, Bach's exquisitely detailed dialogue of pain and despair. This time the music is Brahms, the German Requiem. Brahms ignored the customary text of the Funeral Mass in this requiem and chose words from the Old and New Testaments and from the Apocrypha. He wanted to create a universal text, one not tied to any particular religious tradition. He wrote to the music director the night before it premiered that the term "German" referred only to the language in which it was sung, and that he would have gladly called it "A Human Requiem," a piece that expressed the universal experience of death, but focused on the living rather than the dead.

From the passion to the requiem; such is the journey of grief as well. Last year every thought of Martha brought pain and anguish. I told no one at last year's camp, fearing I could not restrain the tears. I withdrew in silence, searching for a way to imagine her loss receding and not being the centerpiece of my life.

This year I have told one person, my roommate, who saw me slip a booklet of children's Indian masks into an envelope for Liamarie. The story came out naturally in response to her question, "Who's that for?" and I was surprised at my tears as her face softened with sympathy. It is always the same words that get to me. "It was your sister," the last two words holding the meaning and piercing the soft spot deep within that still bleeds when touched. *There is no replacing a sister*, the inflection implies, and the emptiness that follows has no response save silence. But I can breathe into that silence now, and that is the difference.

The music too, is different. It does not begin with "Requiescat in Pace," rest in peace, or "Requiem Eternam," the familiar words directed at the dead. No, its first words are for me: "Blessed are they that mourn, for they shall have comfort. They that sow in tears shall reap in joy."

What have my tears watered this past year? What am I nurturing in all this pain? I am not sure that I know. I am not better in so many of the ways I had hoped to be. I have the same weaknesses and failings. If anything has changed, it is that I am more aware of them now, less able to deny the faults when they emerge. *See, there you go, being critical,* I say to myself. Or, *Enough, no more bragging about the kids.* In my deepest pain, I wanted to believe I would be pricked, lanced like a wound, burned clean and closed, emerging more refined, more aware, more . . . something. But I am the same. My life proceeds on its singular path, and I take that path alone. I do not feel comfort, only the sense that death has cheated us all and left no gifts in its wake.

The music of the Brahms is heavy, the orchestra building the overture to the opening words we sopranos sing over and over, "Selig sind . . . Blessed are they who mourn, for they shall have comfort. They that sow in tears shall reap in joy." Though I cannot feel this joy yet, it feels good to sing it with conviction, as if I can pull it from the depths of the harmonic progressions and inhale it somehow, seeding my soul.

The final movement of the Requiem returns to those words, "Selig sind," but this time they are for the dead. "Blessed are the dead which die in the Lord from henceforth, sayeth the spirit, that they rest from their labors and that their works follow after them."

A promise of rest and more . . . that their works follow after them.

And what of Martha's works? Forty-seven years of a life so full of energy and labor? Do they live in all of us in the ways she shaped us, molded us, stretched us beyond what we might have been on our own? It feels selfish wanting her death to do even more, to continue to work in me from beyond the grave. Perhaps the truth is simpler. Let them be done and complete, leaving those of us who received them to continue our own work, reaping in joy what we have sown in tears. "Selig Sind. Blessed are they." Those words sat with me, like a quiet companion throughout the week.

The trip was full of contrasts for me that marked the passage of time and its influence on my grief. Last year I had no roommate, an accident of fate for which I was profoundly grateful. This year my roommate was Roberta, a bubbly, attractive woman my own age but in a very different place in her life. We liked each other instantly, and I was drawn to her vivacious extroverted playfulness.

She was divorced and, she told me, "seriously looking" for a new man in her life. We giggled like teenagers trying to figure out who might be "eligible" in the tenor section. Whether or not she found a partner, she was going to have fun this week, and her infectious laugh made me feel old and staid by comparison.

She was also a serious singer who had performed this piece before with her symphony chorus in Pennsylvania. Her voice was strong and precise, and I could lean on her vocally when I felt tentative in rehearsals. But when class was out, she was ready to "meet and greet," and, surprisingly, I was charmed. She flirted with a carefree attitude, and her joy was contagious. Usually my introverted self would be exhausted, and probably a bit uncomfortable, but not this time. I think the universe, like the requiem, was reminding me to find joy in my own life. It is time, and though I was not going to join my roommate's lighthearted dance, I could feel her like a pushy angel, giving me a shove in the right direction.

The soloist this year is a young Canadian woman, full-figured, vivacious, and warm. She pulled up her chair to an already packed table at lunch and joined our conversation. When someone asked what she ate before performances, what food she might avoid or select to clear her palate and prepare her voice, she laughed. "I eat everything, and the only thing I worry about is whether I can fit into my dress that night!" I loved her casual comfort with herself, and with a talent that she need not coddle. I listened to her warm up in the shed, fluidly carrying notes above high C with a softness and control hard to imagine. That night she sat through more than a half hour of music, silently straight in her chair. Finally, the fifth movement, her solo, began and she rose, lifting her head as the first phrase broke the silence. Softly at first, it grew, soaring within a few notes to a magnificent high note, which she held gently, letting it expand through the air.

Brahms wrote this movement after his mother's death in 1865, and added it to the Requiem years after the piece had premiered without it. His sorrow lies softly in the soprano's first words:

Ihr habt nun traurigkeit:
And ye now therefore have sorrow:

but I will see you again,
and your heart shall rejoice
and your joy no man taketh from you.

And behind the soprano's words, the chorus enters softly, chanting over slow moving chords, murmuring behind her sorrow:

Ich will euch trosten, wie einen seine Mutter trostet.
Thee will I comfort as one whom a mother comforts.

I am where I belong.

Chapter 40

Touch

>>>>>>>>>>>>

Eighteen months after Martha's death, touch remained the most important communication between Liamarie and me. Whenever we were together, I was aware of the physical space between us. I was aware, because it was a space she monitored with vigilance.

"Sit next to me. Sit in the back seat of the car please, Mary Beth."

Outside, walking on the sidewalk, she observed proximity with radar that was never turned off. "Hold my hand, walk next to me." If she lost out to adult conversation, I saw her head fall slightly; then she quickly assessed the other adults to see who might be available for closeness. When we entered a restaurant, she jumped to the front of the group. "You sit here, Papa, and Mary Beth is here." I was, of course, not her only preference. But on visits, which occurred monthly at best, I was novel enough to lose out rarely to Dad or Mirka. Margaret was my biggest competitor, but any of my children were happy targets for her climbing, snuggling behavior.

At first, the behavior might be hard to distinguish from the normal "orchestration" of five-and-a-half-year-olds, who love to dictate where others must stand or sit, exerting power they rarely feel in adult company. The difference is subtle, but it is there. Unlike others her age, Liamarie's bossiness had little to do with seeing how much power she had or discovering who will acquiesce and who will not. Nor did it reflect the normal desire to design the space around her, putting children together or insisting on gender or family groupings. This push to pattern is developmentally salient at five, a necessary prerequisite as her neurology prepares for reading and language-based learning.

No, for Liamarie, there is one primary purpose to her requests. She wants a design that provides maximum physical proximity to those she wants paying attention to her. She wants to be able to reach out and touch the people she wants most. Chairs need to be pulled as close as possible, and lap sitting is demanded whenever she is not actively eating.

On my lap she is a sensory whirling dervish of activity. She snuggles her head under my chin, strokes my cheek, wraps her arms around my neck, then pulls away laughing and turns to do the same thing on the other side of my face. She shifts her weight constantly, almost bouncing, and leans forward and back, in and out, side to side, over and over again. It is as though she cannot get enough of the feeling of her body against mine, the pressure, the connection, as each time she leans in again and touches me.

And always she wants my eyes on her, following her movement and welcoming her back with a smile and a hug of greeting. If I am distracted, she is apt to turn my face back toward her with the pressure of one finger on my cheek. *See me, feel me, touch me, respond to me* is the message over and over again.

Touch is our first method of communication. The holding, stroking, gentle handling that is so necessary for growth. Infants, given food and basic care but deprived of touch, do not thrive. Their neurology shuts down, and developmental progress is halted. Following World War II, psychologists did not understand that. Orphans awaiting adoption were housed in institutions, and their caretakers were instructed to care for them dispassionately. Do not hold them or rock them or try to relate to them. Don't let them attach to their temporary caretakers, the wisdom of the time advised, so that they will be free to attach to the adoptive parents they would soon meet. But many never met those parents. Without the stimulation of touch or gentle stroking, without the reciprocity of interactive verbalizations, these children retreated into a condition called marasmus. They lay quietly in their cribs, became less and less responsive, and eventually died.

We now know that attachment breeds capacity for attachment. We understand that the earliest experiences of attunement—that reciprocal, non-verbal language of relationship—establish critical groundwork. They build the foundation of a neurology that learns how to attach and a psychology that trusts enough to reach out into the world and expect caring. Early loss disrupts this, but it does not destroy it. I remind myself of this every time I visit Liamarie. My arms are tired, and my lap is sometimes sore with her bouncing, but I do not want to pull back. So we snuggle and wrestle and hug and touch. And through it all, I am grateful for Martha, whose loving, sensate memories are so clear in her daughter.

Children also learn to differentiate the touch of their parents and respond differently to males and females. Mother's touch is not the same as Father's. "Daddy rough and tough, Mommy big and soft," my own two-year-old announced when I was an intern. I was upset, afraid that, despite my best efforts at non-sexist childrearing, stereotyping had already begun. A wise psychiatric supervisor reassured me that such differentiation was normal and healthy. Infants must differentiate first before integration, a more complex function, can occur.

Early on after Martha's death, Herb was frustrated when Liamarie insisted she needed "Mommy's hugs."

"Show me how to do it," he would say, and try to comply with her limited and vague descriptions. How do you convey the uniqueness of a mother's touch, the softness of her stroking and firmness of her hold? In her grief and sadness, Liamarie knew that a hug from her dad was not the same. No less valuable and important, but not the same as a mother's hug.

And so, when we are together, I provide a little dose of the feminine touch, the mothering touch that she misses so much. No doubt she finds it more healing than words. Hold me, cradle me, stroke me, and I will feel soothed and loved and mothered again, at least for a little while.

Chapter 41

Happy Day

>>>>>>>>>>>>

"Hi, Mary Beth, it's Mama's birthday!" Liamarie's voice on the phone was excited and celebratory.

"Well, yes it is, Liamarie. Today was her birthday." I hesitated. Is, was, what is the right tense here? I struggled. Do I say it "was" her birthday, as though her death ends our celebration of her birth? Or will it always be present tense? Today "is" her birthday, even though there is no additional year to celebrate.

I suddenly remembered my mother's disappointment after my father died, and their wedding anniversary was ignored by others. She was truly offended. "He may be gone, but it is still my anniversary," she would argue. *Yes*, I thought silently, *but there is not another year of marriage to mark, to be grateful for, and to celebrate. If there is no marriage partner, there is no anniversary.*

Now, two years after Martha's death, I find myself caught in the same quandary. And I have more sympathy. For more years than she was married, my mother and I have marked her anniversary in some special way, with lunch together or a small bouquet of flowers, as she insisted that my father's death did not change her need to remember that this day is, and always will be, a day of remembrance and gratitude for the one marriage she had in her lifetime.

So too, I think Martha's birthday will be for me. I think I shall choose "is" and not "was" when I speak of it. This is the day she came to this earth. For that I am grateful. To choose the past tense is to give her death veto power over her life, and over our celebration of it.

Besides, Liamarie would not tolerate ignoring her mother's birthday. She made that very clear. Birthdays are not to be ignored in childhood and to do so seemed like insulting her mother's memory. For Liamarie, it was bad enough that her mother had died, but that her mom would not have a birthday either? That was just too cruel. So we tried to celebrate, to remember, and to do something happy in honor of the day her mother was born.

"You want to tell stories?" she asked expectantly.

"Sure, Liamarie." And so I tell her again about the day Martha came home from the hospital, and Ed and I got to name her.

"Was she tiny?" She asked.

"Very tiny, but very loud," I replied, and she laughs.

And I tell her about the day Martha took her doll carriage for a walk.

"She walked and walked, till she was almost a mile from our house," I said.

"Was she scared?" Liamarie asked.

"I don't think so, but she did get thirsty."

"So what did she do?"

"She knocked on a door and asked the lady who answered for a glass of water."

Liamarie laughed. "And then what happened?"

"The lady called the police, and they brought her back to Grandma, who was very worried."

Liamarie loves these stories of her mom as a little girl, doing things she can relate to, things that connect with her own life as a five-year-old. "Your mom was an adventurer," I added.

"But what about presents?" Liamarie interrupted. "We have to have presents."

"You are so right, Liamarie. Your mom would not want us to celebrate her birthday without presents. What do you think she would like us to buy?"

"Something for me?"

"Yes, Liamarie, I think we should both get something . . . something she would have wanted us to have, something that would make her smile. What do you think that could be?" I asked.

She thought for a moment. "A book! Mama loved books."

"That's a great idea. I think you and your dad should go get a new book in honor of your mom's birthday."

"Papa, can we get a book for Mama's birthday?" I can hear her call to Herb.

"OK, so what will you get?" she asked.

"I don't know, Liamarie, but I will think of something," I said softly.

On March 9, Liamarie called again. "I'm calling because it's Mama's death day," she began. The phrase takes me by surprise, and I can hear her hesitancy as she looks for cues as to whether this too is a day for celebration. "So what did you do for Mama's death day?" she asked.

I don't quite know how to answer, and the flood of anniversary thoughts that go through my head are of no use. How do you tell a child this is a day to remember and be sad, as if sadness, especially hers, can be turned on and off according to some date on a calendar? How do you tell her that anniversaries are embedded in us, that they bring on visceral auras of remembrance that have no language, no form, nothing to hold onto. That when loss seeps in, it goes deep, beyond awareness, beyond our memories, and imprints itself like some encrypted message, awakened by a March breeze or the smell of blooming lilacs.

I have sat with patients who begin a session with only a feeling—overwhelming, overpowering—and no conscious awareness of what is behind it. Often I will pose the simple question, "Is this an anniversary time for you? Is there anything important in your life that happened at this time of the year?" A look of shock and sudden awareness betrays the connection, moved from the unconscious to the conscious mind by that simple reminder.

But for Liamarie, this is not yet about unconscious memory. It is also not about sadness or grieving. It is about the simple question of how she can keep the pieces of her mother present in her life. Mama's death day is another piece of her mother, one of the few she has left, and she is asking how we are going to mark it.

"Papa and I went to church," she says.

"Me too, Liamarie. Bill and I met Grandma at church. Lots of times people go to church on this day."

"And I looked in my memory box. But what else should we do?" she asks.

"I know, I'll find some pictures of your mom when she was five or six and send them to you," I offered.

"You mean when she was little, a long time ago?"

"Yes, Liamarie, would you like that?"

"Yes, can I put them in my memory box, too?" she asks.

"Of course," I replied, suddenly aware of how few shared memories fill that box.

"OK," she says. "Bye, Mary Beth, I love you."

"I love you too, Liamarie."

"Happy Mama's death day."

Chapter 42

Two Years

"Grieving is a two-year process," I often tell my patients. Whether a divorce or a death, the developmental stages seem to fill a two-year period before one's emotional state returns to normal.

The first year is the year of letting go, of feeling the loss at every juncture in your life. The pain is reexperienced, burned into the places, the times, the events that articulate your life. Christmas without her, vacations alone, a simple Sunday night telephone call that will never happen again. Whatever the routines and rituals of your life, they are, for the first time, marked with the loss, and, like a branding, the pain of the mark is searing, the imprint permanent.

The second year is different. In it the aloneness and isolation of loss is the centerpiece. Pain is there, but its sharp knife edge is dulled, and it is the cold stark reality of being alive and alone that demands to be addressed. The world retreats from you in this year. The newness of your loss is fading. Offers of support and consolation recede. For others the loss is old news; the expectation is that accommodation has taken place. You should be "used to it" by now. And, in a way, you are. The fact of your loss is like a bad tattoo you've had for a while. It doesn't surprise you any more when you see it, but you keep wondering how you're going to live the rest of your life with it.

"It takes two years before your emotional system returns to normal," I would say with confidence. But "normal" is the wrong word. I shall never use it again when I work with someone who is grieving. Things never return to normal, to what they were before.

They find a way to regulate themselves so that your affect is under control, so that the pain of the loss is not the centerpiece of your life anymore, but "normal" is decidedly not where you are. You are in a new land whose landscape is littered with the remains of the past. You trip over them, sometimes accidentally, and they stop you in your tracks. A picture, a memory, a color may be enough to bring you to your knees emotionally. But your eyes are on the horizon now . . . your focus on the moving forward, not the looking back.

In the second year, you must learn to be alone, to accommodate to the loss and to move forward again in spite of it. I suspect now that this is the crucial year. If we cannot make the turn successfully, shifting from past to future, we may never do so. We can become stuck in the loss, paralyzed by its force, and unable to find a way to proceed. Perhaps this is the year we need a different kind of help from the world—not the loving arms of comforting but the extended hands of invitation, encouraging us to step away from the loss and begin moving again.

This is also the year in which you decide whether the direction of your life is going to be permanently channeled by the loss. Will I become an advocate for breast cancer treatment or ARDS research? Will I challenge the system of managed care that delayed her treatment and probably contributed to her death, or will I channel my anger against the doctors themselves, who let her leave the hospital when she had been running a fever earlier in the week?

This last question is particularly troubling. I certainly saw the guarded looks on their faces when we asked questions as she was dying. *Be careful what you say*, they seemed to be thinking, *be very careful.* Their expressions told me they expected us to sue, even though we had not been accusatory and had given them no reason to suspect we blamed them for the tragic turn of events. They were careful and guarded about how decisions had been made. They chose their words judiciously, careful not to give us anything we might use to criticize or question their judgment.

Herb and I talked about this after her death. He needed to make his own decision about a suit, and there were certainly those around him who encouraged him to proceed. *Get the records, see what it is they aren't saying and why. Find out what those guarded looks are hiding,* others counseled. Herb struggled with this, more tempted than I to investigate.

But I could not go there. For me, the medical staff's guarded looks reflected a more generic concern. A bad outcome in our society has come to mean someone is to blame, and someone must pay. Years before, I had seen a Florida billboard: *Had an accident? No one may be to blame, but someone may be legally responsible.* It horrified me then, and I never forgot it. Have we come so far in our expectation of a tragedy-free life that we no longer require guilt to demand compensation? Are we so entitled to a risk-free existence that someone must pay us when the risks we take do not work out in our favor? And, most importantly, has money become the currency against which all loss is measured?

No, I would not sue Johns Hopkins. Perhaps they had made an error in judgment; perhaps they were chiding themselves for their decisions. I shall never know. I do know this: the people I met worked with us, even coming back on their own time to offer their medical expertise. They cried with us as the truth emerged day after day, and some, I learned later, had to avail themselves of counseling to handle their own disappointment and grief that this young, vibrant woman, who had "sailed through the transplant," had fallen so suddenly and irrevocably.

I chose to believe that they had done their best, and that we will all have to live with the outcome. No amount of money will change that. If I am wrong, no amount of money should assuage their guilt. I know that no amount of money will ease my pain, and I cannot bring myself to put a price on either.

Will I make her death my cause? Another difficult question. Under other circumstances, where I could see a concrete reality to attack, I might be very tempted. If defective procedures or equipment were at fault, my voice would be raised. But this is different. I can still see the materials she shared with me when she was deciding whether to go ahead with the transplant. Under side effects were listed the terrifying words "total organ failure." We had been warned. She took the risk and lost. Courage, I believe, must include the strength to lose and to absorb that loss without the wound alone choosing the direction of my future.

And my life already has a direction. My work and my children are not going to be put aside to crusade for other causes, no matter how worthwhile. I shall support them, certainly, perhaps with a deepened enthusiasm and generosity, but I will return to my own life and move on from there.

Year two . . . I had no idea there was so much to decide.

Chapter 43

Turning Six

>>>>>>>>>>>>

Every year Liamarie's request was the same. The year she entered kindergarten, she asked in the fall, more than six months before Mother's Day. "Will you come to the Mother's Day party at my school, Mary Beth? . . . 'cause I'm the only one who doesn't have a mother." Moving from day care to elementary school highlighted her status as she met new children and quickly learned that, once again, she was alone in this distinction.

The proximity of Mother's Day and her May 10 birthday seemed a cruel coincidence in the first years after Martha's death, but now, as Liamarie turns six, I am grateful that they occur so closely. I can soothe her grief and play the role of joyful mother in the same visit.

Each year the theme of the birthday party is much discussed ahead of time, as we pick out the cups and party favors for her friends. Having her party at home seems to give her the feeling of normalcy she craves. Herb has offered to host her party at a restaurant or party location, as her friends are doing increasingly. She refuses summarily. She wants her friends coming to her own house, where someone who looks like and sounds like a mother will be there to decorate the table and lead the children through the familiar rituals of singing and games. This is a lovely regression for me, back to my own children's days and years of parties at home.

I arrived the night before the party, and we opened all the birthday supplies and assured ourselves we were ready for the event. Then, Liamarie switched quickly to her game, leading me by the hand into the living room.

"Lie down, and pretend you're dead," she instructed. She took the long silk scarf I was wearing from around my neck. "I need this. This is how they fix dead people in Kinga."

"Kinga? Where is that?"

"It's a place I know," she said dismissively. She carefully straightened my legs, pushed my feet together, and crossed my arms across my chest. "And they put this over your face," she said, as she draped the transparent oblong scarf over my face, down over my folded hands, and as far as it would extend to the middle of my calves. She tugged at it, carefully spreading it to cover as much of me as possible.

"And here are the things you will need in heaven," she continued, folding my glasses gently and laying them carefully beside me. Then—"Wait, I'll be right back"—she ran to the next room and came back with her school picture, wallet sized, which she set down next to the glasses.

"How do you know this?" I asked, but she ignored me. She went on busily arranging the scene, adjusting my hands, and smoothing the scarf. "Where is Kinga?" I tried again, but still no response.

The stimulus for this kind of play may be external or self-generated. Her silent response confirms again how little it matters. Children will take from their surroundings the facts and fantasies they need. If none is a good match for the psychological work they are doing, they will create their own. The important question is seldom "where did this come from?" but rather "where is it going?" I decided to be quiet and let her lead. I lay silently for several minutes.

She stood watching me. "OK, you are dead long enough," she announced suddenly and began to tickle my toes to wake me up. She giggled, and I could feel the silliness underneath the story. Then, in an instant, she began laying my body out again, draping the long scarf over my face, "And now you are dead again." I tried adding my own silly touch, blowing the scarf off my face "to be alive again," and she dissolved in delighted giggles. Then in a strong voice she demanded, "Now go back to dead." We repeated this pattern over and over again.

I remembered the play therapy rule: ritual and repetition, repeat and control. This is still the work happening here. Over and over, I was dead, then alive. Over and over, she made me dead, then let me come back. Repetition, the ritual of emotional learning, the rhythm of approaching the affect and then retreating, controlling it, then letting it go—all of this was there in this simple exercise.

But the tone of the play had shifted. There was much less intensity and drivenness about the story. I could insert more, and her flexibility suggested real progress toward resolution. My presence was a reminder of Mom and of death, and our game was no accident. But it was at least as much play as play therapy, the work of resolving her loss.

Once, she interrupted her happy mood to ask firmly, "Will I die before you do, Mary Beth?" Her tone had shifted for this question she is compelled to ask but whose answer frightens her.

"No, Liamarie, I don't think so. You are much younger than I am and will probably live a lot longer." I sense it is not her death but mine she is afraid of. "I think you will be all grown up when I die."

"But what if I'm not?"

"Then I will be very mad, because all the other people who love you will get to do your birthday parties, and make the cake, and have all the fun!"

She smiled at this and wanted to keep it going.

"Like who?"

I start listing her uncles and aunts by name. "And Mamita and Papito," I go on as she smiles.

And the list keeps getting longer as she adds more names— "And Grandma and Mirka and Justin and Matt . . ."—and delights in my reaction.

"No way, Liamarie, I'm not dying yet . . . they can't have all the fun!"

Several times during the birthday weekend she insisted we play "Dead Mary Beth." Each time the story shifted slightly. She experimented with folding my hands, putting a flower on my chest, and laying me out in a casket. But she seemed unsatisfied, uncertain how she wanted to end the story. Finally, she yelled "I know, I know. It's like *Anne of Green Gables*. You are Anne, pretending to be the Lady of Shalott!" She laid me out in a rowboat and pushed it out into imaginary water. "But the boat is starting to sink," she yelled, "you better get to shore!" I sat up quickly and crawled back across the rug toward her. "You can do it!" she cheered me on. From death to life to fantasy to rescue. It was wonderful to see her master the scene and, in the end, we were left laughing in a heap on the floor.

My presence still stirs fantasies of remaking family. At bedtime, as I was tucking her in, she announced, "I think you and Grandma should move here and live with us. You can sleep in my top bunk, and Grandma can sleep with Mirka."

Mirka was with us, and she laughed, "But Liamarie, what about Bill? He would be very lonely." Liamarie was silent for a minute, thinking about this in her bottom bunk perch.

"Well . . . sometimes grown-ups just can't work it out, and they get divorced. It could happen, you know." She looked at me warningly.

We all laughed at this one, even Liamarie, and I gave her an extra hug before saying good night.

Some important growth had occurred. Home is in Virginia now, and her draw is to pull a mother figure there, not to join me in Maine. She had found her center again, and it is with her father, Mirka, and her friends at school. Only one thing is missing, and she played at adding a double dose of mothering by bringing Grandma along as well. The rest of my family was not essential to this particular fantasy so they were disposed of easily with the all-too-common divorce scenario she had no doubt heard in the schoolyard more than once.

Something else had shifted as well; she is missing mothering more than her mother now. The person who was so central to her life has faded. Memories of her are few. I remind myself not to be sad that it is not her mother *per se* whom she grieves. Martha did her job well. The experience of being mothered is embedded in this little girl's heart and soul. She feels it, wants it, and is drawn to it in whatever form the world offers. This is good. She cannot have her mother back. But if she can be open to good mothering, in all its guises, she can get more of what she will need to thrive.

Rest well, dear sister, I want to say, *for in three short years you showed her what loving and nurturing are all about. You laid down a pattern of bonding so securely that she has only wonderful sensate memories of what it means to be mothered. There is no ambivalence in your daughter. She knows what she is missing, feels it to be a wonderful and warm and powerful piece of life. This will keep her open and searching, able to accept my small substitute offerings, until there is once again a real mother in her life.*

Chapter 44

Communication

>>>>>>>>>>

From the beginning, Liamarie's need to stay connected to me was powerful. Right after her mother's death, when she was just turning four, that connection had to be physical. Nothing could substitute for the way she would sink into my lap and breathe in the scent of mother and mothering when we were together. It was physical enmeshment; her body and mine, wrapping our sadness with skin and arms; letting our breath find a common rhythm, exhaling the ache as one. I felt blessed that my body was not strange to her, my embrace familiar enough to bring on the comforting trance of physical connection.

Between visits, communication was difficult. Calls were inept—me asking lots of questions, her responses monosyllabic and distant. Often, I knew I was interrupting a time when she was not thinking of her mom, and that my voice brought on sadness. Emotions are such overwhelming and disregulated things in childhood . . . I did not want to add to the chaos, interrupting good times with triggers of sadness. So much of this process, and my support, needed to be on her schedule, and that was hard to do from afar.

I began almost immediately sending packages, small gifts of a book, a toy, the kind of things a mom might pick up for her child as a surprise. They were not expensive or even things I knew she wanted; rather, they were small gestures of communication that said, *I think of you when you are not here . . . You are special to me . . . You are on my mind and in my heart*. Because Liamarie could not read, I covered the packages with tiny bright yellow smiley face stickers, an immediate signal to her that this was for her and from me.

"A happy face package—for me, for me!" brought an excited smile, and was a much better way to initiate a phone call, more often from her, to talk about something besides our shared sadness.

Whenever I traveled, whether for work or vacation, I sent something as well. Children who have experienced early loss can be particularly sensitive to the fear that any separation might lead to a permanent one. When Liamarie knew I was in Maine, my presence was anchored by that background, and though she missed me, she could imagine me in my home and be soothed. I was where I belonged. But when I traveled, that familiar background was no longer there to anchor my permanence in the world, and that increased her anxiety. I tried to soothe her with connections that meant something to her.

"But where are you going? How far away is that?" she asked.

"I am going to Prince Edward Island, where Anne of Green Gables grew up. You remember her story. I will get you another book from her house when I visit it."

"Do they have cows there? I saw cows yesterday on my field trip."

"There are lots of cows there. They even have an ice cream store named Cows with lots of funny t-shirts of cows doing silly things. Would you like me to get you one?"

"Yes, but send me a postcard of the real cows too."

"OK."

I hoped these small reminders would reassure her that I was safe, that my travels were not pulling me dangerously away from her world, and that I was taking her with me wherever I went.

Halloween was already our holiday. When she was two, Liamarie showed her mother a picture of a tiny green pixie in a book. "I want to be that," she insisted. All the packaged costumes Martha found were enormous on her.

"I can make it," I offered. "Just send me her measurements." I called twice to confirm that the impossibly tiny measurements were correct, and put together a green tulle-skirted pixie costume that delighted her. So after her mother's death, I reminded her that it was my job to do Halloween, as I had done even when her mother was here. Fall phone calls were focused on deciding what her costume was to be, and whether to make or purchase it. By the time she was seven or eight, I was sending a duplicate catalogue for her to peruse, so that we could look at the pages together while we talked on the phone. Each year was different, sometimes ending here in Maine, and sometimes in Virginia on Halloween night, but it was the phone negotiations and excitement around the holiday that provided the natural connection, and a reminder of how important it is to stay in the moment with young children.

....

As Liamarie moved into first and second grade, she often called me in the evening to tell me about her day.

"The boys chase me, and they are so bossy," she complained one afternoon.

"So what do you do?" I asked.

"I run fast, and I boss them back!"

I bought a book of Norman Rockwell postcards and began sending one every week or two. She was old enough to be fascinated with his pictures and the stories they told, so my written message was sometimes only, "What do you think of this one?" and we had one more thing to talk about when we called.

Email was a blessing, but when we first began, Liamarie needed Mirka's help to use it. Dictating did not work well, and her messages were infrequent and stilted. But by second grade she began to be independent enough to email me on her own:

"Hi, Mary Beth, I miss you. When will I see you again? How are Margaret and Bill? Write back soon. Love, Liamarie." This one was repeated over and over for months. She must have practiced to get it right, and each time I saw it, I would quickly respond, knowing Mirka would help her read my answer and keep the conversation going.

Connection. Conversation. Simple presence. One week it's multiplication. She tells me what she is learning, and I send back a few problems for her to try. Nothing major, just the run-of-the-mill chatter of the day, like any parent and child might do around the kitchen table after school. But her emails always end with the plaintive "I miss you" and her full name—first, middle, and last—as if I needed to be reminded.

Chapter 45

Knowing

≫≫≫≫≫≫≫≫≫≫

My first call to the Center for Grieving Children in Portland, Maine, was made in August 1998, just a few months after Martha's death. I had just returned from seeing Liamarie, and her fragile state frightened me. I hoped the Center staff could guide me to a similar resource in the D.C. area. I learned, to my dismay, that there was no equivalent organization in northern Virginia or anywhere nearby. Centers for families suffering loss were few and far between in other states.

"I found one place," Herb said. "They have groups for children who have lost parents."

"I think it's worth a try," I agreed. "She needs to know she is not alone in this experience."

But their first group was a disaster. Five tiny children sat in a circle. Parents sat behind in an outside circle to observe. One little boy spoke. "I want my mommy to come back."

"Your mother is dead," the therapist replied. "She is not coming back. You need to understand. She is never coming back."

Herb watched, stunned, as Liamarie vomited into the center of the circle.

"I took her back, hoping it would get better," Herb told me, "but by the third session she knew where we were headed and started to vomit as soon as I pulled into the parking lot."

I was horrified. I hoped a group experience would be a place for play and creative expression, a refuge of shared experience with other children undergoing similar loss. But this, this was torture. And it violated everything I knew about a child's way of knowing.

"Should we get her a therapist?" he asked.

I was hesitant, as I have always been about using therapy for childhood grief. Often in my practice, I would be approached to work with children whose parents were divorcing or who had suffered a death in the family. They were surprised when I hesitated and asked for more information about how the child was doing and why therapy was being considered.

Grief is not pathology, I explained, and in the eyes of a child, seeing a doctor happens when you are sick, when there is something wrong with you. I wanted first to talk about creating sufficient resources for the child in their home, school, and community to let the grieving happen naturally. Let's watch that process, I would advise, and add therapy only if things are stuck, if the natural process of a loving family and community is not facilitating the grieving as it should. Helping a grieving child is mostly about holding, and we can all offer that.

This is why centers for grieving are so crucial. They do not provide therapy. They do not separate and individuate each person's grief to be analyzed in the clinical hour. Rather, they provide a common atmosphere of loving acceptance that conveys a powerfully important message:

> *What is happening to you is sad but survivable. What you are experiencing is overwhelming but understandable. There is nothing wrong with you or with your feelings, nothing that needs to be fixed or treated. There is only the deepest human experience of loss that has come your way, so much sooner than anyone would have wished for you. We are all here to help you make sense of it, and to find a way to see beyond it.*

"I think we'll have to get a therapist, Herb. You certainly can't take her back there."

Through some mutual contacts, we found a warm female therapist, willing to see Liamarie individually and to give Herb some support in parenting her. Liamarie told me, "Sharon is my happy doctor. She helps me to be happy when I am sad." I breathed a sigh of relief.

I contacted Sharon only once, a few years later, when Herb and I were discussing school choices for first grade. He was drawn to a school for gifted children, but I was hesitant.

"I don't doubt she can do the work," I said to Sharon. "But I wonder if the extra pressure will be good for her. Maybe I'm being too protective."

"Liamarie needs three things in her school choice," she said simply. "Nurturance, nurturance, and nurturance." I was relieved, and Herb's final choice, a bilingual program in a small public school, offered her both the challenge she needed and the nurturance she craved.

Childhood grieving is not like adult grief. It is different because the simple structure of knowing is different for children. For adults, knowing is the cold, hard fact that lies behind our shock and denial and avoidance. Our defenses try to soften the truth, but there is no doubt that, at our core, we know what death is. We know its permanence, its finality. We may not be able to face those facts head on, but they exist for us, and we do not doubt them.

For a child, knowing is not a fact. It is a process. The rules of time and space, cause and effect are evolving. How do you understand "forever" when you do not yet understand days or weeks or years? When the future means only "after my nap" and time is measured as "one Sesame Street." Anyone who has ever tried to explain to a child that Christmas is three weeks away, when the carols are playing and Santa is right there in the store, knows the futility of such abstraction. The only time is now, to a very young child. The only fact is what they see or have experienced.

If Mommy worked in that office building, maybe she is still there.

If she came to my play last year, maybe she will be there again when I walk out on stage.

For adults, these thoughts are about wishful thinking and memory combining to create a fantasy even the most mature of us cannot resist indulging occasionally. For a young child, they are much more than that. They are the testing of the rules of permanence, and object constancy, and cause and effect. And as the rules fall into place, and the abstractions begin to have meaning, one truth is learned over and over anew: *My mother is gone. I will never have her again. She is never coming back.*

And just as this knowing cannot be rushed, or forced, or explained to children before they have the cognitive maturity to grasp it, so too, the sense of what they have lost for the future cannot be known. Imagining being eighteen when one is six has little reality. "When I grow up" is a magical state of being, and when children play with it, they try on adult roles that have little relationship to the person they are now. When I grow up, I will be a fireman. When I grow up, I will be an astronaut. The game is about what they will "do." It is not an anticipatory awareness of who they will be, what they will need, and how they will feel.

We adults grieve the lost partner who will not grow old with us, because we can imagine that aging process and relate it to our feelings and hopes and dreams of the future. We, whose egos are formed, whose values and desires are established, can imagine those needs and wants and thwarted plans. We can think about our emotional selves in the future, and each time we do, we know the reality of the empty space beside us in that picture.

Knowing is a process, I remind myself as Liamarie moves through these early elementary years. A slow and gradual awareness that will deepen as her sense of self is formed, and her understanding of permanence evolves. Today she can grieve that her mother is not here to pick her up at school. But she cannot grieve that she will not be there when she graduates and marries and has her own child. Only time will allow those sadnesses to emerge. *Knowing is a process for children*, I keep repeating to myself. And all of us go through that process with her as the loss becomes real—for today, for tomorrow, for the future. And the pain of that loss is fresh each time her expression says *I get it* in some new way.

By age seven, Liamarie's memories of her mother were faded and soft. She could not recall too many instances of being together, of specific activities they had shared. She had lived half of her life since her mother died.

As memories fade, grief itself is transformed. "I just want to be normal. I just want to have a mother and father like everyone else," was Liamarie's strongest complaint that year. As the person fades, it is the structure of family that is more salient, more obvious with its painful reminders. Everyone else has a mother who shows up for dance class. I do not. Everyone else has two parents to come to meet the teacher. I do not. I am different, and less than. Anger, more than sadness, is the child's reaction at this age. What did I do to deserve this hole in my family? Why has the world done this to me and to so few other children around me?

"I just want to be like everyone else. I'm mad that I'm not normal," Liamarie repeated.

I was cautious in my response.

As Liamarie enters this important developmental phase where identity and self-esteem are beginning to coalesce, integrating the fact of her mother's death is tricky. What does it mean that this essential and powerful piece of support is not present in her life?

The building blocks of self-esteem in early elementary grades become more complex. They have moved beyond the "I am good because I am loved" construct of the preschooler. Now, children are beginning to differentiate one child from another, and to attach that uniqueness to their value. I am taller, faster, kinder than someone else, and I can feel good about that. I am strong. I am helpful. This is how I am different from others and special.

I am motherless. This is how I am different from others and not special.

Knowing is a process, and in that process, the interpretation of loss shifts. The challenge in the elementary years is to help the child move beyond the primary narcissism that says, *I am the source of all that comes to me. I am loved because I am lovable. Good things come to me because I am good.* For in that language, the horrific bad thing that greets you every day is evidence of your own unworthiness.

But the alternative is not very soothing either. To understand that bad things happen randomly, or because adults cannot control your world, even when they try their best, is no consolation. It may mean you didn't cause or deserve this, but it also means that the world is a more frightening place than any seven-year-old wants to face.

"I just want to be normal. It makes me mad. I just want to be like everyone else," Liamarie repeats. And she did not want to hear reasons or reassurances or explanations.

In her words I hear the anger of lost innocence. *Don't make me understand this. I don't want to and can't find a way to know this without feeling bad.*

I wish I could take away her pain and confusion and self-doubt, but I cannot. I can only be with her and say again, "I know, love, I know."

I understood what was happening for Liamarie. She was experiencing an explosion of brain cell growth. Day by day it took her further away from the protected self-enclosed world of the very young child. In that world, she was the center, all of us like planets circling, keeping her safe. What she did not understand she ignored, or trusted us to explain. Her concerns revolved around her own life, her own experiences.

Now approaching eight, she was beginning to understand that her world is part of something much larger that lies beyond the confines of her circle, and that even the adults who love and care for her cannot guarantee or control it all. She could not only imagine that larger world, she was curious about how she fit in it. Though it may have seemed that she was regressing, sliding backward in her understanding of loss, that was not true. She was coming to terms with it at deeper levels of meaning.

"How did my happy, carefree six-year-old become this skittish eight-year-old?" a mother once asked me. "He has a hundred questions he never thought of before, and he seems more anxious."

"He is," I answered, "but not with an anxiety you need to worry about. Just the sudden newness of understanding that he is a little guy in a great big world."

I understood why this was making Liamarie's emotions surface again, and why the questions we had answered a hundred times, now came with fear and anger more than sadness.

....

What was happening for me was harder to explain. Three years. That number kept rolling around in my head, and my mind played with it. The trinity, the trio, the almost home-run triple. Good things come in threes. Three years since she is gone. I wrote, tried to find images to capture what was inside.

I should be at some end point of grieving but I am not. Like a traveler arriving exhausted I look around me and am disappointed. Is this what I've worked so hard to achieve? Have I traveled all this way to find myself in this barren, uncomfortable place?

The soil is sandy, almost desert. An occasional brilliant green draws my eye and lets me know the earth here can support life, even beauty. But mostly it is flat, dry and windy. I breathe lightly here. The sand invades my lungs, a barrier to the kind of deep breath that cleanses, an irritating reminder that I am still alive.

The air has no temperature, not hot or cold. Its only character is its movement, pushing against me with a force that keeps my muscles tight to maintain my balance.

There are guests, but they do not stay long. They step cautiously, sit silently, then dissolve back into their own lives. Truly, I am alone. Only my soul inhabits this place, too comfortable to be desolate, too desolate to be comfortable. I am not unhappy. There are no tears. No wailing rage. I simply sit, looking out and surveying the scene. This is the flat, dusty place of knowing.

I do not live here, but like a retreat it is where I return when my life recedes, even for a moment. Sometimes I crave it, the silence, the simplicity, the blandness of so much emotion gone cold. Like a black hole imploding into negative space, the deadness is a welcome relief from the turmoil that preceded it. But I am not dead either. My soul rests here; it does not hide. It merely sits quietly feeling the wind and the sand and the deadness in the air and reminds me that I am still alive.

Chapter 46

First Communion

›››››››››››

In late March of 2002, I flew in to see Liamarie. A sudden impulse, driven by the plaintive sound of her almost daily emails: "I miss you. When am I going to see you again?" Our visits were stretching out, further than her mind could hold onto. She was here at Christmas, a still-essential ritual for her to be in our house and reminded of our familiar holiday routines. But it had been two and a half months since that visit, and her emails were increasingly focused on one question: "When will I see you again?"

She was ill most of the weekend, fighting a flu that made her happy to stay home and snuggle with me, watching a movie. We went out only briefly, to pick out a First Communion dress. She had called me, pleading, only a week before, "Mary Beth, you have to help me. Mamita wants to buy me a poufy dress for First Communion and *I hate poufy dresses!* They itch and scratch me, and I have to go through the door sideways. But Mamita says First Communion dresses are always poufy, so you have to help me!"

I brought Margaret's First Communion dress, a long linen dress with a cape collar trimmed in antique cotton lace. I hoped tradition would trump a beloved grandmother's privilege without offending, and that we might be able to alter it to fit. But it was all wrong for Liamarie, and as soon as she put it on we knew. The collar fell to her waist and the hem floated in folds around her feet. So, fever and all, we headed for the mall, a silent prayer on my lips to her mother: "Send us in the right direction, and quickly please."

It was at the third store that we found it, a simple satin dress with a wide decorative cummerbund. No sign of the tulle and lace she found so itchy, and the skirt a soft compromise between full and straight. "Oh, Liamarie," I said, "this is just perfect—and your mother would have loved it. It's certainly the one she would have picked!"

She stood silently looking at herself in the mirror. "No, you're wrong," she said firmly, her expression a mix of determination and delight. "She *did* pick it out, and she just showed us where it was."

I went back a few weeks later to watch her wear that dress. Herb's parents were there, and late in the evening, as I cleaned up the kitchen, Mamita came up behind me.

"Heriberto and I have something for you. To thank you for what you do for Herb and Liamarie," she said haltingly. She handed me a black velvet jeweler's box.

"They are not real," she offered quickly, "but they are good."

The single long strand of pearls was beautiful, but it was the words that stayed with me and soothed me that day. Not real, but good. Please let me live up to that.

On the flight back to Maine, Baltimore's inner harbor was visible in the distance, slightly behind the edge of the plane's oval window. It was far enough away to seem mythical, a city recognizable only by the outline of its skyscrapers. *In one of those building she died,* I thought, as the plane accelerated, and the harbor receded behind the fuselage. *Four years ago this week.*

It is nearing time to end the recording, the watchfulness, the self-conscious monitoring. I am well, stronger than I have been in years. Happier too, and more relaxed. My life has simplified enormously in the past two years, and I recognize with sadness that my mother's death in August of 2000 and Matt's leaving for college just a week later are a part of this. I was suddenly the parent of only one child, and with no elderly family members to consider.

For months after my mother's death, I was exhausted. I felt heavy and spent. The weight of four family deaths in four years had drained me even more than I could admit. I found myself wanting only to read and rest. I spent every free moment on the couch with a stack of books by my side, drinking them in like I'd come back from the desert. But recently the fatigue has been lifting, and my life seems open, ahead of me once again.

I am still writing. The 3:00 A.M. impulse to rise and put pen to paper still happens. But that too is changing. It is less about grief and more about gratitude. Grief and gratitude seem to be sisters as well. Without gratitude for what has been, grief cannot be assuaged; without the depth of grief, the fullness of gratitude is incomplete.

I am grateful for her cancer. It is a strange thought, but I cannot say it any other way. Without the cancer, we would not have bonded so closely in her last year, would not have let each other in so fully. It had to be something so life-threatening that we—so different in personality, but so alike in our self-containment—would reach out and let intimacy take us where it did.

I am grateful that she did not live a compromised life. That last month, watching her fight on the respirator, I struggled with this. What if her lungs were forever damaged? I imagined her living permanently on a respirator, or riding a wheelchair, an oxygen tank at her side. Was that life a fair bargain with death? I have come to a place of gratitude about this as well. She took the risk to have a full and healthy life, and, if that was not to be, I am grateful she was not asked to compromise. It is some consolation to envision the worst it could have been and know she was spared that.

I am grateful she never woke. In the beginning that was hard to bear, that I could not speak to her and know that she was in there and aware of my love and support. But now I am grateful that she was never conscious enough to know that she had lost her bet, and that saying good-bye was all that was left to do.

She would not have liked long scenes of crying and remembrance around her bed. She'd probably have kicked us all out periodically so she could be alone with her dying. With us there, she'd have been reflective. Mostly I imagine long silences broken by practical instructions about the house, Liamarie's future, the life she was not going to share but would still want to shape. I could not have stayed strong as she said her good-byes, and I cannot imagine watching her feel that much pain. Perhaps cowardice is to blame, but I am grateful she slipped quickly from full awareness to unconsciousness and never woke. She may have been aware behind the sedation; she may have known and felt all the things I wanted to spare her. But we did not have to know it together, and I want to believe that was easier for her. It was for me.

I am grateful to Herb for his openness, his willingness to let me help. He may have needed my expertise and my parenting experience, but I needed the healing that could come only from being involved in Liamarie's life, and he gave me that.

I am grateful for my South Freeport friends, who have always made children a community affair. From preschool days— when we had a babysitting co-op—to middle school, the "South Freeport Kibbutz" gave me at least ten people I could call at a moment's notice to pick my child up at school, have an unscheduled overnight, or provide transportation to a game. These families knew my children well enough to be more than chauffeurs, but living reminders that there are others who will care for you in simple ways when times are difficult.

I am grateful for my patients. Most never knew what was happening in my life. I am a believer in boundaries in psychotherapy. They allow the patient to be the center of the small universe of the therapy room, and to have their feelings toward me contaminated as little as possible by my real life. But I have always broken this rule in small ways, with deliberateness on occasion. Sometimes this happens because my practice is home-based, and knowledge of my family intrudes in a way that is unavoidable. When my daughter gets off the bus and walks down the driveway, one cannot help but see her. "Is that your daughter?" some ask, and it would not be setting a boundary to refuse an answer; it would simply be rude. Boundaries are there to protect treatment, not to make people feel unworthy to be in your life. So I answer.

So too, with this. When Liamarie lived with us, a few people came to know that and wondered why. I don't know if I always made the right choice of whom to tell, whom to shield. The choices were conscious and deliberate, but that doesn't guarantee wisdom. But I am grateful for their patience, their compassion, their willingness to offer sympathy, even as I redirected us back to our work together. I needed to know that I could walk that fine line between graciously receiving support, and gently reasserting the purpose for which we meet. It was that as much as anything that gave me hope that the sadness was not swallowing all of me. I could still do my job and be trusted to do it well. I am so grateful for that.

Looking down on the skyline I had seen so often, I also felt a bit embarrassed. There are so many things I might have done better. It is only in retrospect that we see ourselves clearly, and the picture, for me, was not a pleasant one. I saw my solitary stubbornness, my persistent exhaustion that brooked no alternative, not even those that might have made my life easier. I felt embarrassed that I couldn't have figured out a better way to survive.

Chapter 47

Mastery

≫≫≫≫≫≫≫≫≫

In Liamarie's elementary and preteen years, she came for a week of vacation every summer. We planned it well ahead of time, so we could enjoy the anticipation, talk about plans, and hint at surprises that might be in store. Mirka, who was by then a beloved part of the family, usually came with her. She provided a soothing presence for Liamarie and a help to me. Mirka knew Liamarie's routines and habits, and could easily switch from playmate to disciplinarian when the need arose. "Come on now, Liamarie, you know your papa doesn't allow that," she'd say. All I needed to add was silent support.

Inevitably, sometime during the visit, Liamarie would ask to "play in your office." She may have been seven when this began, and by then she had her own experience of therapy and knew how to orchestrate her game.

"You have to sit out here first," she'd say, "while I do my work."

I sat silently in the waiting room. She gave me a little piece of paper with my name and my problem written in crooked printing. I waited until she opened the door, and invited me in.

"You can sit on the couch," she said, then perched up on my office chair with a pencil and paper in front of her as she took the slip from me and began the interview. There were many variations.

At first, her writing was sometimes hard to translate: "Jena I chabod filings," one reads.

I began with a shrug and a "guess it's my feelings" mutter.

"Are they choked?" she asked. Another paper is clearer: "Mariana Conte . . . sad she takes care of animals."

"I like taking care of animals," I began, "but sometimes it makes me sad."

By age ten, the writing was clear: "Kathryn Lakers. Her brother died she is sad."

....

Liamarie usually began the conversation.

"So, you are Emily, and you are mad all the time," or

"I heard you get in trouble in school a lot," or

"Teachers tell me you are bossy with the other kids."

I took on the character, sometimes with exaggerated bravado. "Yeah, so why not . . . the other kids are not as smart as me . . . why shouldn't I be the boss?" I'd challenge. Other times I played a softer character, one who shrugged and could not answer her questions easily. She drew me out, suggesting what I might be feeling, and where she wanted the character to go. A few times I tried giving a "wrong answer," one that took the story in a different direction, but Liamarie looked over at me as if I'd broken the rules of a game and should know better. "That's not right," she'd say quickly and redirect the dialogue.

As she got older, she added some grown-ups to the patient list: "Amy Elizabeth . . . boss is being mene," reads one.

Wherever we began, we ended up telling the same story. Always her questions led carefully back to her own story, played out in variations:

"Did anything bad happen to you when you were little?"

"Do you miss someone special in your life?"

"Is there something different about you that might make you mad a lot?"

No matter how creative the presenting problem or my elaboration of it might be, the purpose of the game was clear. All things could be traced back to the one cataclysmic loss in her life. All conversations were about expressing that idea in the multiple colors and forms of childhood experience.

I resisted the game. I'm embarrassed to say there were times I begged off, not wanting the familiar ritual that seemed to soothe her.

For her, it was about mastery. She took my chair and, in the language of play, expressed her own path through the challenges of growing up without a mother. In my role, she was not overly empathic, but rather compassionately practical. "Now look," she counseled me one afternoon, "it's OK to be sad, but you can't be mean to other kids. They just won't like it. Maybe you should find a grown-up when you feel like that. They could hug you or just stay with you while you are sad."

Over the years from seven to eleven, the faces of Liamarie's struggles and successes were easy to find embedded in the dialogue and the characters we created. There was the child who felt it was her fault that her family was "different" and she had no mother. She was mad at the world and at her father for not being able to fix this instantly. And the child who was terrified that fixing it would bring new problems, like sharing her dad with a new mom, who might not like her and might steal her father's affections.

Later there was the child who worried that if death had happened once, it could steal in and ruin her world at any moment. She wanted not only reassurance that this was an unlikely possibility, but also a long, long list of the levels of protection that were there for her as she wondered over and over, "And what if she died . . . and what if he died . . . and what if they died?" until there was no answer except the trust a grieving child must find that her world loves her enough to keep her safe.

So why did I resist? Why did this game make me uncomfortable when so many others had not? I did not understand at first. In truth, it was no different from so many earlier games we'd played, from the lobby floor at Johns Hopkins to her Virginia home. Why was this different for me?

Part of it was that this crossed the mother/therapist boundary for me more directly than anything before had done. Of course, her play was expressive at three and a half and four, and, understanding its symbolic language, I tried to respond to it in a therapeutic way, but always in my role as loving aunt and substitute mother. I never wanted Liamarie's time with me to be about treatment or evaluation, just about a loving response to her experience and the welcoming arms of family.

But there was a deeper source of resistance for me as well. I had hidden out in my office, escaped into my competence and professional responsibilities when I was grieving, and I did not want to give that up. Walking up the stairs to the office was difficult some days, but more often than not, it had been a relief. With each step I put aside my own life, compartmentalized and distanced myself from the whirlwind of emotion in my home and in my heart, and hid.

The focused conversation of therapy was a blissful relief and reassuring confirmation that life would go on. If I could enter that hypnotic state of engaged presence—listening, reacting, probing, challenging—then the grief had not destroyed everything. It is a delicate dialogue, a dance of conscious and unconscious awareness that makes the therapeutic process work. Entering that dance requires putting away distraction and letting the mindfulness of the moment carry you forward. I loved escaping into it. More than that, I loved knowing I could escape into it. It gave me some relief from my own pain for an hour or two, and a chance to look beyond it into someone else's. I had not realized how much of an escape it had become until Liamarie wanted to incorporate it into her healing ritual, and to bring the real story of her pain, and mine, into that room.

There were other rituals that evolved over time. Pizza night with Bill became a surprise boat trip to Eagle Island to see the Peary Museum, and later a daring invasion of the Mount Washington Hotel. "Just stick with me, and look like you belong here," he whispered as they snuck past the concierge, and into the side room where the historical markers told the stories of early American history that so fascinated her.

The trip to our favorite jewelry store in the Old Port saw a child's simple pendant evolve into dangling earrings at thirteen, but the ladies' lunch that followed was always marked with Liamarie's "Remember when . . . remember when . . ." taking our conversation back in time and reprocessing her life story in the context of soothing ritual.

I knew that, as Liamarie matured, those rituals would evolve. That there would be summers to come when she would be too busy with camps and high school and her own expanding life to come to Maine. But I prepared myself for that with a reminder that that is what healing means. Visiting the past is healing only if it gives us strength to let us grow into our future. Liamarie will always be my fourth child, the child of my heart, whom my sister entrusted to me so many years ago. I will try to live up to that commitment as she grows. But she may become someone else's daughter in time, and this too is as it should be. Resolving grief is about loving enough to let go, and when that time comes, I trust Martha will help me do that as well.

Chapter 48

Two Weddings

Liamarie had just turned nine when Justin and Sandra were married. An in-between age, a bit old to be a flower girl but young to be a bridesmaid. Sandra is the oldest of thirteen cousins in her extended family, and relates to them with ease, so I left the negotiations to her. "Liamarie, Justin and I want you to be in our wedding, and you can pick what you get to be. You can help us with Willa, the little flower girl, who might need a bigger girl to walk with, or you can be a junior bridesmaid if you prefer."

"Well, I don't care what you call me, but I'm telling you this: *I'm not walking with a boy!*" That settled it. On May 17, 2003, she was the "senior flower girl" in an elegant Manhattan wedding.

She looked lovely in her white dress, a blue sash highlighting her still tiny frame. Her hair was long now, and tiny cornrow braids pulled it back from her face until it cascaded down her back. She got lots of compliments but seemed subdued when she joined us for pictures.

"Is she excited?" I asked.

"Yes, but last night she cried," Herb replied. "I finally got her to tell me that she is afraid they'll have grandchildren and she'll lose you." In all my excitement about the wedding, I had forgotten this. This change, any change to her support network would always trigger hypervigilance. *How might this make things worse? How might this take more from me?* This is not selfishness, only the natural consequence of losing a nurturer so early in her life. I can be compassionate and reassuring, but not without a deep sadness that this is the burden on those tiny shoulders, and I cannot, no matter how I try, take that away.

But I can ask the photographer to take one special picture of just the two of us.

....

Herb was still alone. Although he had dated some, there was no one who met his requirement. "Papa says we're a package deal," Liamarie was fond of repeating. And I knew he meant it. Sometime before, Liamarie had spoken about a woman he was seeing. "I know she doesn't really like me," she said softly. "But it's OK because she makes Papa happy." The relationship ended soon after that.

Fifteen months after Justin and Sandra's wedding, on a summer afternoon in a rustic chapel on the shore of Lake Michigan, Liamarie was part of another wedding. This time she was the maid of honor, dressed in a soft, flowing, floral print dress that needed to be altered slightly to accommodate her budding figure. At ten and a half, she was no longer the wiry stick-thin child of a few years ago. Her face was fuller, softening with the beginnings of adolescence, and this made the resemblance to her mother more apparent. Her cheeks were full and round, and her smile, that perfect duplicate of her dad's grin, was transforming into a gentler, deeper version of Martha's.

This time it was her dad getting married. His last name was already hanging outside his new in-laws' Lake Michigan cottage, where the married names of all of their daughters were burned into wooden plaques, strung together on chain, and hung on a post near the front door.

The rustic log church had no electricity. Simple white candles on the windowsills bathed us in a soft light. A string quartet with a full-size harp backed Margaret's pure soprano. The last phrases of The Lord's Prayer build . . . "For Thine is the kingdom, and the power, and the glory . . ." until the final high note saturates the space with a power that vibrates in my skull. No one breathes.

Linda and I were still getting to know one another. I'd watched her handle raucous cross-examination at a Virginia cookout a few months before, when Herb brought her to meet his friends. George was there, the man who had driven me to Johns Hopkins that first night. And Patti, who stayed with Liamarie the evening of the wake, and who did so many favors during Martha's chemotherapy. Ian and Donna, friends for decades now, who had shared Martha and Herb's political journey, hosted the event at their home. Seeing them all together again was strange for me. It was as if they were Martha's representatives, the jury that would pass judgment on this new person in Herb's life.

But the atmosphere was festive, the grill fired up, and the close quarters conducive to laughter and happy memories. When Linda, a tall striking blonde with a beautiful smile, arrived, they seduced her with compliments and teased Herb about his good fortune. Then the real grilling began. They poked, they prodded, they teased her about being a career woman in her forties who had never married. She took it all in stride and told me later she was touched by the depth of concern she felt behind the questions.

"They really care about Herb and Liamarie," she said. "I respect that."

Toward the end of the evening, someone asked how they'd met. Herb told the story. They sat together on a plane, shared some airline snacks, and complained about business travel. His enthusiastic descriptions of his daughter drew Linda in, and he pulled Liamarie's picture from his wallet and told their story. When the flight ended, she suggested they meet again. Herb professed confusion.

"Well, what did you think she meant?" his friends taunted.

"No, really," he protested, "I couldn't see her expression. The sun was in my eyes, coming in through the airplane window, and it was blinding. I couldn't see her face. She gave me her card, and I didn't know if she meant for business or a date."

"Oh, come on, Herb, you know better than that," Ian chided. "That was Martha saying, 'Herb, wake up. I've given you six years to do this on your own. Do I have to put a halo around her so you get the message? *This is the one!*'" The group erupted, Linda laughing as freely as the rest.

That night, I was reassured by Linda's openness, and her willingness to be vetted by Herb's friends and feel the love behind that process. But on their wedding day, it was something else that gave me comfort. It was the look in her eyes when the ceremony was over, and she reached over, took Liamarie's hand, and the three of them walked back down the aisle together.

Chapter 49

Quinceañera

>>>>>>>>>>>

May 2009

Fifteen small white votive candles are clustered together on a table beside the dance floor. Each is set carefully in a clear glass holder. A book of matches is hidden discreetly in the display.

There are probably seventy teenagers in the room. Their electric energy saturates the space, soaks up the band's vibrant Spanish sound and deposits it onto the dance floor. There are only half as many adults, and we let the teenagers lead the way through the evening's events. Their party clothes glitter in the strobe lights but are no match for their faces—glowing, vibrant, full of promise.

Liamarie is at the center of the group. Her fuchsia ball gown's striking color and porcelain doll detailing give it an energy only a fifteen-year-old could carry off. And she is doing it tonight. Holding court at the center of the room, she is radiant. A tiara sits atop a profusion of dark brown curls that would make any starlet jealous. Her broad smile and sparkling expression show no traces of timidity, only confidence and delight. There is no question that she is the Quinceañera and that this is her night.

The evening began at the church, where Liamarie stood before the congregation to read prayers honoring her commitment to Christian values, and celebrating her symbolic entry into womanhood. Her voice was strong and sure, and the congregation's warm applause felt like a large extended family welcoming her with pride. Her court of seven girls, identically dressed in white and gold semi-formal dresses, and their escorts, squirming a bit in suits and ties, watched attentively. As Mass ended, they poured out into the street, anxious to get to the restaurant and to the party portion of the evening.

This is all new for me. There is no Irish equivalent to this Latino celebration that feels like a cross between a Jewish bat mitzvah and a sweet sixteen party. I know there are more rituals to come, but I do not know exactly what to expect as we head to the Spanish restaurant Herb has hired for the evening. Its name, Carnivale, is a fitting moniker for this place, whose vibrant décor overwhelms you as you walk through the door. Mardi Gras colors glisten against black edging on the walls and ceiling, balloon bouquets rise from every table, and strobe lights make the electric reds, oranges, and greens pop. The band is already warming up the group, and the DJ wields his mike with a Mohawk haircut and authority. This is going to be fun.

There are several choreographed dances, and the DJ guides us through the list. First, the formal dances for the quinceañera and her court. The teenagers' expressions betray their determination to get the steps right. The dance reminds me of the quadrilles of the Middle Ages, and I wonder how the choreographer got this group of preppy Chicago teenagers to do this with such seriousness of purpose. They go through the patterned routine without a catch, and are relieved and delighted at the adults' enthusiastic applause.

When the DJ announces the presentation dance, I stand on the sidelines and watch Herb, arm raised delicately to take his daughter's hand. His expression of pride makes him four inches taller tonight as he leads Liamarie to the center of the dance floor. They are both graceful and tender and perform flawlessly. Where did the time go? I wonder. Can she really be fifteen?

My reverie is interrupted by the DJ announcing the presentation of gifts. I am a part of this and have gotten my instructions. As her godmother, I will present Liamarie with a silver bracelet, a symbol of the unbroken circle of life. The audience is quiet and attentive as I put the bracelet on her arm.

Herb's parents, now in their nineties, bring an instant hush over the crowd, as Papito pushes Mamita's wheelchair into the center of the room to present Liamarie with a rosary and a Bible, symbols of their Catholic faith. There are other gifts as well, a necklace from her new grandparents, who have only known Liamarie five years but have welcomed her into their warm Midwestern family with open arms and open hearts. And a symbolic pair of high-heel shoes, replacing the flat shoes of girlhood and placed on her feet by her father, kneeling before her in a scene out of Cinderella. In the dim lights of the restaurant, all of these rituals proceed carefully, and the crowd's response is softened by their tenderness and significance.

Finally, Liamarie approaches the candles. There are fifteen votive candles, and as she begins to light them, there is a sense of expectation in the room. The candles represent those who have been important to her, who have in some way lighted her path toward this day. Carefully, she pulls out a single sheet of paper, on which she has written a few words to accompany each candle presentation. Her parents have told me that this part of the night is hers alone. They do not know to whom she will give the candles or what she will say. Liamarie's words are simple and pure. They tell the story of her life as only a child could know it.

There is a candle for Mamita and Papito, who "kept my Spanish heritage alive for me," and for her Uncle Al, who "loved me through all my awkward stages and could always make me laugh." There is a candle for "the gang of four," as she calls her best friends here in Chicago, who welcomed her as a sixth grader, adjusting not only to a new city and a new school, but to a new family as well. They are all sophomores in high school now, but her gratitude for their friendship makes them jump with delight. There are candles for her Chicago extended family: new grandparents and new aunts, uncles, and cousins, who embraced her with love and affection five years ago when Herb and Linda were married.

There is a special candle for Linda, who "stepped into the role of mother so beautifully," in Liamarie's words. Linda steps forward, and her adoring expression leaves no doubt about her feelings toward her adopted daughter. The audience here knows all these relationships and applauds with enthusiasm as she presents each candle.

Her words for her dad speak a profound truth in a simple phrase: "To my dad, who works harder at being a great dad than anyone ever could know." In an instant, a hundred images flash through my mind. She is so right.

The guests are quieter when Liamarie turns to offer candles to a group unfamiliar to this audience. She presents a candle to several couples who have made this trip from Virginia, and honors them for supporting her and her dad in the difficult days after her mother's death and "never letting go of us as our lives moved on." Many of them I have not seen since Martha's funeral, and they are clustered together tonight as they were so many years ago. They were Martha's best friends, who drove her to treatments, made her food, and sat with her when she was dying. Their loyalty brings them to this night in Martha's memory, and they are visibly touched as Liamarie calls them to the front.

A candle for their children, now an impressive group of college students who jump with enthusiasm as she reminds them how they introduced her to Marx Brothers movies, took her out into the woods to play, and made her feel like her life had not ended when her mother's life did.

There is a candle for Mirka, whom Liamarie calls "my nanny who became my big sister, and who practically raised me." I remember Mirka growing from the timid Polish farm girl into Liamarie's advocate and a respected voice in the decisions about Liamarie's life and needs. Mirka moved to Chicago when Herb was married, and lived nearby, postponing her return to Europe and staying for almost a year to help Liamarie make the transition. Though she cannot be here tonight, I know she will hear about every detail in the days to come. Liamarie places Mirka's candle carefully back on the table near the group that has formed behind her, all holding their candles.

Liamarie lifts the next candle and holds it outstretched. "And this is for my mother, who has always been a guiding light in my life, and whose spirit is looking down on us tonight." *Oh yes*, I think, *her spirit is here.* But not only to watch. I see it in the faces all around me, in all of us who tried to let her strength and courage become our own in the years after her death.

By now the tears in the room are flowing freely, and I see faces glistening all around me. There is no more need to hide mine as the ritual ends and the audience applauds this lovely young woman and the group of people she has standing behind her.

I am there, just behind her, as I have been since the presentation began. When she called my name, I found myself standing before her, accepting the first candle of the night. Though she began with a smile, her voice choked as she spoke, and her brown eyes locked with mine in a moment that erased more than a decade. Her words could not have been simpler, nor more perfect.

"To Mary Beth, my aunt and godmother who became my second mother, and who took care of me when nobody else could."

Epilogue

We cannot afford to forget any experiences, even the most painful.

— Dag Hammarskjöld

Kaleidescope

There is part of our story I have not told. I cannot weave it into the narrative because I am not sure if it is true. That's not true. I know that pieces are true. Sharp fragmented pieces that exist in my memory like the remains of a mirror tossed onto a tile floor, shattered, glittering, impossible to order or sequence. They look different each time I come across them. I walk around them, circling, afraid to get too close. Sometimes the sun will catch a piece, and the glare will blind me. I retreat. Sometimes the shadows blend pieces together, hide one beneath another. I pick one up and, startled at what I see below, drop it. It breaks again. More pieces. Will I never know? I wonder.

I know that Bill called from the family room one night as he was watching the news. "Have you seen this? Mary Beth, did you know this?" I remember I was irritated. *Don't ask me. Don't talk to me about this. There is no room in my head for this information. Keep it out. Go away.*

I know that I refused to remember the name of the researcher. I don't know if I ever knew it, don't remember if Martha ever told me his name. But after her death, I could not know it.

I know that when Herb called, I didn't want to talk to him. Was it days later, maybe weeks after the news hit the papers? "Have you heard?" His voice was shrill. "That's the guy. I know it."

Go away. Calm down. Stay focused.

I don't know if I said these words. Only to myself, I think.

Like all traumatic memories, mine were recorded under strobe lights, flashes of truth that would not stay still. Is it real? Your mind's eye wonders, even as the pictures flash before you. They disappear as soon as you try to grab hold of them, or their force pushes you away and makes you recoil in horror.

I can hear a familiar voice, NBC Nightly News. "The Upcoming May 1999 meeting . . . reports will show no benefit . . . across the board . . . shocking the research and treatment communities . . . questions are now being raised . . . questions."

No thank you. I don't want to hear this. Turn it down. It's too loud. Make it go away.

....

Kaleidoscope images. Broken colors shift. Bill's concerned face. Silence. Herb's scream. Me pushing it all away.

It was enough to take in that the treatment did not work. Hard enough to hear the report that the results were definitive. "The results of large-scale US and European studies are in," the announcer says, "and the overwhelming evidence supports a failure of bone marrow transplant studies to show improved survival in women with aggressive tumors."

Enough. I can live with this. She could have lived with this. She knew the answer might be no. "That's why we need the research," she would have said, "to get an answer."

A weird fragment of relief. An incongruous feeling of comfort. This would not have saved her. Maybe her death was easier than the one she would have had when her cancer returned. Bizarre contorted comfort.

Enough. It is enough to know she risked her life for something that would not have made her well. I keep saying this over and over. She risked her life—no, she lost her life—doing something that would not have made her well. "No difference. No statistical improvement in recurrence rates or long-term survival," the reporter says with no inflection at all. I do not want to talk to Herb about this. He is distraught, broken, voicing all the questions I cannot find words for. Should she have waited? Should we have discouraged her?

But it is not the research failure I cannot absorb. It is the rest.

"Questions are now being raised about the South African research on which these American and European programs were based."

The newscast is too loud. I can hear it from downstairs. Turn it off. I cannot know this.

························

In the spring of 1999, this was as far as my wounded brain could go. I could not look at those broken pieces of glass, the shattered story of research and hope and doubt and deceit. I could not put them together. Any piece I touched made me bleed. The researchers were wrong. The preliminary promising results we had pinned our hopes on were an illusion. The disappointment of this was huge. *She would be here right now*, I thought, *if she had said no to this. She would be alive.*

But as the months followed that initial disappointing news, the specter of something much larger emerged. It was the thing I could not hear, could not take in until years had passed. Most people didn't mention it, or were careful how they phrased it. "They're not doing BMT for breast cancer anymore, right? They found out there was some problem with the research, is that it?"

What did I say in response? I cannot remember a single time. My denial, my blocking was so complete I just shifted the lens, turned the kaleidoscope a quarter turn inside my head, and smiled. "I guess so. I don't really follow the research."

Is that what I said? Or did I ever tell the truth? Did I ever say they discovered that a world-famous South African medical researcher lied, that he made up data, that he perpetrated a fraud on the international medical community? I don't think I said those words to anyone because I could not say them to myself.

But I know that I knew. I know because of a yellowed piece of newsprint in my jewelry box. It's an Ellen Goodman column from the *Boston Globe*, and for more than ten years, Ellen's ageless face stared back at me whenever I opened the box. I cannot date the article. I put it there a year and a half, maybe two, after Martha's death. I remember reading it once, inhaling its poison, and not being able to breathe out for days. So I clipped it, folded it neatly, and let it sit there as I ignored it, day after day, year after year.

Oh yes, you. The lie.

Each time I saw it, I flashed on Martha sitting across from me at my kitchen table. "There was one really good study in South Africa, really good results," she had said. "Others haven't been able to replicate them yet, but that's why these programs are so important. Programs have been established across this country now, Phase II and Phase III clinical trials, and Johns Hopkins is a part of that." Her eyes punctuated the statement. I can still see her face and hear her voice rise at the end of the sentence.

"Preliminary results are promising."

The yellowed newsprint tells another story. It tells of a sloppy, poorly documented, and ultimately falsified set of data that set the stage for Martha and so many other women to risk their lives unnecessarily. It tells of a researcher who published results in 1995 of a randomized study demonstrating that bone marrow transplants led to improved long-term survival for advanced metastasized breast cancers. When programs in France and the United States were not finding similar patterns of success in their newly formed studies, the same South African doctor gave notice of ongoing further research, to be presented at the May 1999 meeting of the American Society of Clinical Oncology that would show effectiveness for aggressive non-metastasized high-risk tumors like Martha's as well. And it tells of an audit of both of those studies in 2000 that found missing files, fabricated patients, and no evidence of the results that had been so widely touted around the globe.

I can justify my denial. I can tell myself some version of what I did say to others: "We are focusing on Liamarie now. We need all our energy to help her. No, I haven't kept up with the research." I think the truth is much less altruistic. The truth is that keeping the pieces separate allowed me to function. The truth is that knowing it all in one connected narrative was too much to bear.

It was not until 2009 that I was able to put all of the pieces together. It was then that I read *False Hope: Bone Marrow Transplantation for Breast Cancer* (Rettig, R.A. et. al. Oxford University Press 2007). The book, by four prominent medical authors, details the complex and convoluted story of how bone marrow transplant came to be the great hope of breast cancer victims in the nineties. Falsified data was a foundation stone in that process, but the cultural, financial, and political forces that attached themselves to that data played a significant role in creating a climate where application of the treatment jumped ahead of randomized clinical trials, and the belief that it worked superseded the proof that it worked. It was in this climate that Martha was encouraged to consider this treatment, to participate in a Phase II study, and ultimately, to take the risk that took her life.

Within a year after her death, the questions began. That newscast I could not hear occurred on March 9, 1999, the first anniversary of her death. The medical community was shocked that the data they were about to present in their May ASCO meeting were so uniform. Two large United States studies and one from Sweden showed the same results. No statistical difference in survival or recurrence rate for women who were enduring this painful, expensive, and life threatening procedure. A smaller study done in France concurred. Only one research paper differed.

Werner Bezwoda was the name I could not remember. Werner Bezwoda, MD, who at that same 1999 meeting would report his randomized study of 154 women with high-risk aggressive tumors like Martha's. Like his 1995 study on women with metastatic tumors, his results were positive and stunning.

In October 1995, his research had been published by the prestigious *Journal of Clinical Oncology* (Bezwoda et. al. 1995). An accompanying favorable editorial was written by John Kennedy, MD, Martha's transplant physician, who had been doing research on bone marrow transplants for multiple solid tumors at Johns Hopkins University since 1989. His endorsement called the Bezwoda study "provocative and encouraging," and concluded, "It is probably fair to say there is a qualitative superiority to the high-dose regimen" for breast cancer. The stage was set for the growth of this treatment protocol across the country.

But by 1999, it was the uniqueness of Bezwoda's results that stood out. "Why can't we replicate these South African results?" researchers across the world were asking. "Why are our centers not finding the same long-term outcomes that his studies did?" Twenty thousand doctors and researchers registered to hear the results from around the world at the May 1999 ASCO meeting. They were stunned, horrified. No one except Bezwoda had good results to report.

Pressure rose to do a formal audit of the Bezwoda research, and in January of 2000, a team of doctors was dispatched to audit his work. For months the team was delayed and turned back. Soon they knew why. Records were missing, protocols fabricated, and controls nonexistent. The researcher, described as South Africa's leading oncologist, was fired instantly from his University of Witwatersrand position for scientific fraud.

....

She died because you lied.

There's still a voice in me that wants to simplify, to demonize, to blame. But it is much softer now. I know that there is plenty of blame to go around. Bezwoda deserves our condemnation for his lies. But we all wanted to believe them. Doctors and patients jumped on this hope before the truth was in. Somewhere between thirty and forty thousand women received bone marrow transplant procedures in the 1990s for metastatic breast cancer and for high-risk aggressive primary tumors. Fewer than a thousand of these were in randomized clinical trials. The enthusiasm about the procedure spread so quickly that few women wanted to risk joining a study that might place them in a control group with no treatment. Few doctors wanted to discourage women who were willing to try something that promised a long-term cure. It was not until that May 1999 meeting of the American Society of Clinical Oncology that the results of large-scale randomized studies would finally be presented. Not until a year after Martha's death would the medical community meet the standard it should have set years before, the requirement that empirical data from more than one researcher show this treatment to be effective.

Martha's was one of the treatment-related deaths reported at that meeting.

Acknowledgments

I will not try to list all of those whose skill and encouragement enriched this work. Through the Maine Writers and Publisher's Alliance I found The Stonecoast Summer Writers Conference, the Haystack Writer's Workshop, the Writer's Week in Hoth, Ireland, and the Black Fly Writer's retreat. In these places, total strangers offered notes, suggestions, and occasional tears that kept this project alive. Richard Hoffman's memoir workshop at The Writer's Hotel in NYC introduced me to even more of these generous souls, who honed my skill as an essayist and storyteller.

A few names will have to represent them all. Special thanks to the poetic genius of Megan Grumbling and Cynthia Eyster, the unflagging encouragement of my Merrymeeting Writer's group… David, Sybil, Judy, Chris, Liza, and Deb, and to Jennifer Caven, who copyedited early drafts of this with loving attention to detail.

Suzanne Strempek Shea and Susan Conley pored over many drafts, teaching me craft and pushing me to be a better writer. My agent, Anne Depue, always seemed to ask just the right "wise question" and Joan Dempsey, my friend and #1 cheerleader, showed me what commitment to writing really means.

The team at She Writes Press offered professional wisdom, publishing expertise, and a community of women writers who eased my way into the whole new territory of becoming an author.

I am forever thankful to Herb and Liamarie for permitting me to tell their story, and to Justin, Matt and Margaret, for opening their childhood's pain to the world.

Martha's courage stands behind every word in this story. Her silent reprimand got me through more moments of self-doubt than I can count.

Some years ago, my husband said his job was to keep me sane, so that I could go up to my office and do the same for others. As I lived this story, and re-lived it in writing the book, he proved the truth of those words. Without him, none of this would be real. Gratitude is too small a word.

About the Author

Mary E. Plouffe, PhD is a clinical psychologist with thirty-five years of experience as a clinician, teacher, and consultant. She has served on the faculty of Maine Medical Center psychiatry residency training program, the Maine Board of Examiners, and The Collaborative School, and has provided consultation to public and private schools and courts. Her essays have been published by NPR, *On the Issues Magazine*, *Brain, Child Magazine*, *Survivor Review*, and *Mothers Always Write*. Find additional information at www.maryeplouffeauthor.com.

Author photo by Fitzgerald Photo

SELECTED TITLES FROM SHE WRITES PRESS

She Writes Press is an independent publishing company
founded to serve women writers everywhere.
Visit us at www.shewritespress.com.

Four Funerals and a Wedding: Resilience in a Time of Grief by Jill Smolowe. $16.95, 978-1-938314-72-8. When journalist Jill Smolowe lost four family members in less than two years, she turned to modern bereavement research for answers—and made some surprising discoveries.

Falling Together: How to Find Balance, Joy, and Meaningful Change When Your Life Seems to be Falling Apart by Donna Cardillo. $16.95, 978-1-63152-077-8. A funny, big-hearted self-help memoir that tackles divorce, caregiving, burn-out, major illness, fears, and low self-esteem—and explores the renewal that comes when we are able to meet these challenges with courage.

A Different Kind of Same: A Memoir by Kelley Clink. $16.95, 978-1-63152-999-3. Several years before Kelley Clink's brother hanged himself, she attempted suicide by overdose. In the aftermath of his death, she traces the evolution of both their illnesses, and wonders: If he couldn't make it, what hope is there for her?

Green Nails and Other Acts of Rebellion: Life After Loss by Elaine Soloway. $16.95, 978-1-63152-919-1. An honest, often humorous account of the joys and pains of caregiving for a loved one with a debilitating illness.

The Beauty of What Remains: Family Lost, Family Found by Susan Johnson Hadler. $16.95, 978-1-63152-007-5. Susan Johnson Hadler goes on a quest to find out who the missing people in her family were—and what happened to them—and succeeds in reuniting a family shattered for four generations.

From Sun to Sun: A Hospice Nurse's Reflection on the Art of Dying by Nina Angela McKissock. $16.95, 978-1-63152-808-8. Weary from the fear people have of talking about the process of dying and death, a highly experienced registered nurse takes the reader into the world of twenty-one of her beloved patients as they prepare to leave this earth.